The
Thatc
Government

The Thatcher Government

PETER RIDDELL

Martin Robertson · Oxford

First published in 1983 by Martin Robertson & Company Ltd,
108 Cowley Road, Oxford OX4 1JF.

British Library Cataloguing in Publication Data

Riddell, Peter
    The Thatcher government
    1. Great Britain— Politics and government—1964-
    I. Title
    354.4107'2'09   DA592

    ISBN 0-85520-602-0
    ISBN 0-85520-603-9 Pbk

Typeset by System 4 Associates, Gerrads Cross
Printed and bound in Great Britain by
Whitstable Litho Ltd., Whitstable, Kent

To my mother
and to the memory of my father

Contents

Preface

Thatcherism has undoubtedly caught a popular mood in Britain. But it is not all-conquering, and there are many internal contradictions — over public spending and taxation, over defence commitments and the welfare state — which will have to be resolved over the next few years. This book aims to discuss the aspirations, performance and prospects of the Thatcher administration. The perspective is the summer of 1983, thus the book looks back at the record of the first term and forward to likely problems and possible achievements of the second. The emphasis is primarily analytical — explaining the nature of Thatcherism, its implications for particular policies and its impact upon Britain. While Mrs Thatcher's personality, in all its vivid contrasts, is naturally central, this is not another biography of her. There are already plenty. Similarly, this is not intended to be a blow-by-blow account of 'what really happened'. I hope there are insights and revelations, but they are incidental to the explanation and assessment.

Above all, this book is not a contribution to any inter- or intra-party debate. There are some forceful books on this theme by traditional Tories such as Sir Ian Gilmour and Chris Patten — though almost nothing recently from the Thatcherites (perhaps they are too busy privatizing). And there has also been a plethora of polemics from the left, often of high quality. I do not aspire to unattainable objectivity; I hope merely not to be partisan. Naturally, I have views — a sympathy with the necessity for the broad change of direction in economic policy which began in the mid-1970s under Labour and has been sustained and extended by the Thatcher administration. I believe that some hard decisions on economic and industrial policy were inescapable, but I disagree with many features of their implementation and am out of sympathy with many of the social priorities of Thatcherism.

This book concentrates on the main themes of Thatcherism — the attempt to change direction in economic policy, to shift the frontiers between the public and the private sectors, to revive enterprise, to restore law and order, and to assert Britain's interests in the world. This may be an ambitious (possibly an over-ambitious) aim, but I am all too aware of what has been excluded or discussed only in passing. There is very little on Northern Ireland, Scotland and Wales, on constitutional issues, on training, on agriculture and fisheries, on planning, on energy and on transport. All these matters are important, but they have not been central to the changes of the period.

The sources for the book have reflected the privileges and opportunities offered by my observation post. Throughout the period I have been working as a journalist on the *Financial Times*, writing about economics up to the summer of 1981 and since then about politics. In a sense, my contacts with politicians, civil servants, economists and businessmen are the main input. I am grateful to all of them for their insights and indiscretions. In addition, during 1983 I have had a number of more specific conversations about the themes of this book with Conservative MPs, both Ministers and backbenchers, and with civil servants. Most must necessarily remain anonymous, though they are none the less appreciated for that. However, I would like to single out Sir Geoffrey Howe, who talked to me twice during his busy pre-Budget period, and Adam Ridley, then his special adviser, who helped to clarify the background to Conservative preparations in Opposition.

I have made a point, where possible, of identifying sources in the case of speeches, Commons select committee reports (an increasingly important help to any commentator on contemporary British politics and society), articles and books, all of which are listed in the bibliography. I have also made considerable use of the leaked papers produced during 1982–3, especially those associated with discussions about the medium-term expenditure outlook, since they highlight the dilemmas which will be faced by the Thatcher administration in its second term. The titles I have given people are generally those of 9 June 1983, ignoring subsequent ennoblement.

I am naturally grateful to the two editors of the *Financial Times* over the period, Fredy Fisher and Geoffrey Owen, for giving me the opportunity to observe and write about the phenomenon of Thatcherism. The main economic and political commentators of the paper, Samuel Brittan and Malcolm Rutherford, have influenced my thinking during countless conversations over the years, and I would like to thank Samuel Brittan for showing me the draft of part of his new book, *The Role and Limits of Government*. A number of friends and colleagues have commented on parts of the book — notably James Naughtie, Margaret van Hattem and Michael Cassell. I am also particularly grateful to Martin and Helene Hayman for their support and advice, while their three sons, Benjamin, Joseph and Jacob, provided welcome diversions at critical points during the writing. Finally, I would like to thank Michael Hay of Martin Robertson for his encouragement and responsiveness and Elizabeth Bland for her sensitive treatment of my sprawling typescript.

All authors absolve everyone else of responsibility for what they have written. I am no exception: even if much of the light has come from elsewhere, the prism is mine.

Peter Riddell
August 1983

1

A Portrait of Thatcherism

The mission of this Government is much more than the promotion of economic progress. It is to renew the spirit and solidarity of the nation.

Mrs Margaret Thatcher
Conservative Political Centre Summer School, Cambridge
6 July 1979

We offered a complete change in direction — from one in which the state became totally dominant in people's lives and penetrated almost every aspect to a life where the state did do certain things, but without displacing personal responsibility. I think we have altered the balance between the person and the state in a favourable way.

Mrs Margaret Thatcher
Interview in The Times
5 May 1983

For more than thirty years every British Government has had a different answer to the question of economic and industrial decline. The Thatcher administration has adopted a novel approach. It has tried to change the question. Instead of the Government being regarded as primarily responsible for solving Britain's problems, the onus has shifted to the people. In the process the post-war consensus about economic management has been challenged. All the old certainties about, and expectations of, political behaviour and the impact of high unemployment have been shaken. Paradoxically, this narrowing of the Government's role has been coupled with an assertion of strong prime ministerial leadership. The most striking consequence has been the Conservatives' landslide victory in the June 1983 general election. So dominant is Mrs Thatcher herself, and so mesmeric is her influence, that it is often difficult to assess the real achievements behind this shift in the terms of the political debate.

This book aims to see whether the Thatcher administration of the 1980s has changed, or could change, the direction of British politics. If so, the administration would rank alongside the Liberal Government elected in 1906 and the Attlee administration of 1945. There are two central questions. First, will the changes in attitudes and industrial behaviour trumpeted by Ministers have a lasting impact, or will they amount to no more than a short-lived response to the deepest recession for fifty years? Second, has the Government created sufficiently widespread consent, as opposed to acquiescence, to promote a new 'settlement' about how the economy and society should be run to match that of the previous thirty years?

The Challenge of Thatcherism

There is no doubt that the Thatcher administration has challenged the previous consensus, the legacy of Keynes and Beveridge. The 'settlement' of the late 1940s and 1950s, enshrined in the word 'Butskellism', reflected attitudes shared by the major parties towards the need to ensure full employment, the broad scope of the welfare state and the public sector.

The 'settlement' had started to break down from the early 1970s onwards, first under the Heath administration's short-lived 'Quiet Revolution' and, most significantly, after the first oil price shock in 1973–4. The Wilson and Callaghan Governments also tacitly abandoned any attempt to attain full employment, even if they maintained the pretence for their followers. The key shift towards a broadly monetarist approach and tougher controls on public expenditure occurred under Labour from 1976 onwards. So the continuities after the 1979 election have in some respects been greater than either the Tories or Labour have found it politic to admit.

Yet both Tory and Labour administrations up to the late 1970s were concerned principally with repairing the post-war 'settlement', not with challenging it.

The open assault on the stated assumptions, as opposed to the practice, of the Keynes/Beveridge era began only after the 1979 election. According to Nigel Lawson — one of the foremost polemicists for, and practitioners of, economic Thatcherism — the Conservative Party embraced the social democratic delusions of the efficacy of Government action and of the idea of equality throughout most of the post-war era, but the Thatcher administration's approach after 1979 represented a rejection of these 'false trails' (Lawson, 1981). Since then there has been a deliberate attempt to change direction — to shift the frontiers between the public and private sectors, to stimulate enterprise and property owner-ship and to encourage the private provision of education and health.

Conservative leaders claim that events since 1979 have marked a 'turning of the tide' and the 'rebirth of Britain' (Lawson, 1982). Sir Geoffrey Howe, the patient Fabian of Thatcherism, has talked of a 'Conservative consensus' in attitudes towards economic and industrial policy, in line with the practice in other countries (Howe, 1982). According to this view, the Thatcher administration has at long last faced up to Britain's deep-seated economic and industrial problems, notably inflation and the size of the public sector. Nigel Lawson has referred to the 'new realism' — a wide-spread recognition that no Government can guarantee full employment and that only a limited amount can be done by Government directly to affect the level of unemployment. Similarly, the abandonment of incomes policy has helped to restore managerial authority and has taken the politics out of wage determination, leading to the discovery by workers that 'trade union emperors wear very few clothes.'

The evidence for these claims is still highly contentious. After all, the economic record since 1979 seems to point to continuing decline and a less than coherent strategy. Manu-facturing output dropped by more than one-sixth and has so far staged only a partial recovery. Profit margins have been at around record low levels, and competitiveness in international markets deteriorated sharply in 1980–1. Moreover, for all the rhetoric about rolling back the frontiers of the state, public spending has risen as a percentage of total national income, as has the personal tax burden. But, say the Thatcherites, the corner has been turned: in particular, inflation is now at its lowest level for fifteen years, creating the conditions for further advance. Admittedly, times have been hard, but after long overdue adjustments output and productivity are clearly improving, and attitudes in industry have changed.

No one disputes that the cost has been high. Unemployment has risen by roughly 2 million to more than 3.25 million since 1979, and large numbers of companies have been forced out of business. A key question is whether the reduction in inflation and the (probably necessary) shake-up of British industry could have been achieved with less suffering, perhaps through a modification of the basic strategy.

The Thatcher administration has undoubtedly now seized the political initiative, but it has not yet won the argument. Its view that there is no workable alternative has never been entirely persuasive, even inside the Conservative Party. Mrs Thatcher and her allies have appeared dominant in large part because of the divisions of the Opposition. Without the bitter splits in the Labour Party and the rise of the SDP/ Liberal Alliance, the Thatcher administration would not have been able to win back, and to hold, the political initiative in 1981–2.

The Conservatives' landslide win in 1983 was a direct reflection of Opposition divisions. The Tory share of the vote in the 1983 election fell slightly by comparison with that of 1979 and was smaller than those of the party's previous victories since the Second World War. There was therefore no upsurge of popular support for Mrs Thatcher and her administration. Nevertheless, the victory was remarkable, especially given the economic circumstances. Mrs Thatcher's administration was the first since 1959 to be re-elected after being in office for a full term. The electorate appears to have been sceptical about the other policies on offer and at least half-persuaded that no Government could offer an easy way out of high unemployment. The 1983 election may therefore have been a rare case of a campaign's being lost by an Opposition: voters appeared willing to give the party in power longer to finish the job.

There is a danger, however, of drawing too many long-term conclusions from the 1983 election. Some commentators have been talking about a new Thatcherite majority, just as some US observers mistakenly concluded that there was an emerging Republican majority after the Nixon landslide in the 1972 American presidential election. Electoral opinion nowadays is too volatile to make such long-term projections. Anyway, the major lessons of the 1983 election were for the Opposition parties, not for the Government.

The Thatcher administration will have to produce more tangible proof of an end to decline if it is to maintain its political position. The light cannot always be at the end of the tunnel. The 1983 election did not suggest there was yet any new consensus about British society and the management of the economy – even if there have been important changes in attitudes in industry. Indeed, Mrs Thatcher and her administration have aroused as much bitter antagonism as fervent support.

Intense debate continues about methods of economic management, about the operations of the welfare state and about the balance between central and local government. There is no sign of anything comparable to the cross-party agreement about the economy that emerged in the decade after 1945. Professor Samuel Beer, a long-standing observer of British politics, has written of the need to mobilize 'wide and lasting consent' if changes are to last (Beer, 1982). Many Thatcherites would reject such a search for consensus, preferring the sharp edge of the 'conviction' approach. But without such consensus the achievements of Thatcherism could be overturned once the electorate's preferences change.

Defining Thatcherism

Is there a coherent strategy that has been followed by the Conservative administration since 1979? It is tempting to dismiss the use of the word 'Thatcherism' as the perennial, but misleading, search both by politicians for an easy label to put on opponents and by commentators for a way of simplifying the complexities of politics. For instance, the Thatcher administration has not followed a pure free-market or monetarist programme, though strands of both have clearly been important since 1979. The works of Hayek and Friedman are seldom quoted at meetings of the 1922 Committee of Tory MPs. Indeed, Professor Milton Friedman, the leading guru of academic monetarism, complained in an interview with the *Observer* in September 1982 about the extent to which monetarism was popularly equated with Mrs Thatcher 'to cover anything that Mrs Thatcher at any time expressed as a desirable object of policy'. Some of Mrs Thatcher's most forceful personal interventions have been to counter market forces by trying to hold down interest rates and gas prices.

Yet both supporters and critics of the Conservative administration believe there have been a clear theme and style since 1979. Moreover, these have been different both from those that went before and from those currently being offered by the Opposition parties. Politics may be determined more by chance and accident than by plan, but there may still be a distinctive approach to such events. And however difficult it is to define, Thatcherism does have a meaning for those in the political world.

Any explanation turns inescapably on Mrs Thatcher herself. Her leadership has been the key influence in the Conservatives' success. A Market and Opinion Research International survey in late March 1983 showed that for many people the foremost reason for supporting the Tories was her strength of character, which was cited by 33 per cent of the sample.

Mrs Thatcher's views, prejudices and style have determined the Government's actions more than any other single factor. As Sir John Nott, the Defence Secretary from 1981 to 1983, remarked of her contribution to the Falklands victory, 'without [her] it would have been impossible.' This is not to say that the Conservative Government has followed a blueprint drawn up by her or that she has always got her own way. She is not Lenin. The administration's record has been marked by the usual twists and turns of all politics, and the standing of both her and her Government has also fluctuated sharply.

Thatcherism is essentially an instinct, a series of moral values and an approach to leadership rather than an ideology. It is an expression of Mrs Thatcher's upbringing in Grantham, her background of hard work and family responsibility, ambition and postponed satisfaction, duty and patriotism. Her views were 'born of the conviction which I learned in a small town from a father who had a conviction approach', as she put it in an interview in January 1983 on London Weekend Television's *Weekend World* programme. The striking feature of Mrs Thatcher's approach has been its consistency. The same themes have cropped up again and again in speeches and interviews throughout the past decade – personal responsibility, the family and national pride. The key lies in her use of language, especially off the cuff in interviews. Words like freedom, self-respect, independence, initiative, choice, conviction, duty, greatness, heart and faith recur. As one of her close aides has remarked, she is like an open book in revealing her thoughts and concerns.

Quintessential examples of Mrs Thatcher's approach have been her attitudes to borrowing and to Victorian values. Speaking at the Lord Mayor's Banquet in November 1982, she noted that she had been criticized for

talking about the principles of financial management of a nation as if they were like those of a family budget. Some say I preach merely the homilies of housekeeping or the parables of the parlour. But I do not repent. Those parables would have saved many a financier from failure and many a country from crisis.

(Curiously, Mrs Thatcher has also claimed to be in the tradition of Keynes, though he was always careful to distinguish between the finances of housekeeping and of a nation.) And in her *Weekend World* interview in January 1983 she argued:

[Victorian values] were the values when our country
became great....As our people prospered, so they used
their independence and initiative to prosper others, not
compulsion by the state. Yes, I want to see one nation,
but I want everyone to have their own personal
property stake.

These and subsequent remarks stimulated a lively debate.
Historians pointed out that a central feature of Disraeli's
Conservative administration in 1874–80 was the use of the
state, not personal initiative, to promote social reform via
legislation on public health, housing, pollution, the sale
of food and drugs and trade union rights. The charm of
Victorian values probably also look less alluring to people
living in towns with nineteenth-century sewers and hospitals
in need of urgent repair work that cannot be undertaken
because of a lack of public money.

Mrs Thatcher's other main theme has been a sense of
mission to save Britain. In her final election broadcast in
1979 she said:

Somewhere ahead lies greatness for our country again.
This I know in my heart. Look at Britain today and you
may think that an impossible dream. But there is
another Britain. It is a Britain of thoughtful people,
tantalizingly slow to act, yet marvellously determined
when they do.

By November 1982 Mrs Thatcher was able to claim that the
years of doubt and denigration were over:

We have learnt not to run away from difficult choices.
Doubt whether we resolve our problems is giving way to
knowledge that we can, and to resolve that we will.

In defining Thatcherism these values are far more revealing
than specific policy proposals. Indeed, when it comes to
policy Mrs Thatcher has not been an original thinker. Most of
the Conservative Party's programme has come initially from
other people: her contribution has been to take up and

articulate these themes. She has been described as populist, reflecting her view that as a woman, as a mother, as an outsider in the establishment political world, she understands how ordinary people feel about and react to issues such as law and order, family morality and the trade unions.

Perhaps most important of all is her style, dominant and certain. In conversation — and, by all accounts, around the Cabinet table — she presses her points home insistently, convinced of her rightness and wearily contemptuous of other views. There is no hint of traditional Tory scepticism in her approach. This was evident constantly during the 1983 election campaign, when Mrs Thatcher at times appeared to be the domineering headmistress ordering around her ministerial colleagues and the media alike. She is not a good listener and is not sparing of reputations. In the early days of her administration Whitehall frequently buzzed with stories about the Ministers whom she had told to shut up in front of officials, the ultimate loss of face in the mandarin world. And few present will ever forget her public humiliation of Francis Pym during the 1983 campaign, when she interrupted him during a press conference. (This incident was rightly seen as a prelude to his dismissal as Foreign Secretary.) Mrs Thatcher is also a workaholic. She seldom relaxes. She absorbs a brief at great speed and is able to pour out figures and arguments on the issue of the moment, as she shows in her mastery of the twice-weekly Prime Minister's questions in the Commons.

Her single-mindedness is aptly reflected in the Soviet Union's description of her as the 'Iron Lady', a sobriquet that, like many similar ones, she soon turned to advantage. Mrs Thatcher arouses strong responses: to Denis Healey she is 'La Passionara of middle-class privilege', while to Paul Johnson, now a zealous convert from the left, she has got 'a bit of the bulldog breed' in her. Yet even sympathizers have had their doubts. Ferdinand Mount noted in late 1979 'a certain impatience with subtlety of feeling, a lack of sympathy with people unlike her and a definitely limited range of experience'. Mr Mount's comments did not, however, prevent her from appointing him head of the Downing Street policy unit in the summer of 1982 — or him from accepting. Moreover, while Conservative backbenchers habitually adopt public-school slang, some of the nicknames that they have invented for her (the 'Leaderene', 'Attila the Hen', the 'Boss', 'Boadicea') suggest more than a hint of nervousness about her.

Mrs Thatcher has been an acute party politician, aware of rank-and-file and backbench feelings. But her political antennae tend to be of the crude *Daily Telegraph* kind — sensitive to murmurings in Finchley but not in Falkirk. In Whitehall and within the Cabinet she has certainly responded to external pressures. Lord Carrington, as Foreign Secretary, had the reputation of being able to persuade her, generally after much time and effort, that 'political realities' should come ahead of her instincts. Francis Pym was less successful.

The Place of Thatcherism in the Conservative Party

Both critics and supporters would be mistaken to regard Thatcherism as synonymous with Conservatism and its success as inevitable. Neither assumption is accurate. Mrs Thatcher has needed all her political faculties to achieve her recent dominance. As the next chapter indicates, she won the leadership of the Conservative Party in February 1975 by what amounted to a *coup d'état*. She won, in spite of the votes cast against her by the vast majority of her senior colleagues, in what Julian Critchley, that most biting of Tory MP commentators, has called 'the Peasants' Revolt'. The views of Mrs Thatcher and Sir Keith Joseph, her ideological mentor, were unorthodox then and are still far from universally accepted within the Conservative Party.

The clue to the success of Thatcherism lies in the tribal nature of the Conservative Party. As a tribe the party responds to leadership — as long as that offers a chance of success — but it is ruthless when faced with actual or prospective failure. The party's support for its leader is therefore conditional. When Edward Heath appeared to be a loser in 1974–5 and something had obviously gone seriously wrong, the party welcomed a bold challenger, Mrs Thatcher. Like its support for Mr Heath and his approach in the early 1970s, the party's loyalty is founded on the fact that Mrs Thatcher is the leader and has so far provided success.

Mrs Thatcher has, however, a more natural constituency among the Conservative rank and file and the new generation of MPs than had some former leaders. She is the voice of the suburban and provincial middle classes. Conservative Party conferences are full of her people with her prejudices, which is perhaps why some of the more fastidious, or snobbish, Conservative MPs stay away from her speech on the final day of conferences — 'all that idolatory and Elgar'.

Ideology and policy, as I have remarked, are less important in explaining the dominance of Thatcherism, which is anyway influenced by different, and often conflicting, creeds ranging from monetarism, via moral authoritarianism, to an anglicized view of Gaullism. And Thatcherism has been only one of many strands within the Conservative Party. This is a treacherous area in which those with internal party points to argue have frequently become embroiled in rival interpretations of history. Appeals to the thoughts of past leaders by Conservatives have become almost as frequent, and as futile, as references to what the young or the old Marx would have said about a particular problem.

The search in the past for precedents to support current views has been reflected in the labels conferred on various groups. Is Sir Ian Gilmour, who was sacked from the Cabinet in September 1981, in the Tory tradition, as he has argued with considerable elegance, or is he a wealthy Whig aristocrat with a guilt complex about the unemployed? The 'wets', so called for their alleged softness on economic and social issues, would like to appropriate the word Tory, but Enoch Powell also sees himself as a Tory, though many regard him as holding some of the views of a nineteenth-century liberal — which, to complete the confusion, was how Sir John Nott, a supporter of minimalist government, described himself in a *Guardian* interview in September 1982. Sir John went on: 'So is Mrs Thatcher. That is what this Government is all about.' But that was a partial, not to say somewhat impish,view.

This may be to adopt too intellectual and rational an approach. Most members of the Conservative tribe belong for reasons of family, tradition and instinct, not because they have made a distinctive ideological choice. This applies as much to Conservative MPs as to local activists. Francis Pym was nearer the mark in a *Guardian* interview in November 1982: 'In the Conservative Party there are many mansions. It is a hugely broad-shouldered party.' Mr Pym, himself consciously in the paternalist tradition, thought there was an element of truth in what John Nott had said about the style and approach of Mrs Thatcher. 'But that is not a description of the Conservative Party as a whole. I think it is a description of the Government.'

Even among MPs it is more helpful to talk about a spectrum of views and groups, differing on particular issues. This has been reflected in the difficulty which commentators and fellow MPs have encountered in attempting to classify the 100 new Conservative Members elected in June 1983. Within a parliamentary party of 397 there are probably no more than between 80 and 100 Members committed to a free-market and monetarist position over economic issues. One hesitates to describe them as Thatcherites, since Mrs Thatcher herself does not take a clear-cut or consistent view of these matters. There is, however, probably a group of roughly this size which is closely in tune with her broad social outlook and identifies clearly with her and her aspirations. In that sense they are Thatcherites. In contrast, there are perhaps 50 or 60 'wets' who are very doubtful about the economic strategy that has been followed since 1979.

The majority of Conservative MPs have no such firm commitment. They follow the leadership, with varying degrees of enthusiasm. Many do not have particularly strong views on monetarism, but they did feel that something had gone awry in the mid-1970s and that the Heath approach had run into the sand. This feeling coincided with a general disenchantment about the growth of public expenditure and the power of the trade unions. Many MPs therefore responded to the policy lead and the promise of a new direction offered by Mrs Thatcher and Sir Keith Joseph. Even within the Cabinet the largest single group can best be described as comprising men of office — loyal but not zealots. For every keen supporter like Norman Tebbit or Cecil Parkinson there is a Patrick Jenkin or Tom King, a type that defies rigid classification but has been recognizable in every Conservative Cabinet for the last half-century. However, the Thatcherites, the close allies of the Prime Minister, have been growing in numbers and influence.

Mrs Thatcher's position appears unassailable only in retrospect. At the start of her administration she and her supporters were in a minority in the Cabinet. And her approach has at times isolated her from many of her colleagues, who have been more concerned with departmental and external pressures. It was only in 1981 that she started to establish her dominance over the Cabinet as a result of two shuffles of her ministerial team.

Her ascendancy in the country became evident somewhat later. In the summer and autumn of 1981 her position had been weakened by the impact of the recession, which was deeper than expected, by the tough spring Budget and by the summer riots in the inner cities. There was even talk of a possible coup against her leadership, although this was only backbench gossip, and the plan never had a serious chance of getting off the ground. By December 1981, after two spectacular by-election losses to the SDP/Liberal Alliance, a Gallup poll put the Conservatives' rating at 23 per cent and the proportion expressing satisfaction with Mrs Thatcher's performance at a record low, 25 per cent. Within a year the Conservative position had been transformed, largely because of Britain's victory in the Falklands war in the early summer of 1982.

Throughout these events the distinctive feature has been Mrs Thatcher's determination, her combative style and her rejection of consensus. There have certainly been a number of modifications of policy, and at times it has been difficult to discern any clear overall strategy in respect, say, of the Government's approach to nationalized industries or local authorities. But on the central issue, economic management, the long-term aim and thrust have been consistent. For all the short-term shifts, the strategy was not, after all, changed in 1981 in response to the sharper than expected rise in unemployment. There was no U-turn.

Mrs Thatcher summed up her approach during an American television interview conducted a week after her 1983 election victory. She said:

When the ratings were very bad it was an acutely difficult time for us, and nevertheless I knew that we had to
do certain things economically in order to get things
right in the longer run. There are certain right ways to
go, and you have to stick to it long enough to get
the results. We were doing that: then along came the
Falklands, and one applied just exactly the same
principles....It was the same approach to both problems. They saw the kind of results it produced in the
Falklands, and I think they began to realize that it was
the right way to go at home as well...I think people
like decisiveness. I think they like strong leadership.

A Comparison with 'New Right' Policies in the USA

All this has made Mrs Thatcher and her Government stand
apart, both at home and abroad. After the 1979 election
there was much talk of the Thatcher experiment. Academic
economists referred to the UK as a laboratory test for
monetarism and as a guide to the rise of the New Right.
These trends had already become apparent with the widespread adoption of monetary targets in the late 1970s and
with the passage, in a referendum in California in June
1978, of Proposition 13, limiting property taxes. Republican
and conservative US commentators were enthusiastic about
Mrs Thatcher in her first year of office. They cited her as an
example to be followed before the election of Ronald Reagan
as President of the USA in November 1980.

The honeymoon was short-lived. By the time President
Reagan took office in January 1981 supporters and members
of his administration were distancing their economic policies
from those of Mrs Thatcher. George Gilder, one of the most
vocal apologists for the New Right in the USA, warned people
to heed the 'cautionary tale' of Mrs Thatcher, who had
'failed to combine her reduction in basic monetary growth
rates with a reduction in government taxing and spending'.
American criticism became more muted in 1982, when the
Reagan administration ran into much greater economic
problems of its own as the Federal Budget deficit soared.

Most comparisons between the Thatcher and Reagan records are misleading. Admittedly, there were similarities in the rhetoric used by Mrs Thatcher and President Reagan before they came to power; they both voiced their intention to reverse a generation of economic decline and to rein in public expenditure (apart from defence). Yet the differences have been more significant. The Thatcher administration has never accepted the supply-side theories advocated by some Republicans and American economists such as Arthur Laffer. When he was Chancellor of the Exchequer Sir Geoffrey Howe fully endorsed the importance of reducing marginal rates of tax to improve incentives. But he never believed that large cuts in personal taxation would stimulate the output or supply side of the economy sufficiently rapidly to raise tax revenues and so offset any initial rise in public borrowing. The British view has been rooted in a traditional idea of sound finance, as its critics have lamented. This has been that personal tax cuts should accompany, but should not anticipate, reductions in public expenditure and should therefore not raise public borrowing.

Differences of tradition and style have also existed between the Republican Party in the USA and the Conservatives in Britain. For instance, while Mrs Thatcher's speeches have a large moral content, issues such as abortion and religious education have not become official party policy. There has been no Moral Majority in British politics, and British MPs have not been eagerly displaying their credentials as 'Born Again' Christians.

Domestic Interpretations of Thatcherism

In Britain Mrs Thatcher's approach has posed a challenge to all shades of opinion and has led to widely differing interpretations. It has been impossible for anyone to remain neutral. Mrs Thatcher's 'conviction' approach has forced, and has been intended to force, a response. There has been a tendency, particularly on the left, to make Thatcherism seem more clear-cut than it is — to devise an ideology from what is in practice a series of values and instincts and a political alliance. Both opponents and supporters of the Thatcher administration have created more of a pattern from disconnected events and policies than is warranted. Yet their responses do help to define the nature of the Thatcher administration.

The supporters of the Thatcher administration regarded its election in 1979 as a new beginning, an end to the period of retreat and the steady encroachment of state power. Mrs Thatcher was the focus of the expectations of a wide variety of groups — academic monetarists, advocates of a free-market approach, fervent tax-cutters, enemies of the public sector, lobbyists for public money for the police, the armed forces and parts of private industry. In some respects the aims of these discrete groups overlap. Monetarists, for example, tend to favour an extension of the market approach. But some of the aims conflict. Calls for higher expenditure on particular projects are generally incompatible with a desire to reduce expenditure in total.

The hopes of these groups have so far been only partially satisfied, as was reflected in the title of a symposium of essays by economists, *Could Do Better* (1982). Professor Harold Rose of the London Business School, who is also group economic adviser to Barclays Bank, argued that 'the crucial weakness of the Tory Government's venture is that what was rightly intended to be a radical economic policy has been accompanied by an excessively cautious political strategy.' He cited, in particular, the Government's slowness in changing both trade union law and methods of financing the welfare state. Other free-market economists have attacked the Government's failure to curb the rise in public spending sufficiently. Business organizations such as the Confederation of British Industry have at times been critical about the impact of the Government's strategy upon manufacturing industry, but the Institute of Directors, which has close links with the Thatcherite hierarchy, has been supportive, apart from urging more zeal.

According to its more committed supporters, the Thatcher administration has not yet transformed the British economy and society, though it is travelling along the right road. Indeed, the verdict cannot be other, with the public sector still as large as before and only partial and controversial signs of a turn-round in the economy.

The response of the Tory critics, the upholders of the party's traditional approach, has been confused. There has been considerable private concern, occasional limited public rebellion and expressions of doubt but, in general, acquiescence — acceptance of office when it has been offered. Mrs Thatcher has taken the wind out of her critics' sails by having the initiative and through her obvious rapport with the party's rank and file. Rebellion has appeared futile, especially as the few 'wets' in the Cabinet have generally been ineffectual. So the approach of doubters has been to sound warnings on particular symbolic issues of the moment. Many of them have believed that Thatcherism is an aberration from the party's non-ideological traditions and that there will be changes as a result of the eventual reassertion of pressures towards the middle ground.

A complementary view has attempted to reassure: 'Do not listen to the rhetoric. Watch what we do and spend.' This case has been put particularly by ministerial 'wets', partly as a justification for their involvement in the Thatcher administration. For them the Government's practice has been more in line with Tory traditions than has its rhetoric. That in essence is what Peter Walker was saying when, as Minister of Agriculture, he pointed to his extensive interventionist policies in agriculture. The same approach has been implicit in Kenneth Baker's work as Minister for Information Technology in supporting a whole range of 'new' industries.

For those outside the Conservative tribe Thatcherism has appeared to be a bogey. The biggest shock has been for the centrist establishment — the world of senior civil servants, lawyers, top bankers, university lecturers and pundits. These have recoiled from the style as well as the content of Thatcherism, from its deliberate rejection of the consensus cherished by so many of them. Their doubts have been reinforced by Mrs Thatcher's own evident dislike for the institutions in which many of them work — the Foreign Office, the BBC and the Bank of England. The establishment has been accustomed to Governments coming into office with ambitious and what it considers to be ill thought out plans. But normally these have been modified after a couple of years — generally following an economic crisis of some kind — and there has then been a move back to the centre. This shift has not happened with the Thatcher administration, which has left the old establishment bewildered.

The classic expression of establishment dissatisfaction is the Social Democratic Party. The formation of the SDP may have been primarily a reaction to changes within the Labour Party. But the extent of its initial support from dons, lawyers, retired civil servants and the more avant-garde type of businessman suggests that the SDP also represents a revolt by part of the establishment against Thatcherism, a rejection of the polarization of British politics. These people have attacked Thatcherism as freely as those on the left. Many remain attached to the post-war 'settlement' and have been concerned particularly about the Government's alleged fatalistic claim that nothing can be done about unemployment. Significantly, Dr David Owen, the SDP leader since June 1983, was one of the first non-Conservative politicians to recognize that Mrs Thatcher had struck a popular note and changed the terms of the political debate.

The trade unions and the Labour Party have been left largely stranded by the advance of Thatcherism. Their response has been a mixture of anger and incomprehension. Official statements have spluttered with frustration, reflecting both impotence in the face of rising unemployment and the unions' succession of defeats in the vast majority of industrial disputes since 1979. For many in the Labour movement the argument has been that sooner or later voters would see through Thatcherism and would revolt against record unemployment, turning to the alternative of massive reflation. Yet the 1983 election exposed the weakness of that analysis and forced Labour politicians to recognize, in many cases reluctantly, that Mrs Thatcher had won the initiative in the economic argument.

Some of the most percipient insights into Thatcherism have come from Marxists and others on the intellectual left, especially in periodicals such as *Marxism Today* and *New Socialist*. The analyses of Eric Hobsbawm, Stuart Hall and Andrew Gamble (brought together in Hall and Jacques, 1983) have underlined how Mrs Thatcher has changed the ground rules of British politics by highlighting the potential of the populist radical right in the face of a demoralized and divided left. Andrew Gamble has argued that 'unless Labour can recapture the "popular" from Thatcherism, it will remain on the defensive, ideologically and politically, and threatened by decline into a permanent minority position' (Gamble, 1983a). Since the 1983 election Andrew Gamble has said that the result means that 'the New Right has won the battle to shape the new consensus on how to respond to the recession. The new agenda of public policy will reflect their priorities, and the opposition parties will be pulled along in their wake' (Gamble, 1983b).

These Marxist commentators have conferred on Thatcherism greater coherence and consistency than it has had in practice. Many of the actions taken since 1979 — ranging from the increased aid to British Steel to the tighter Whitehall controls on local authorities — were much more a response to the failure of earlier policies and to short-term pressures than the implementation of a carefully worked out blueprint. This accounted for many of the discrepancies between the Conservatives' election manifesto of 1979 and what they did over the next four years.

Moreover, the manifesto for the 1983 election was notably short of specific commitments. It was no mandate for reconstructing the welfare state. The Thatcher administration's critics said this was election window-dressing. They pointed to alleged secret manifestos — to the Think Tank and Treasury papers on the public expenditure and taxation implications of maintaining current welfare services leaked in late summer 1982 and to ideas, considered by the Family Policy Group of senior Ministers, for strengthening individual, as opposed to collective, responsibility. But several of these suggestions have already been rejected, and there is no sign yet that there is the political will to implement such far-reaching changes.

The preferred Conservative tactic seems to be almost Fabian: the inevitability of gradualness, with, for instance, a trade union Bill every two years. All this could, of course, add up to major changes over time. Left-wing commentators such as Gamble (1983b) have argued that the Thatcher administration is consciously undermining the institutions on which the political strength of the Labour movement rests by limiting rate increases sought by Labour-controlled councils, by proposing the abolition of Labour-run metropolitan authorities, by reducing the number of council tenants, by privatizing major nationalized industries as well as major public-sector services, and by reforming the internal procedures of trade unions. Apart from the major electoral impact of the sale of council houses (a masterly political move), none of these actions has yet permanently undermined the Labour movement's base, though they might do so over time if the proposals are now implemented.

Thatcherism has so far meant primarily bold rhetoric, a new style and a determination to persist with a difficult economic policy. It has not yet meant a shift in the frontiers of the public sector or changes in the welfare state comparable with those of the late 1940s. The terms of the political debate may have been changed, but Britain's economy and society have not yet altered course.

2

Preparing for Power

What we need now is a far greater degree of personal responsibility and decision, far more independence from the government and a comparative reduction in the role of government.

Mrs Margaret Thatcher
Conservative Political Centre lecture
October 1968

It was only in April 1974 that I was converted to Conservatism. I had thought I was a Conservative but I now see that I was not one at all.

Sir Keith Joseph
Reversing the Trend, *1975*

The Leadership Election

Mrs Thatcher became leader of the Conservative Party in February 1975 principally because she was not Edward Heath, not because of a widespread commitment to her views. She was the only serious candidate willing to challenge Mr Heath at a time when the majority of Tory MPs wanted a change.

Yet Mrs Thatcher and her allies were determined to set the Conservative Party on a new course. She had a distinctive set of political values which were consciously different from the post-war consensus of state intervention and collective provision. Her victory coincided with, and stimulated, a reappraisal of Conservative principles and policies. But her actions in Opposition were more cautious and conciliatory than her rhetoric. There was a continuing contrast between the 'conviction' politician and the shrewd tactician, which was reflected in the continuities with past policies and the avoidance of too many ambitious commitments in the Conservatives' 1979 election manifesto.

The Conservative Party had been shell-shocked after the two election defeats of February and October 1974. Not surprisingly, these prompted a good deal of introspection, both about the political direction of the party and about the position of Edward Heath as leader. Something had clearly gone seriously wrong. To many MPs the Heath administration had been a failure. Apart from taking the UK into the EEC, it appeared at the time to have succeeded in little else; its period in office had been marked by a series of major changes of policy or U-turns. Moreover, the administration had left office in humiliating circumstances, with its authority shattered.

The pressures for change intensified after the October 1974 defeat, when there was the prospect of a fairly lengthy period in Opposition. Mr Heath had already alienated many MPs by his high-handed approach, and his failure to win power made him seem an electoral liability. The question of replacement turned not on whether but on how and who.

The existing rules for the election of a Conservative leader did not provide for a re-election procedure, but Mr Heath agreed to a review of the rules following a messy confrontation with the officers of the backbench 1922 Committee. The review proposed that there should be an annual election of the leader; that to be elected on the first ballot a candidate should have not only an overall majority but also a lead over the runner-up equal to 15 per cent of the number of MPs eligible to vote; and, most significant, that further candidates could enter the contest on the second ballot if the first were not decisive. This was seen as creating a considerable initial hurdle for Mr Heath.

The line-up of candidates was completely unexpected. Close colleagues of Mr Heath, such as Willie Whitelaw and James Prior, had ruled themselves out as long as he was determined to remain leader. This left Sir Keith Joseph who, even before the October 1974 election, had signalled his misgivings about the Heath administration, during which he had headed the Department of Health and Social Security. Sir Keith delivered a series of speeches expressing his regrets both about his own actions and about those of the administration as a whole. Enoch Powell commented on Sir Keith's recantation, 'I have heard of deathbed repentance. Perhaps it would be more appropriate to refer to post-mortem repentance.' Sir Keith was never, however, a likely successor. A shy, sensitive and self-doubting man, he appeared to have insufficient steel or political skill. His real role was to open up the policy debate. Indeed, Sir Keith quickly eliminated himself as candidate for the post of leader in October 1974, shortly after the general election, after a row about a speech that he had given in Birmingham in which he referred to a threat to the 'human stock' because of the higher birthrate among poorer families and parents of low intelligence.

Sir Keith soon put his backing behind Mrs Thatcher. She was the only former member of the Heath Cabinet who had drawn close to him and had supported his analysis after the February 1974 election. She emerged as the main challenger once Mr Edward du Cann, the chairman of the 1922 Committee, made it known that he was not interested for personal and business reasons.

Mrs Thatcher's appeal rested primarily on the fact that she presented a clear-cut alternative to Mr Heath. MPs campaigning on her behalf said that she would return to the party's first principles, would listen more closely to her followers and would be aggressive. She was helped by an impressive performance during the debates on the Finance Bill during the winter of 1974–5 — benefiting, ironically, in the same way as Mr Heath had when leading the opposition to the 1965 Finance Bill.

Mrs Thatcher won by a large margin on the first ballot, having forced Mr Heath's withdrawal after the first round. Her victory was a case of 'who dares wins' rather than the result of an upsurge of positive enthusiasm for her. Opinion polls quoted by Professor Anthony King (in Penniman, 1981) showed that while most voters believed that Mr Heath should resign as leader, Willie Whitelaw was clearly preferred as his successor. Mrs Thatcher never attracted the support of even a significant minority of those questioned.

Changes in the Intellectual Climate

The election of Mrs Thatcher turned out to represent much more than a rejection of Mr Heath. It marked a change in style and the start of a battle of ideas. Mrs Thatcher, Sir Keith and their sympathizers wanted to alter the whole climate of politics. Looking back from the peak (or trough) of 1980, David Howell, then a member of Mrs Thatcher's Cabinet, commented:

> Some time in the mid-seventies, amidst the grandiose absurdities of incomes policies and industrial strategies, it began to be seen by the Tory Party that policies built on this static view of society, with its so-called social partners, its stratified corporate rituals and its odd vocabulary so alien from everyday living, just would not do. (Quoted in Norton and Aughey, 1981)

Mr Howell was, ironically, one of those most closely associated with Mr Heath's managerial approach.

From the mid-1970s onwards the views of what became known as the New Right assumed prominence in intellectual debate and were associated with Mrs Thatcher and her allies. It was the heyday of the counter-attack against collectivism. Economists such as Hayek and Friedman were the new prophets. In the contest of ideas the Conservative Party appeared to be making the running and could no longer be called the stupid party, as was highlighted by the enthusiastic involvement of converts from the centre/left such as Hugh Thomas and Max Beloff (both later made life peers) and Paul Johnson.

Sir Keith Joseph's role was to interpret the New Right and to set the intellectual tone. This was partly achieved by his formation, with the support of Mrs Thatcher, of the Centre for Policy Studies. Sir Keith argued that the Conservative Party had been seduced into error over the previous thirty years by compromising too much with socialism. He drew a distinction between the middle ground, a mid-point between the two main parties, and the common ground, the area on which most voters agreed. He said that in pursuing the illusory middle ground, Conservatives had been drawn into accepting the collectivist policies of previous Labour administrations as a new consensus, so, in a ratchet-like way, Conservative policies had gradually been driven away from the market approach. He also attacked the pursuit of equality as a goal, since it sapped a sense of responsibility.

Sir Keith urged instead an unapologetic reassertion of the virtues of capitalism, the profit motive and the entrepreneurial spirit. The need, he said, was to recreate the conditions for the 'forward march of embourgeoisement which went so far in Victorian times'. Monetarism fitted in as the 'pre-essential for everything else we need and want to do' (these and later quotations from his Preston speech, September 1974). His starting point was the Heath Government's concern with the notion of full employment, which, he said, involved a false reading of the true extent of voluntary unemployment. This had prompted the Heath administration to try to spend its way out of unemployment, a course of action which had only a short-lived impact on the level of unemployment but a permanent effect on the increased stimulation of inflation.

Moreover, Sir Keith argued, in conditions of excess demand, inflationary tensions could not be cured by incomes policy. He said: 'Incomes policy alone as a way to abate inflation caused by excessive money supply is like trying to stop water coming out of a leaky hose without turning off the tap; if you stop one hole, it will find two others.' The answer lay in sound money. 'The next Government should adopt a broad but gradualist strategy to phase out excess demand — and stick to it, refusing to be stampeded.' This, he said, would involve moderating the trend rate of growth of the money supply and the budget deficit, so that after a lag, perhaps of three or four years, the rate of inflation would start to ease. But a great deal would depend on the attitude of the trade unions.

Monetarism alone would not be enough, however. Speaking

at the London Business School in January 1976, Sir Keith said that unless state expenditure was cut, restriction of the money supply would 'strangulate the private sector and precipitate recession'. (This turned out to be a prophetic comment on the problems faced in 1979–81.) Sir Keith argued that without such a contraction of the state, there would be no scope for tax reductions and the restoration of incentives to produce 'the climate for entrepreneurship and risk-taking that will alone secure prosperity, high employment and economic health'.

These lengthy extracts from Sir Keith's speeches show that by the mid-1970s all the key beliefs were present which guided the Thatcher Government after 1979. Many of the campaign arguments of the 1983 election could have been drawn directly from Sir Keith's Preston speech nearly nine years earlier. His thesis was a distillation of the work of several New Right writers. Indeed, Sir Keith circulated a reading list of many of their works, as well as some of his own, among his civil servants at the Department of Industry when he became Secretary of State in May 1979.

The New Right is not a monolithic group. As Nicholas Bosanquet (1983) has argued, there have been differences in the emphasis that has been placed by its adherents on the role of the state and on the scope for macroeconomic management. But there are some common themes. Bosanquet has suggested a thesis and an antithesis. The former is represented by the New Right thinkers' belief in society's natural tendency to order and the economy's to grow, inequality as the inevitable and tolerable result of freedom, and the centrality of the capitalist entrepreneur as the guarantor of growth. As the antithesis, the New Right has highlighted the pressures in democracy towards centralization, the concern of politicians with buying votes and the power of interest groups opposed to the market, rising public expenditure, the failure of the welfare state, the pressures for bureaucracy, and the failings of trade unions.

These arguments were made known to a wider public in Britain mainly through the publications of the Institute of Economic Affairs, a market-oriented research body formed in 1957. One of its most distinctive contributions has been the work on the welfare state of its two leading lights, Lord Harris and Arthur Seldon. Their case has been that state-financed monopoly services are not related to the true preferences of consumers and tend towards inefficiency, inflexibility and bureaucracy. Harris and Seldon have urged the ending of the public monopoly in the provision of welfare and educational services, the encouragement of competing supplies and the introduction of direct charging for certain health services and of educational vouchers for schools. They have backed their case with a series of public-opinion surveys. These have indicated a distinct switch away from support for the present system of the welfare state towards the option of contracting out. As they have argued (Harris and Seldon, 1979), the percentage expressing a readiness to pay for a choice of services rose sharply between 1965 and 1978, though there have tended to be ambiguities in all such surveys. The change in the intellectual climate was revealed in 1981 when the Institute published a symposium of essays entitled *The Emerging Consensus...?*

The impact of these ideas was reinforced by a more general questioning of the past-war 'settlement' during the late 1970s. There were doubts about the scope of government and the power of trade unions, underlined by the inflationary upsurge in 1974—5. Books appeared with such titles as *Why is Britain Becoming Harder to Govern?* (1976), *The Future that Doesn't Work* (1977) and *Can Government Go Bankrupt?* (1979). The public debate was also influenced by the broadly monetarist (though certainly not Conservative) views expressed in the weekly columns of Samuel Brittan in the *Financial Times* and of Peter Jay in *The Times*.

Conservative Party thinking at the time was heavily influenced by a series of newspaper articles and a book, *Britain's Economic Problem: Too Few Producers* (1976), by two Oxford economists, Robert Bacon and Walter Eltis. They argued that a growing shift of Britain's resources from the production of marketed goods and services to unmarketed goods would reduce investment, employment and the growth rate while stimulating inflation and obstructive union behaviour. This view complemented work undertaken by Adam Ridley, the head of the economic section of the Conservative

Research Department and a former Treasury and Think Tank official. He argued that the growth of the public sector and the consequent rise in the proportion of take-home pay going in taxes had pushed up wage demands and inflation.

This thesis was strongly contested by other economists, who argued that the chain of causation might be the reverse — that is, that the weaknesses of the productive sector had in part stimulated the growth of the public sector. Moreover, the share of total national income absorbed by public expenditure and taxation in Britain was in the middle of the international range. Some critics argued that the public sector should be the engine of economic recovery, a view that opposed Conservative theory and much of Labour practice after 1975.

The doubts were not confined merely to commentators and Conservative politicians. In a speech in January 1976 Roy Jenkins, then Home Secretary, questioned whether the recent growth in public expenditure had reached a point at which it was possible to 'maintain the values of a plural society with adequate freedom of choice'.

This debate was matched by what the Labour Government was itself doing. A series of reviews produced cuts in public expenditure or, at any rate, in future planned levels of spending. After the breakdown of the economic consensus in 1973—4, under the impact of the oil-price shock and the acceleration of inflation, there was also a drift to monetarism. This was enshrined in Britain's letter of intent as part of the International Monetary Fund loan of December 1976 and in the announcement of formal monetary targets. Admittedly, monetarism as practised by Denis Healey when Chancellor was of an idiosyncratic kind. It was one element of a tripod which also included incomes policy and a modified version of the earlier demand-management approach. But City and other commentators looked with favour on Mr Healey's performance, particularly between summer 1976 and spring 1978.

Approaches to Policy-Making

Mrs Thatcher began her review of Conservative policies against this background of intellectual debate and policy

changes. Her approach, which was a combination of provocative rhetoric and cautious practice, was dictated both by
circumstances and by her instinct. A majority of the Shadow
Cabinet almost certainly did not vote for her in the leadership election, but she dropped only two prominent Heath
supporters — Robert Carr and Peter Walker — and there were
strong links with the party's traditional approach in the
persons of Mr Whitelaw, Mr Prior, Lord Carrington and
Sir Ian Gilmour.

Her instinct was not to make too many new commitments.
She believed that Edward Heath had adopted too rigid a
programme, with too many promises, in Opposition before
1970. What was needed, according to Mrs Thatcher, was
the formulation of a distinctive philosophy and of fresh
policies with which to deal with all the unexpected problems
of power.

There were obvious similarities between Mrs Thatcher's
period as Opposition leader between 1975 and 1979 and
Mr Heath's from 1965 to 1970. The 1979 election manifesto
contained many pledges like those in 1970 — promises to
cut public spending and income tax, to end nationalization,
to restrict immigration and to raise defence spending. But
all Conservative manifestos of the past twenty years have
contained such commitments.

More significant were the differences. Mr Heath was
interested in techniques for modernizing Britain — in improving the performance of the economy and in institutional
reforms (for example, in the machinery and structure of
central and local government). Detailed policies were made
public in Opposition, particularly those associated with tax
reform and industrial relations, in an attempt to build up
the image of a credible alternative Government. In contrast,
Mrs Thatcher was more concerned with principles and
doubted the usefulness of institutional changes. Her views
coincided with a more widespread scepticism about what
Government itself could do to deal with problems. Her
priority was the reassertion of the principles of Conservatism.

Mrs Thatcher did not, however, avoid controversy. Like
Mr Heath a decade earlier, she and her Shadow team were
criticized for being ineffectual in attacking the Government,

the perpetual cry against all Oppositions. She was also accused of occasionally producing policy off the cuff — for example, her suggested use of a referendum in serious strikes. Her attempts to become better-known did not always work. There were stories of her lecturing groups of businessmen; a dinner at the Bank of England was particularly frosty. Her immediate circle was also criticized for being too tendentious and lightweight.

The main internal criticisms were related to the increasing stress on monetarism. In May 1976 Peter Walker questioned the overwhelming emphasis upon monetary policy, while Edward Heath remained in favour of an incomes policy and in 1979 argued that 'to rely solely on monetary policy to solve these problems [of inflation] could work only in a closed society'. Sir Ian Gilmour warned in *Inside Right* (1977) against too dogmatic a commitment to an abstract theory such as monetarism, which might entail deserting the party's broader and more flexible traditions.

The divisions should not be exaggerated, however; they were mainly below the surface. Indeed, one of the few open challenges came from among Mrs Thatcher's normal supporters when, in the autumn of 1978, there was an unsuccessful attempt to rally the party against the continuation of Rhodesian sanctions. Fortunately for Mrs Thatcher, there was no substantial group of Heath loyalists. Mr Heath was increasingly isolated from his former supporters. He was regarded as a bitter and bad loser, in contrast to Lord Home, who had offered him loyal support after resigning the leadership in 1965.

The differences were more of mood and style. Professor Anthony King (in Penniman, 1981) listed distinctions between economists and politicians, hawks and doves, and his own preference, ideologues and pragmatists. Robert Behrens (1980) has suggested the labels 'diehards', for those rejecting the post-war consensus as a deviation from the principles of limited Government, and 'ditchers', for those prepared to make accommodations and to accept the necessity of an interventionist approach. None of these labels caught on, and it was not until after 1979 that the terms 'wet' and 'dry' became commonly accepted in the political world. But in practice leading Conservatives knew on which side they and others were.

In general, unity was maintained. The autumn 1976 policy statement, *The Right Approach*, won general support after some skilful drafting. Similarly, a year later *The Right Approach to the Economy* combined the traditional Conservative theme of boosting enterprise with a commitment to strict monetary control. The authors were Sir Geoffrey Howe, Sir Keith Joseph, James Prior and David Howell, with Sir Angus Maude as editor. It proved possible to compromise over differences of emphasis on incomes policy and industrial relations in view of the agreement on most points.

Policies were decided by the leadership, though Mrs Thatcher consulted widely, especially among backbench MPs. At one stage there were over sixty policy groups, whose work was formally channelled through the Advisory Committee on Policy, chaired by Sir Keith Joseph. In practice, decisions were taken by a small group of members of the Shadow Cabinet, led by Sir Keith. The Centre for Policy Studies played a maverick role in this process and had rather strained and distant relations with the Conservative Research Department under Chris Patten. The Centre's stated task was anyway in theory a longer-term one; its brief was to step back from everyday events and to change the climate of opinion. Its influence was probably brought to bear more on the broad agenda of discussion than on detailed policies.

With respect to specific policies the initiative came much less from Mrs Thatcher and Sir Keith than from the various spokesmen. Mrs Thatcher was chiefly the interpreter of Conservative principles, while Sir Keith's contribution was to herald the change of direction in the intellectual climate. Many of the key proposals in the 1979 manifesto came from the economic reconstruction group under Sir Geoffrey Howe.

Sir Geoffrey's focus then, as it has remained with remarkable consistency since, was the need for sustained explanation and dialogue to secure widespread support for monetary discipline. His reconstruction group included the main spokesmen on economic and industrial affairs, and other major influences were Professor Brian Griffiths from the

City University, stockbrokers like Peter Lilley and Gordon Pepper (both from W. Greenwell and Co.) and the economic work of the London Business School under Professor Terry Burns, later to be the Government's chief economic adviser.

Public Expenditure and Counter-Inflation Policy

The Conservatives' work in Opposition, much of which never appeared publicly, concentrated in particular on the control of public expenditure. The review was among the most comprehensive ever undertaken by a party in Opposition. One step was to look qualitatively at the way in which spending was controlled, via proposals for cash limits (adopted by Labour in 1976) and for improving efficiency and eliminating waste. But most significant was the Shadow expenditure review conducted by a group under Nigel Lawson, then a Treasury spokesman, to mirror the annual exercise in Whitehall. Bilateral discussions were undertaken with the spokesmen shadowing spending departments. The aim was to identify options for expenditure savings and to set down suggested totals for particular departments. This exercise was supposed to be consistent with returning, as nearly as possible, to the real (inflation-adjusted) total of spending in 1977–8.

The hope of the Conservative Treasury spokesmen was that it would be easier to negotiate with Shadows than with Ministers backed by Civil Service briefs. But the process was not always smooth, since some were reluctant to make commitments before taking office. However, the Shadow spokesmen had to obtain Sir Geoffrey's approval before announcing new commitments, in the hope of limiting the number of pledges in the manifesto. Nevertheless, there were commitments to increases in expenditure on defence and on law and order. The main targets for cuts were the industry and employment budgets, housing subsidies and financial transfers.

The policies for reducing inflation reflected Sir Geoffrey's preference for persuasion and education. The framework was to be set by the published target of a steady reduction in the rate of growth of the money supply and a parallel steady reduction in the size of public-sector borrowing and in the public sector's share of the national income. The sensitive question was what to do about pay after the problems of 1970–1. It was accepted that monetary policy alone would not be enough and that the Government had to have some view, not least in the public sector. There was, however, general scepticism among Conservative policy-makers about setting general targets or norms for pay bargaining.

Drawing from the West German experience of 'concerted action', Sir Geoffrey stressed the importance of securing in industry the widest possible understanding of monetary policy and its implications for employment. As part of the proposed 'open budgeting', Sir Geoffrey argued for some kind of forum in which the major participants in the economy could sit down together. He suggested the National Economic Development Council as the most appropriate body, including a representative from the Bank of England. An extended role for Parliament in such discussions was also envisaged.

Public-sector pay posed the trickiest problems. In a speech to the Bow Group Economic Standing Committee in May 1976, Sir Geoffrey said:

> In the nationalized industries the main discipline should come from the imposition of strict cash limits on any funds available from the Exchequer and from the enforcement of strict commercial targets. But in the directly employed public sector we also stand in need of some more coherent bargaining arrangement than the series of ad hoc solutions.

These were fine-sounding aspirations, but in practice until the election the emphasis in public statements was principally on cash limits, with managers and unions being left to balance jobs and pay rises within these figures. But this view left unresolved many of the practical problems posed by the strength of public-sector unions and the nature of the pay round.

The so-called enterprise package of measures designed to stimulate business expansion and to provide personal incentives was of a familiar Conservative kind. There were proposals to lower income tax at all levels, financed in part by an unspecified transfer to indirect taxes such as Value Added Tax; to reform capital taxation; to encourage wider ownership and capital accumulation; and to reduce regulations.

Sir Geoffrey added his idiosyncratic flavour to the package with a suggestion — made in a speech on the Isle of Dogs in the East End of London in June 1978 — of enterprise zones to help the worst affected urban areas. The idea was to set up test areas which could be developed with as much freedom as possible. He suggested that the key features of these zones might be the removal of detailed planning controls apart from a basic minimum, freedom from rent controls, possible partial exemption from rates, a guarantee to businesses of no changes to tax laws to their disadvantage and the absence of state grants in the area. Sir Geoffrey said it was worth taking some risks to create 'an environment that is positively hospitable and inviting to enterprise'.

In retrospect, a surprising feature of the Conservatives' economic policy statements is the limited amount of discussion of the exchange rate. Admittedly, the issue was not ignored. In a speech to the Oxford University Business Summer School in July 1977, Sir Geoffrey suggested that one way of using North Sea oil would be to initiate a 'virtuous spiral' of declining inflation 'by allowing the pound to strengthen, thus moderating domestic cost increases, reducing the rate of inflation, in turn further strengthening the exchange rate and so on'. He noted that if the pound rose too much, 'we could risk destroying all the trade benefit of our oil revenues by pricing our other export and import competing industries out of their markets.' If there were any signs of such an excessive appreciation relative to domestic costs, Sir Geoffrey said, 'it would probably be appropriate to begin relaxing exchange controls.' This turned out to be an over-optimistic assessment of the extent of exchange rate pressures, but it was one of the few detailed discussions of the issue.

Industrial Policy

The dominant feature of Conservative industrial policy in Opposition was its absence. There was certainly plenty of discussion about what to do about regenerating business, but there was a conscious attempt, encouraged particularly by Sir Keith Joseph, to avoid any suggestion of an industrial strategy like that of the Labour Government. The emphasis was on the enterprise package and the removal of regulations. Yet the Conservatives still faced the problem of what to do with existing state support for ailing private-sector companies and for nationalized industries. The approach was negative, reining back state agencies such as the National Enterprise Board and repealing interventionist legislation such as the planning agreement provisions of the 1975 Industry Act.

The statements became increasingly cautious as the general election approached, particularly under the influence of James Prior, who talked of the need for 'some form of casualty clearing station'. Similarly, both Mrs Thatcher and Mr Prior pledged during the election campaign to continue helping the BL motor group and to back Sir Michael Edwardes, its chairman, in his efforts to turn the company round.

There was considerable discussion in Opposition about what to do with nationalized industries, but there were few public commitments. A study group was set up under Nicholas Ridley, Financial Secretary to the Treasury after 1981. In a speech to the Selsdon Group in October 1982, he pointed out that five years earlier *The Right Approach to the Economy* had noted: 'The long-term aim must be to reduce the preponderance of state ownership and to widen the base of ownership in our community. Ownership by the state is not the same as ownership by the people.' But that was about the only public reference before 1979 to what became known as 'privatization'.

The 1979 election manifesto referred to the sale back to the private sector of the recently nationalized aerospace and shipbuilding concerns, together with the aims of selling shares in the National Freight Corporation and of disposing of the National Enterprise Board's shareholdings. But there was little hint of the scale of activity which developed after 1979. The issue was discussed, but there does not appear to have been a clear view of the potential. There was also acute political sensitivity over possible accusations about the sale of public assets, especially the British National Oil Corporation (BNOC). This involved Lord Carrington and Tom King, the Shadow Energy spokesman. A commitment to sell off BNOC was opposed on the grounds that it would be wrong to dispose of such a valuable asset, given both British strategic interests in safeguarding oil supplies and legal problems over participation agreements. The result was that the manifesto referred merely to a 'complete review of all activities of BNOC'.

Industrial Relations

After the 1974 débâcle the Conservative leadership faced particular problems over industrial relations. The issue of how a Conservative Government would get on with the unions was often raised. The generally accepted conclusion was that the Conservatives should not attempt major across-the-board legislation, though there were differences of opinion about the extent and rate of change. James Prior, the party's employment spokesman, said in February 1979 that there should be 'a recognition that the law has a part to play in industrial relations, but there is a need to ensure widespread public support for such legislation'. A month later he affirmed that 'the greatest challenge facing the Conservative Party is to demonstrate that it has undergone an education in political thought so that it can recapture its traditional trade union vote'.

The debate turned in part on how the Tories were to respond to the legislation introduced by the Labour Government, which both repealed the laws passed by the Heath administration and extended the favoured position of trade unions. The Conservatives' reaction was generally cautious, promising a return to the 1974 position on the closed shop and picketing but favouring ambiguity in other respects (for example, over the issue of unfair dismissal). In general,

James Prior wanted to avoid outright confrontation and to win the consent of union leaders to a series of limited measures to deal with the specific problems of industrial relations.

In 1977 *The Right Approach to the Economy* recognized that a simple attempt to ban closed shops would not work. Consequently, it proposed that such agreements should be made only with the consent of a majority of all the people involved, via a secret ballot, and that people should not be forced to join a union against their will. The emphasis was on voluntary agreement with a code of practice and legislation as a back-stop. This pledge hardened during the 1978–9 'winter of discontent'. The Conservatives' general view was that picketing rights should be limited to those in dispute at their own place of work. There was also a promise to change the law on the payment of social security benefits to the families of strikers.

Objections to the gradualist approach of James Prior surfaced several times before 1979 and included, ironically, criticism from Norman Tebbit, his successor as Employment Secretary in September 1981. Differences arose over the closed shop and the Grunwick affair. The key points of disagreement were union recognition and the position of the Advisory, Conciliation and Arbitration Service. Sir Keith Joseph strongly attacked the report of the Grunwick court of inquiry under Lord Scarman, arguing that the recommended reinstatement of the sacked workers at Grunwick was giving in too much to law-breakers. Mr Prior, on the other hand, broadly favoured a solution based on the Scarman report. Their public dispute, and the support of a vocal section of the Conservative Party for Sir Keith's views, underlined the tensions in the party.

Whatever her personal feelings, Mrs Thatcher supported a pragmatic approach and, in general, backed Mr Prior's line. In any event, the bitterness of the 'winter of discontent' and the breakdown of the Labour Government's relations with the unions took some of the pressure off the Tories. Their response was to propose legislation for postal ballots for union elections and strikes, for the withdrawal of the right to strike in public utilities and for changes in the law on the closed shop and on picketing.

Preparation of the Manifesto

There was a good deal of anguish inside the party on other issues, such as immigration and Scottish devolution. On immigration Mrs Thatcher had, for example, alarmed many of her colleagues by her remarks in January 1978 about popular fears that Britain might be 'swamped by people with a different culture'. She talked of keeping 'fundamental British characteristics' and appeared to hold out the prospect of a clear end to immigration. After lengthy discussions, Willie Whitelaw's official policy on immigration promised a new definition of citizenship, limitations on the rights of dependants to enter Britain and the setting up of a quota system to control all entrants for settlement. There was also considerable discussion of constitutional issues, with open splits within the Scottish Conservative Party over devolution. But many of the divisions had in practice narrowed after the referendum in March 1979, and it proved possible then to produce a policy line acceptable to most party leaders.

Many of the main policy issues had already been decided by the summer of 1978, and a draft manifesto was prepared in case there was an election in the autumn. It was written by Chris Patten and Adam Ridley and edited by Sir Angus Maude. The emphasis, in line with Mrs Thatcher's own, was on principles, with only a limited list of detailed proposals. The postponement of the election until after the winter prompted few changes by the time of the election in May 1979. Some promises were dropped, and, following the 'winter of discontent', there was greater emphasis on tough action against strikers. The manifesto represented a treaty that papered over differences of view about, for example, incomes policy, while also fulfilling its traditional role as a rallying cry to the party.

The events of the winter had made it easier for Conservatives to appeal for a change of direction in Britain. The collapse of authority and the evident paralysis of decision-making in Government underlined the Tories' message, which championed the rule of law and the need for a new beginning. After the defeat of the Labour Government in the Commons on 28 March, these themes dominated the ensuing campaign. The main new developments were the pledge to honour the awards of the Clegg Commission on public-sector pay (later bitterly regretted by some Conservative Ministers) and the prominence accorded to promises to sell council houses to sitting tenants and to cut income tax. Mrs Thatcher said that substantial cuts to be made in income tax in the first Budget would be 'a start, only a start'.

Labour vehemently attacked these Conservative promises. Party leaders questioned how cuts in income tax could be financed without a sharp rise in indirect taxes, which would push up the cost of living. During the campaign Tory spokesmen hedged on this issue and on how far prescriptions and other public-sector charges would be increased.

The 1979 Election

The result was a decisive win for Mrs Thatcher and the Conservatives, who gained a majority of forty-three over all other parties after the largest swing of votes from the other main party since 1945, particularly among young working-class men. Yet was this a watershed election? Did it mark as notable a turning point in the attitudes of voters as Mrs Thatcher's rhetoric claimed? The Nuffield study of the 1979 election (Butler and Kavanagh, 1980) suggested that the result might not prove to be a watershed, in the sense either of marking a fundamental shift among voters and the permanent balance of political parties or of overturning previously established ideas. The study argued that the events of 1979 offered a good example of a Government losing an election rather than an Opposition winning it. After all, the Conservative share of the vote (44 per cent) was the lowest for any post-war Government except that of 1974.

Moreover, there did not appear to have been a major change in public views on policy. Opposition to trade union power, nationalization and high taxation were not new developments. Labour was still preferred on the key issues of the cost of living and unemployment. But the Conservatives managed to have a greater advantage on the issues of taxation and law and order, while Labour was no longer seen as having a special ability to deal with industrial relations.

Professor Ivor Crewe (in Penniman, 1981, and elsewhere) and others have drawn attention to the growing divergence between the attitudes of Labour voters and the party's policies. A majority of those who identified with Labour in 1979 backed Conservative proposals for the trade unions, the sale of council houses and tax cuts, while support for nationalization and increased social expenditure had declined sharply since the 1960s.

This did not, however, confirm the Conservative argument that the 1979 election signalled a popular revolt against the post-war 'settlement'. The endorsement of voters seems to have been limited to a handful of obviously populist proposals on tax, crime and council house sales. There was little evidence of an upsurge in enthusiasm for the ideas of the New Right. Professor Crewe cited a poll conducted in May 1979 showing that 70 per cent of all voters (and 55 per cent of Conservative supporters) were in favour of retaining government services such as education and welfare, even if it meant that taxes could not be cut. Similarly, 79 per cent believed that government subsidies that were necessary to protect jobs were a good idea. This suggested a pragmatic attitude, not a fundamental ideological shift.

The test for Mrs Thatcher was whether she could turn the big swing in votes, especially among skilled workers, into more permanent support. Whatever happened subsequently, particularly during the year that elapsed between the Falklands war and the landslide election victory of June 1983, there was evidence in May 1979 not of a deep popular commitment to the Conservatives' goals but simply of a belief that it was time for a change. None the less, the Conservatives came to power with an assured parliamentary majority and were faced with a demoralized Labour Party.

3

Thatcherism in Government

It must be a conviction Government. As Prime Minister I could not waste time having any internal arguments.

Mrs Margaret Thatcher
Interview in the Observer
25 February 1979

What attracted me to work for [Mrs Thatcher] was her absolute commitment, a slightly reckless feeling that she had to achieve real change even though it meant, as a politician, living very dangerously. She had a sort of mission-orientated approach, a taskforce-orientated approach.

Sir John Hoskyns
BBC interview
December 1982

No one can deny that in the last few years we have come close to abandoning our traditional approach to politics in favour of the belief that our job was to impose a certain type of economic analysis on the nation — to become a pressure group for a particular economic theory. Nothing should be further from the minds of Conservative leaders than such a task.

Changing Gear: What the Government Should Do Next
Proposals from a Group of Conservative MPs
September 1981

Most Governments lose momentum during their life. The Thatcher administration gained momentum during its first term. There were, of course, accommodations and compromises, but the Government was still full of ideas and vigour after its election victory in June 1983. The key was Mrs Thatcher herself — determined, impatient and never waivering. Thanks to her political skill and quite a lot of luck, she strengthened her control over her Cabinet. As a result, well before the 1983 election the critics, the 'wets', had been rebuffed and reduced largely to impotence. The crucial event was not the Falklands war, as is often supposed, but the debates in 1981 over economic policy and the Cabinet reshuffle of that September. It was then that Mrs Thatcher's ascendancy began to be established.

For all her promises to form a Cabinet of like-minded people, Mrs Thatcher's choices in May 1979 were cautious and traditional. She included almost all her previous Shadow Cabinet, which in turn had been largely inherited from Edward Heath, and from the backbenches she even brought in Peter Walker, the symbol of Heathite interventionism, as well as Lord Soames, the archetypical Tory patriarch. It was a Cabinet with a mixture of the old paternalist wing (Carrington, Soames, Whitelaw, Pym, Gilmour and Carlisle) plus the economic Thatcherites (Howe, Joseph, Nott and Howell). Significantly, the latter group was in the key economic departments, with the exception of James Prior at Employment. But most of the Cabinet did not keep Milton Friedman's works as their bedside reading.

Mrs Thatcher was justified in arguing that all the Ministers shared a general view about the need for a change of direction. As she said in an interview in the *Observer* in May 1983, 'We all wanted strong defence, more resources for law and order, lower taxation, more private enterprise, less government control. Aiming in that general direction, we were all conviction politicians.' The goals, at least as stated in these terms, were not the problem. The snag was how to work out priorities, how to reconcile apparently conflicting demands and how to respond to unforeseen events. As Mrs Thatcher admitted in that interview, 'On the details, how far we should aim to go, how quickly, of course, there were different views, and these were thrashed out in the Cabinet.' These were pretty fundamental details.

The Thatcher administration certainly began ambitiously.

Its programme for the first 1979–80 session contained proposals for legislating on picketing and the closed shop, for restructuring the National Enterprise Board's activities, for extending the rights of local authority and new town tenants to buy their own houses, for awarding the fourth television channel to the Independent Broadcasting Authority, for the amendment of the law on nationality and immigration and for the liberalization of regulations on long-distance coach routes. This was all sound pro-free enterprise stuff, to which virtually no one in the Conservative Party would object. However, these proposals came to be dwarfed by the problems of containing public expenditure and by the deepening recession. These difficulties confronted the Cabinet week after week from the end of 1979 onwards. First it would be one nationalized industry seeking an increase in its external finance limit to deal with the financial pressures caused by falling demand, and then another. And all the time Sir Keith Joseph would be wringing his hands over the dilemma.

Above all there was the annual public expenditure review, starting in the summer and reaching a climax in the decisions of October and November for the following financial year. Later chapters discuss the economic consequences of these debates, but politically they proved to be a severe test for the unity of the Cabinet and for the determination of Mrs Thatcher and Sir Geoffrey Howe, the Chancellor. The discussions were conducted in an atmosphere conducive to leaks, secret briefings and coded speeches that made frank debate impossible. Part of the problem was institutional. Spending Ministers were reluctant to cut their own budgets. Mark Carlisle was already fighting to defend education in the autumn of 1979, and Francis Pym was engaged increasingly in a fractious conflict with the Treasury during 1980. Moreover, as the recession deepened and unemployment rose, many Ministers were reluctant to agree to further financial stringency.

Confirmation of the Strategy

The pressures came to a head in 1981. The traditional view — as seen by many Opposition politicians and by many economists — was that the Government had to choose between maintaining a tight fiscal policy and reverting to the previous post-war response of expansion in face of the worsening economic outlook. There was never really a choice, however, since Mrs Thatcher and her associates were determined to avoid being accused of making a U-turn similar to that of the Heath administration. For them there was no alternative. So the real debate was narrower — whether to modify policy here and there, to give a higher priority to reducing unemployment than to fighting inflation. But even that was heresy and economic nonsense to the Thatcherites. After the protests of some of the 'wets' against the tough spring Budget in 1981 Mrs Thatcher attacked them. She 'wished they had more guts': 'What really gets me is that those who are most critical of the extra taxes are those who are most vociferous in demanding extra spending.' Mrs Thatcher's speech writers were at their most inventive as they applied their skills in order to put across the same message — 'The lady is not for turning' was one gem — and to a somewhat startled annual dinner of the Confederation of British Industry in June 1981, she quoted an American general from the First World War who said, 'Retreat? Hell, no, we've only just got here.' That was the kind of talk that delighted some and alarmed others.

Yet there were changes. Public spending rose well above planned levels; the nationalized industries got more money. All this was seized upon by some politicians and commentators as evidence of a series of U-turns, but more significant was how little altered. The priority was still to reduce inflation and to contain public-sector borrowing. The Government's monetarism might be battered and suspect to the purists, but the practice was a long way from what Keynes would ever have approved. It might be difficult to find much coherence in these events, but the broad strategic aims of Thatcherism remained the same.

Why did Mrs Thatcher win? The main reason was that the 'wets' were never clear about what they wanted to do, nor did they have the will to press their case. Their objection to the existing strategy was instinctive rather than ideological. They felt that there was something wrong with so clear-cut a theory as monetarism. To them no economic theory should be predominant. Politics matters more to traditional Tories, who are sceptical about all attempts to impose scientific rules. As the Tory MP authors of *Changing Gear* (the manifesto of the younger 'wets') wrote, 'One job of the Conservative Party is to protect our citizens from experiments by theorists whose beliefs can never be scientifically proved.'

Within this framework the 'wets' were never in a position to offer a cogent alternative to the strategy put forward by Mrs Thatcher and her colleagues. Almost by definition, they gave only a series of ad hoc responses. Moreover, as Mrs Thatcher's earlier quotations noted, they did not disagree with the need for a change of direction in policy. Their concern was about the pace of change. So their criticisms and suggestions seemed limp in the face of the certainty and confidence of the Thatcherites. Moderation was not a strong rallying cry.

The other weakness of the 'wets' was political. Indeed, it was sometimes difficult to define who the 'wets' were. Apart from the core of clear doubters in the Cabinet, such as James Prior, Peter Walker, Sir Ian Gilmour and Mark Carlisle, how did a loner like Francis Pym fit in, and what about the super-manager Michael Heseltine? Mr Pym urged flexibility but did not join in the cabals with Mr Prior and Mr Walker, while Mr Heseltine maintained a certain distance. Similarly, Lord Carrington deliberately did not involve himself in most issues of domestic politics as part of an unstated pact with Mrs Thatcher whereby she respected his judgement on foreign matters. The networks were too loose to be effective. At times it seemed as if Ministers did not talk to each other, and the 'wets' were successful only when allied with other members of the Cabinet.

This was evident on two occasions in 1981. The first was after Sir Geoffrey Howe told Ministers, on the eve of the Budget, of his tough measures involving a sharp increase in the tax burden. This was partly to offset the impact of the Cabinet's decision the previous November to agree to only half the cuts sought by the Treasury. Peter Walker, James Prior and Sir Ian Gilmour considered rebellion and even resignation. But they were taken by surprise and acquiesced.

The main result of this row was an agreement to hold regular Cabinet debates on the economic strategy. The other example of unity among the 'wets' came at the first of these debates and during the initial discussion of the public expenditure review in the summer of 1981. Then James Prior again repeated his pessimistic view of the state of the economy and was joined not only by Peter Walker and Michael Heseltine but also by the old paternalists such as Francis Pym and Lord Hailsham. Even John Biffen and Sir John Nott, previously regarded as strong Thatcherites, expressed scepticism about Treasury plans for further cuts in public spending. Lord Hailsham was reported as saying that there was now a choice between being 'a Hoover or a Roosevelt', and he knew which he would be. After considerable haggling the autumn decisions raised public expenditure £5 billion higher than it was intended to be in the original plans.

The rise had much more to do with inescapable upward pressures on expenditure exerted by the recession (increasing the deficits of nationalized industries and expenditure on unemployment) than a successful campaign by the 'wets'. In so far as Cabinet reservations during the summer discussions played a part, it was through the assertion of departmental interests by both 'wets' and 'drys'. At the time Mrs Thatcher prided herself on her flexibility, though she was undoubtedly irritated by the rise. In retrospect, the Cabinet battles of 1981 look much more like a sensible, if at times petulant, accommodation by Mrs Thatcher and her economic Ministers in the face of the realities of the recession rather than any abandonment of the underlying strategy.

Similarly, the 'wets' were ineffective on the backbenches. There were perhaps fifty or sixty of them, but there was little co-ordinated action. Some dined together, cracked jokes and sniped at Mrs Thatcher and her circle, but they generally held back from open rebellion. Their forte was subtle and heavily masked criticism in witty articles and speeches. The prevailing ethos of the Conservative Party was against them; loyalty counted more than doubt. They knew Mrs Thatcher had gauged the mood of the Conservative activists correctly and that there would be little support for any challenge. And by 1981 an election was within sight, and the rise of the SDP/Liberal Alliance was worrying the 'wets', especially as many of them were, by chance, most exposed to the Alliance's advance in their constituencies.

Mrs Thatcher was always in a strong position to exploit the weakness of her critics. She had the power of the premiership, and she used it skilfully. For all her later — and undoubtedly genuine — anguish about sacking Ministers, she was extremely adept at shifting the balance of her Cabinet. She followed 'salami tactics' — she dismissed them one or two at a time. First to go, in January 1981, was Norman St John-Stevas, one of the most innovative leaders of the Commons in recent years, probably because he was a little too outrageous and indiscreet. He was replaced by John Biffen, who was a true believer but had been insufficiently tough as Chief Secretary to the Treasury. Sir John Nott took over from Francis Pym as Defence Secretary in view of the latter's resistance to defence cuts. Then in September 1981 Sir Ian Gilmour, Mark Carlisle and Lord Soames all went. Neither they nor Mr St John-Stevas were seen by Mrs Thatcher as potential leaders of rebellions. And their subsequent interventions in the Commons proved her right. The former Ministers, and particularly Sir Ian, have certainly made critical speeches, but they have been infrequent and never part of a sustained campaign. By contrast, Mrs Thatcher has retained in her Cabinet those who might prove a threat from the backbenches, such as James Prior and Peter Walker. In the place of the deposed Ministers, and as part of a wider reshuffle, Mrs Thatcher promoted to the Cabinet some of her closest supporters. They were in general like her, self-made professionals and businessmen, notably Norman Tebbit, Cecil Parkinson, Leon Brittan and Nigel Lawson. She put her men into the key departments, removing not only 'wets' but also the less effective 'drys'.

Mrs Thatcher's position has rested not just on Cabinet reshuffles but also on the support of Willie Whitelaw, the Home Secretary until 1983. He was the link with the traditional landed and paternalist side of the party and with the partly associated group of 'wets'. As long as she had his support, Mrs Thatcher was safe. Mr Whitelaw was the man to sort out any trouble — for example, by chairing the small group of Ministers (known as the Star Chamber) which adjudicated over public spending battles between the Treasury and other departments. His support headed off any potentially successful revolt. Indeed, it was on one of the few occasions when Mrs Thatcher openly offended Mr Whitelaw, over law and order at the Conservatives' Blackpool conference in 1981, that her leadership appeared to be under threat. Then a challenge to her position was actually mooted, though it did not materialize. It was also during that autumn that the backbenchers were most restless with revolt or threatened revolt over unemployment benefit, rates referendums and heavy lorries. The opinion poll ratings both for Mrs Thatcher and for the Conservative Party were at their lowest, and the Alliance was winning by-election victories at Croydon North West and Crosby. Yet after these pressures, the endless discussion over public spending and Cabinet changes, Mrs Thatcher's position was secure, though only up to the general election. Her critics were in effect saying, 'It is up to you to get us out of this mess.' And if she had failed, the traditional loyalties of the majority of Conservatives might have been tested, and the party might have rallied to one of her critics.

The events of 1981 also represented a renewal of the strategy, despite the short-term modifications. Mrs Thatcher had grown frustrated over the problems of dealing with the nationalized industries. She believed as well that some of the sponsoring Ministers had 'gone native' and had been captured by the industries, so she changed around all the industry Ministers in the September 1981 reshuffle. Patrick Jenkin went to Industry with a brief to sort out BL and British Steel. Most significant of all, Nigel Lawson arrived at Energy and took up the long-nurtured plans of David Howell, his predecessor, for selling off North Sea oil and gas interests. He pressed ahead with considerable vigour, angering some of the chairmen of the energy industries but winning the praise of the Prime Minister. All this was linked with the intention of broadening and deepening the privatization programme. As discussed in more detail in a later chapter, the new Ministers were charged with transferring as many as possible of their operations to the private sector. Only a limited number had gone by the time of the 1983 election, and the frontiers between the public and private sectors had changed only slightly, affecting mainly some commercial and manu-facturing operations rather than the core public utilities. Nevertheless, the Ministers appointed in September 1981 were actively preparing plans for these central public-sector activities.

After 1981 a new impetus could also be seen in the dis-cussions among Ministers about the labour market. A number of leaked documents in the weekly magazine *Time Out* showed that during the autumn of that year several Ministers were concerned about what they saw as the limited amount that had been done to lighten the burden of employment legislation on small businesses. Sir Geoffrey Howe circulated a paper headed 'Abolishing or Restricting Wage Councils'. He favoured the idea of 'widening the differential between the wages of trainees and skilled people'. On the same theme, Patrick Jenkin wrote to Norman Tebbit in February 1982, noting that Wages Councils were a particular bane for smaller firms and that exemption for small business would be 'a demonstration of the Government's concern' which would have 'a value out of all proportion to its real economic sig-nificance'. Mr Jenkin argued that exempting small firms would 'make unemployed people with no experience more attractive to take on', a particularly important consideration 'as the numbers of long-term unemployed grow'. Obligations under an International Labour Organization convention have ruled out abolition of the Councils, at least until the treaty runs out in 1985.

A similar awareness that unemployment was likely to remain high for some time was evident in discussions earlier in 1981. In a paper in February the Think Tank (the Central Policy Review Staff) warned, correctly, that by 1983 un-employment would be above 3 million and that the prospect for young school leavers was bleak: 'The effect in terms of future training skills, attitudes to work and opportunities for crime and other forms of social disruption is undoubtedly a matter for justifiable concern.' At the same time the Downing Street Policy Unit under Sir John Hoskyns prepared a parallel paper which noted:

We all know that there is no prospect of getting
unemployment down to acceptable levels within the
next few years. [Consequently] we must show that
we have some political imagination, that we are willing
to salvage something — albeit second-best — from the
sheer waste involved. There are many people who would
like to do something, even if it is of marginal economic
value.

Subsequent discussions led to the announcement of the
youth training scheme, with places for 460,000 16- and 17-
year-olds; to the young workers scheme for subsidizing
employers who take on young people at low rates of pay;
and to the community programme for the long-term unemployed, mainly in their early twenties.

These moves on privatization, the labour market and
training show that 1981 marked almost a new beginning
for the Thatcher administration. They reflected an awareness that the seriousness of some of the problems had not
been appreciated in 1979 and that new initiatives were
required.

This new drive was maintained in the following years —
though with increasing public discretion as the 1983 election
approached. The Falklands war in the spring and early
summer of 1982 consolidated Mrs Thatcher's position within
her Government and strengthened it enormously in the
country. However, the Conservatives' standing had been
improving before the start of the conflict; the last opinion
poll before the Argentinian invasion showed that the Conservatives had recovered from their low point of the previous
December. Mrs Thatcher's handling of the Falklands crisis led
to a further sharp improvement. According to surveys by
Market and Opinion Research International, the Conservatives'
rating rose from 34 per cent in March 1982 (itself up from
27 per cent the previous December) to a peak of 48 per cent
in June 1982, the month of the Falklands victory, and then
back down to the 42—3 per cent level in the second half of
1982. Similarly, satisfaction with Mrs Thatcher's own performance recovered from a low point of 25 per cent at the
end of 1981 to 36 per cent in March 1982 before leaping

to 59 per cent that June. It then fell back to the upper 40s, which was higher than at the time of the 1979 general election.

Mrs Thatcher attempted to take advantage of the 'Falklands factor' domestically. In a speech to a party rally on Cheltenham racecourse on 3 July 1983 she said: 'We have to see that the spirit of the South Atlantic — the real spirit of Britain — is kindled not only by war but can now be fired by peace.' She urged that the example of the taskforce must be taken to heart: 'Now is the time for management to lift its sights and to lead with the professionalism and effectiveness it knows is possible.' The 'Falklands factor' may not have directly changed attitudes on the shop floor, but it did serve to underpin Mrs Thatcher's general style of forceful leadership and single-mindedness in pursuit of her goals, despite the many tactical shifts. This clearly paid off in electoral terms in June 1983.

The Falklands also made Mrs Thatcher invulnerable within her Government, although it is easy now to forget how badly the war started for her, with the resignation of the three Foreign Office Ministers headed by Lord Carrington. She was forced to appoint Francis Pym as Foreign Secretary, despite their strained relations, and her position looked shaky in the first week after the Argentinian invasion. But the campaign and victory changed all that. The criticisms of the 'wets' had already been faltering at the time of the March 1982 Budget, which appeared to offer a little to everyone. But after the Falklands their doubts about economic policy were expressed only rarely and quietly. At the 1982 Conservative conference in Brighton the 'wets' were almost invisible, confining their criticisms to a couple of fringe meetings. The main conference was an extended victory roll for Mrs Thatcher. It was the same in the run-up to the June 1983 election. The predominant voices during the campaign were those of Mrs Thatcher and her allies, notably Cecil Parkinson and Norman Tebbit.

Mrs Thatcher moved the Cabinet a little more in her direction after the June 1983 election. Admittedly, the Thatcherite but accident-prone Transport Secretary, David Howell, was dropped but, more significantly, she sacked Francis Pym as Foreign Secretary. Yet this could turn out to be a shrewd move, in that Mr Pym, as a former Chief Whip, is by instinct a loyalist and by temperament a solitary political operator. Despite a formidable warning shot across the Government's bows in his first speech from the backbenches in June 1983, he did not look about to raise the standard of rebellion. The key offices of state were all held by her supporters and allies — Sir Geoffrey Howe at the Foreign Office, Nigel Lawson as Chancellor of the Exchequer, Leon Brittan at the Home Office, Cecil Parkinson at the newly merged Trade and Industry and Norman Tebbit still at Employment. Similarly, the other changes in the Government were carefully judged, bringing into the Cabinet supporters such as Peter Rees and Michael Jopling but leaving just on the fringes successful moderates like Kenneth Baker and Douglas Hurd. The departures from the Government were generally of middle-aged, middle-ranking Ministers who seemed unlikely to go any further and would be generally unmourned (and, sooner or later, rewarded with knighthoods).

Mrs Thatcher was careful, however, not to repeat Mr Heath's mistake of entirely excluding dissenting voices. The more talented younger 'wets' in the Government remained, and a couple more were brought in. Of the thirteen MPs who signed the *Changing Gear* pamphlet in September 1981, four were Ministers in mid-1983, two more were whips and all the rest were or had been parliamentary private secretaries.

The view of the 'wets' was that Thatcherism was likely to be in the ascendant for some time. It was therefore better to join in and try to influence events discreetly from the inside. There were also pockets of 'wetness' such as the Northern Ireland Office, where James Prior's team included Nicholas Scott and Chris Patten. Higher public spending to help the unemployed was regarded as respectable there, in part as an anti-riot measure.

Mrs Thatcher and the Whitehall Machine

Yet how did the Government work in practice? The best comparison is perhaps with a sixteenth- or seventeenth-century court, the sovereign surrounded by courtiers (her exotic band of official and unofficial advisers) and men of business (her senior officials) and regarding with distinct suspicion outsiders (any doubter being seen as 'not one of us'). The 'court' is possibly less that of Boadicea than that of Elizabeth I. Downing Street has not been a place for those without strong nerves. Meetings can be fractious and tend to be dominated by the Prime Minister herself, interrupting, correcting and hectoring. She has ticked off Ministers — no matter how grand — in front of their civil servants. And, to the embarrassment of all concerned, she has snubbed Ministers by sometimes turning in exasperation to junior officials for their views on highly political subjects.

Mrs Thatcher's approach has involved a curious ambivalence about the Civil Service. She has made no secret of her dislike for the public sector in general, yet she has been unstinting in her praise for private secretaries and officials with whom she has worked closely. Indeed, during her first term she developed a distinct style of appointments in the Civil Service, singling out for promotion officials who had either worked for her or impressed her during briefings. For instance, Clive Whitmore, her principal private secretary throughout most of her first term, was promoted to Permanent Secretary of the Ministry of Defence. Peter Middleton, the civil servant most closely involved in the design of the Medium-Term Financial Strategy and a monetary policy specialist, was promoted to head the Treasury, aged 48, while his former colleague David Hancock, who had co-ordinated EEC matters in the Cabinet Office, was sent to become Permanent Secretary at the Department of Education and Science. And there were other examples. Such appointments led to charges that the Civil Service was being politicized, but these were generally wide of the mark. Some of the new appointees were not Conservative sympathizers — if, indeed, it was possible to discern their political views at all. They were promoted really because they were strong characters who looked as though they were determined enough to implement the Government's priorities for its second term. Mrs Thatcher wanted in key positions officials whom she knew and trusted. Whitehall sceptics also noted that many of the new Permanent Secretaries were ex-Treasury men, thus underpinning that department's influence.

Mrs Thatcher made some more overtly political appointments elsewhere in the public sector and faced considerable
controversy over the choice of Robin Leigh-Pemberton as
Governor of the Bank of England in succession to the distin-
guished Lord Richardson. Yet one of the most adventurous
of the outside appointments — that of Sir Terry Burns as
the Government's chief economic adviser when in his mid-
thirties — was also the most successful, in part because he
had a professional reputation and was not seen as a partisan
figure.

In addition to conventional Civil Service support, Mrs
Thatcher has also sought a wide range of political advice.
The role of the Policy Unit in Downing Street — first under
Sir John Hoskyns and then under Ferdinand Mount — has
been more strategic than tactical; its brief is to look in
particular at the problems of nationalized industries and
public-sector pay. There have also been special advisers
such as Sir Alan Walters, the economist who arrived in
early 1981, while from late 1982 Sir Anthony Parsons has
been foreign affairs adviser following his successful period
as British Ambassador at the United Nations during the
Falklands war.

Mrs Thatcher has kept open lines to free-market and
pro-business thinkers outside the Government through
some of these advisers and people such as Lord (Hugh)
Thomas and Sir Alfred Sherman of the Centre for Policy
Studies. And further out there have been a number of groups
constantly urging more privatization, more competition and
more attacks on union power. These have included not only
the academic Institute of Economic Affairs under Lord
(Ralph) Harris but also the newer, maverick Adam Smith
Institute and the increasingly political Institute of Directors.
The latter, under Walter Goldsmith, has become an active
lobbyist for private enterprise and against the public sector,
and has been engaged in rivalry with the more corporatist
voice of manufacturing, the Confederation of British Industry.
The emphasis on authority in Conservative thinking has been
represented by a group of somewhat arid dons writing for
the *Salisbury Review*; the associated discussions of the
Conservative Philosophy Group in Lord North Street have

had no significance apart from giving Mrs Thatcher a chance to have some good arguments.

Some of these bodies have certainly been influential. Their leaders have access to Mrs Thatcher and her ministerial supporters, have pressed for their policies and have generally acted as a conscience. They have also in part been an echo chamber, since Mrs Thatcher likes to have her own prejudices reinforced. She appreciates new plans as long as they fall within her own broad ideological framework. That is one reason why she found the Think Tank increasingly irrelevant to her needs and why she disbanded it just after the 1983 election. It is perhaps a worrying sign that such a non-partisan warning voice should be absent. Someone has to say unpalatable things. As it is, the influence of some of her advisers, such as Sir Alan Walters, and of free-enterprise bodies has infuriated officials and non-Thatcherite Ministers, who have had these ideas pushed at them. Some of the activists at the Institute of Directors and the Adam Smith Institute were among the new Tory MPs elected in June 1983 — for example, Neil Hamilton, Michael Forsyth, Michael Fallon and Robert Jones. They could form a lively group pressing the Government to go further. But the role of these bodies and individuals should not be exaggerated. Mrs Thatcher makes up her own mind and she has a shrewd political sense of which free-market ideas will go down with the public and which will not.

What all this has amounted to in practice is a highly personalized style of government, in contrast to James Callaghan's formal approach. It has meant that problems have not been discussed openly, in some cases because Ministers have wanted to avoid the bother of long-drawn-out argument if possible. Yet Mrs Thatcher's style has also had its strengths. She can be decisive and clear-headed. The classic illustration of both the positive and the negative aspects of the Thatcher administration's approach was the Falklands war. The Franks Report points up vividly the absence of collective discussion about the Falklands issue during the fifteen months leading up to the invasion. Despite increasing gloom about the position, Lord Carrington and his officials did not feel that it was worth while to bring the matter up at the overseas and defence committee of the Cabinet. The Foreign Office clearly hoped that talks with the Argentine could be kept going and did not want to provoke the political row at home that would have resulted from their pointing out that the way forward was blocked. Similarly, it is extraordinary that Mrs Thatcher's note on the need for contingency plans, written less than a month before the invasion, appears to have prompted no action.

Yet after the invasion Mrs Thatcher proved to be an effective war leader, with her small War Cabinet and efficient service and Whitehall machine. She even won the admiration of the service chiefs for not dithering (which they regard as the usual trait of politicians) but instead making up her mind clearly and decisively after hearing their submissions. Despite her wish to transfer the Falklands spirit to the home front, however, politics is usually less clear-cut. It requires open discussion, compromise and even, sometimes, consensus – not features for which Mrs Thatcher's style of government is noted.

4

Economic Policy: the Record

The Conservative Party decided that the elimination of inflation should take precedence over all other economic objectives, and the development of policy since 1979 is a reflection of that decision.

Sir Douglas Wass
Permanent Secretary of the Treasury, 1974–83
Farewell interview in The Times, *31 March 1983*

It has become abundantly clear in the period [the 1970s] that Governments themselves cannot ensure high employment, so that it would be misleading to present the change of emphasis in objectives as 'ending the post-war commitment to high employment'. Governments can create the conditions in which it can be achieved, but whether it is achieved depends on the responses of management and labour.

Treasury memorandum to the
Treasury and Civil Service Committee of the Commons
June 1980

Any detached observer of Britain looking solely at the economic indicators for the past decade might easily conclude that the most successful period of economic management along broadly monetarist lines was between 1976 and 1978, with a marked deterioration after 1979. In the earlier period the rate of growth of the money supply was in single figures and generally within the published target range; public spending fell in real terms; the economy expanded and unemployment showed little overall change. By contrast, in the two years after 1979 the rate of monetary growth accelerated to well above the target range; public spending rose; output fell sharply and unemployment soared.

Such a comparison is, of course, an over-simplification. It omits a good deal, such as the change in external pressures and the deterioration in the record in the year before the 1979 election. But the contrast shows that May 1979 did not mark as significant a watershed in the British economy as both supporters and critics contend. Just as the Middle Ages did not suddenly end and the Renaissance begin in 1485, so the starting point for monetarism was not in 1979. Two eminent mainstream economists, Professor Robin Matthews from Cambridge University and J. R. Sargent, group economic adviser to the Midland Bank, note in their introduction to the CLARE Group essays (Matthews and Sargent, 1983) that 'it would certainly be hard to guess from the statistics alone whether there had been a change of Government, and if so when.' They point to the element of continuity in macroeconomic policy despite important changes in incomes and exchange rate policy.

This chapter examines the various phases of economic policy under the Thatcher administration, starting with the initial implementation in 1979—80 of the approach worked out in Opposition, followed by the crisis of the strategy in 1981 and, finally, the more flexible stance adopted in 1982—3. After this narrative the overall record up to mid-1983 is assessed. The next chapter considers whether various alternative approaches might have worked better and discusses the prospects for the second term.

The Healey Era

The Thatcher administration has substantially altered the emphasis of economic policy, but many of the main themes were present in the Labour Government's approach from 1975—6 onwards. It was then that the seemingly inexorable rise in public expenditure was first challenged, that cash limits were first applied to such spending and that targets for the growth of the money supply were first announced. All the essentials of what became known in March 1980 as the Medium-Term Financial Strategy were contained in the Letter of Intent sent by Denis Healey as Chancellor of the Exchequer to the International Monetary Fund in December 1976. There were pledges gradually to reduce the share of resources taken by the public sector and to curb public-sector borrowing in order to restrain monetary growth. This statement was, admittedly, written under severe external pressure to secure a big loan and to restore international confidence after the recurrent sterling crises of 1976. And after the 1979 election some Labour leaders were quick to disown the post-1976 policies and the famous comment made by James Callaghan in September 1976 about Britain not being able to spend its way out of recession.

The key changes in official thinking had, however, occurred before the negotiations with the IMF in the autumn of 1976. Treasury Ministers and their advisers had already pressed for, and in part secured, tighter controls on public expenditure. And by 1975–6 the money supply had already become a significant, though as yet largely tacit, influence on decisions about Government borrowing and interest rates. The effect of the sterling crises of 1976 was to make this change more explicit with a published money supply target. This was seen as 'an overriding constraint upon policies which might otherwise fail to stop inflation reaccelerating to 20 per cent per annum and more', according to John Fforde, then a director of the Bank of England, in a revealing discussion of the past decade in the Bank of England *Quarterly Bulletin* (Fforde, 1983). He noted that within this 'overriding constraint' other aspects of policy continued to be conducted broadly along Keynesian lines. This approach was maintained until the 1979 election, and the course of the money supply proved to be the key influence on various policy decisions in 1977–8, though the containment of inflation also rested on the increasingly shaky incomes policy.

If there has been a Thatcher experiment, it was launched by Denis Healey. Indeed, Sir Geoffrey Howe, as Chancellor of the Exchequer, was always torn between stressing his strategy's continuity with the past and its new features. Denis Healey's monetarism was, however, improvised and never had deep roots within the Labour movement. It was the response of a clever and flexible man to the breakdown of the post-war consensus on economic management and to external pressures. In contrast, the Conservative approach has been based on belief. Whereas under Mr Healey monetary policy had been juggled alongside incomes policy and measures to hold down unemployment in an uncertain mix, the early Conservative approach was more straightforward. There was a vision of how the economy did (or should) work, and it was applied. John Fforde described this as the replacement of monetarily constrained 'Keynesianism' by 'monetarism', although this term referred more to the rhetoric used than to the substance of the initial change.

Remedial Measures: the First Tory Budget

Earlier chapters have discussed the change in the intellectual climate after the mid-1970s and the Conservatives' preparations for power. In brief, their conclusion was that no Government could secure high employment. Previous attempts to boost the economy through the injection of monetary demand had led to higher inflation, not more jobs, in the long term. Similarly, measures to protect employment had merely cushioned declining industries and hampered the drive for improved efficiency. The result had been low growth of output and a poor productivity performance by international standards, with steadily rising unemployment from the mid-1960s onwards. At the same time the rate of profitability of British industry had been falling steadily, from about 8 per cent to between 2 and 3 per cent during the 1970s, notably in manufacturing. Many of these developments were seen as the result of rigidities in the labour market, in turn reflecting the privileged position of trade unions.

The Conservatives' answer was that all any Government could do was to reduce inflation and to remove market distortions, thus creating a framework in which managers and workers had the opportunity to succeed. Economic growth and high employment were up to the people, not the Government. After coming to office in May 1979, the

Conservatives attempted to tackle all these objectives at once. Public spending was to be cut; direct taxes were to be reduced; and public borrowing and the rate of monetary growth were to be contained. Meanwhile, various controls imposed by the Labour Government were abolished. These measures added up to a programme of vigorous action broadly along the lines of plans prepared in Opposition.

The snag was that there had been considerable changes in both external and domestic circumstances since the end of 1978 when the Tory plans had been largely finalized. The Iranian revolution had already begun to change the international scene, leading to the second oil shock and soaring prices. This both pushed up costs and cut the rate of economic growth. But, unlike the first oil shock in 1973–4, Britain was fast emerging as a major producer of oil from the North Sea, and this enhanced the attractions of sterling for overseas investors. Domestically, the rate of earnings growth in the private sector had begun to accelerate from 1978 onwards – to nearly 15 per cent by the time of the 1979 general election – as the Callaghan administration's pay policy broke down. In addition, the disputes during the 'winter of discontent' had started to raise the level of pay settlements in the public sector. And the Commission on Pay Comparability under Professor Hugh Clegg, which had been set up to end these disputes, was soon awarding increases of between 15 and 25 per cent. To many Tories' later regret, the party had promised to honour the Clegg awards during the election campaign.

By the time of the election, therefore, there were large inflationary pressures in the pipeline. While the published twelve-month rate of increase of retail prices was around 10 per cent, the underlying rate over the first few months of 1979 was nearer 15 per cent and rising. In addition, there were signs that public expenditure was climbing out of control as a result of both the rise in public-sector wages and the holding down of prices in a wide range of nationalized industries in the few months before the election.

None the less, only six weeks after the election Sir Geoffrey Howe produced one of the boldest Budgets in recent history. (The results prompted one Treasury Minister to argue, admittedly some time later, that all Chancellors should be legally barred from introducing a Budget within six months of coming to office. They should be forced to pause and think.) The key measures were a reduction in the top marginal rate of tax on earned income from 83 to 60 per cent, a cut in the basic rate of income tax from 33 to 30 per cent and a higher threshold for the investment income surcharge. These concessions were financed in part by a large switch to indirect taxation through the replacement of the previous split rates of Value Added Tax (VAT), 8 and 12.5 per cent, by a single rate of 15 per cent and by rises in other indirect taxes. In addition, the volume of public spending was reduced below the level planned by the previous Labour Government by £1.5 billion (or about 2.25 per cent) in 1979–80, while cash limits on expenditure were set to squeeze out another £1 billion, and a similar amount was to come from the sale of public-sector assets.

Several measures were announced with the aim of boosting incentives and enterprise, the supply side of the economy. The impact of various capital taxes was, for example, lightened significantly. In addition, pay, price and dividend controls were ended, and the beginning of a phased removal of outward exchange controls was announced. This process was taken a stage further in mid-July and completed, with the removal of all remaining controls, three months later, at the end of October.

The money supply was at the centre of the strategy. This was the intermediate target in relation to the ultimate aim of reducing the rate of inflation. There were no specific output and employment objectives. It was hoped that the announcement of the Government's monetary policy would influence expectations about prices and jobs and hence would affect wage bargaining, especially in the private sector. In the public sector unions were told to negotiate within the cash limits setting out the total rise in money available on a particular programme. The main difference between this and the Labour approach was the absence, at that stage, of any attempt directly to influence the level of pay settlements. There was no formal incomes policy; there were no norms, no guidelines or even broad hints. Instead, there was a target range of 7 to 11 per cent (down from 8 to 12 per cent in the previous year) for the annual growth of sterling M3, the broadly defined money supply, which consists of cash and bank current and deposit accounts.

This target was intended to be the predominant guide to the setting of short-term interest rates as well as an important influence on budgetary decisions. To reinforce these changes at a time of considerable uncertainty about the state of the economy, Minimum Lending Rate (MLR), the official guide to the general level of interest rates, was raised on Budget Day from 12 to 14 per cent.

Attempts to Implement the Strategy

The rest of 1979 and 1980 was spent trying to achieve these targets. The biggest problem was that the rise in VAT and in other indirect taxes immediately added between three and a half and four percentage points to the retail prices index. There was also a sharp increase in nationalized industry prices and other public-sector charges as part of the drive to curb public spending and to reduce these industries' deficits. All this came on top of the inflationary pressures that were already present. The Government tried to reduce the impact of the rise in prices caused by the Budget measures by introducing a new tax and prices index. This took account of changes in direct taxes as well as in retail prices and hence showed the favourable impact of the big cut in income tax in the June 1979 Budget. The index was devised against the advice of official statisticians and was always regarded as a gimmick. It had no discernible effect on wage bargaining and backfired the following year, when the burden of direct taxation rose.

By the early autumn of 1979 it had become clear that the Budget objectives were incompatible. Bank lending to the private sector was continuing to increase much more sharply than expected, while public-sector borrowing was also high as a result both of the income tax cuts and of strikes which had delayed the collection of VAT receipts and telephone bills. Consequently, the money supply was growing by more than the target range. There was then a crisis of market confidence, which led to a reaffirmation of the Government's commitment to a tight monetary policy. MLR was raised by three points to a record 17 per cent, in order to 'show that the Seventh Cavalry had really arrived', in the words of one Treasury Minister.

Record interest rates worried Conservative supporters, especially as Treasury Ministers were warning that it would be wrong to expect further substantial cuts in income tax in 1980. Attention switched to public expenditure. A White Paper in November 1979 had proposed cutting £3.6 billion (or nearly 5 per cent) from the Labour Government's spending plans for 1980–1, though this left the volume of expenditure at roughly the level expected for 1979–80 and therefore well up on earlier years. After the outcry over the rise in MLR the Government decided to revise its plans for 1980–1, less than a month after the White Paper had been published, and to seek further cuts in the hope of containing public-sector borrowing. This resulted in the deduction of a further £680 million from earlier plans, though the saving was partially offset by higher debt-interest payments.

The March 1980 Budget attempted to set the policy on a clear course via the innovation of a Medium-Term Financial Strategy that provided explicit guidelines for several years ahead. This was introduced despite the caution of many in the Bank of England and of some Ministers, who were reluctant to take the risk of making such public advance commitments. Targets were set for 'a steady deceleration in the rate of monetary growth over a four-year period, buttressed by a gradual reduction in the size of the underlying Budget deficit, which in turn is to be achieved by a steady reduction in the real level of total Government expenditure'. The theory was that an excessive public-sector deficit (the gap between spending and tax revenue) added to the supply of financial assets in the economy and so made it necessary to raise interest rates if the growth of the money supply was to be kept in check. Hence the need for a tight fiscal policy. The 1980 Budget proposed not only cutbacks in public spending but also a rise in the personal tax burden.

The going was not smooth, however. On the monetary side

the ending in the summer of 1980 of the so-called 'corset restrictions' that had been placed on the growth of the bulk of the banks' deposits meant that some banking activities which had been previously diverted from the official indicator of sterling M3 now fell within this measure again, which sharply inflated the published figures. The result was confusion, as well as a bitter inquest personally initiated by the Prime Minister, which seriously strained relations with the Bank of England and led to an inconclusive monetary review. The main impression was that monetarism was not as simple as some initial statements in 1979 had implied.

The recession was also turning out to be much deeper than expected. Manufacturing output dropped significantly from early 1980 onwards, and adult unemployment rose by 836,000 to 2.13 million during 1980, the largest rise in a single year since 1930. Part of the problem was the international downturn, but this was exacerbated by the competitive pressures caused by the earlier rapid growth in labour costs and by the sharp rise in sterling. The exchange rate rose during 1980 by 12 per cent on average, compared with other major currencies, after a 9.25 per cent increase during 1979. Britain's competitive position deteriorated at an unprecedented rate between the end of 1979 and the middle of 1981. The resulting pressures raised public-sector borrowing by increasing the cost of unemployment benefits and reducing tax revenues, while the demand for bank loans increased from companies facing an intense profits and liquidity squeeze. These trends in turn raised the rate of monetary growth.

The Government responded in its autumn 1980 economic statement by trying to provide reassurance — by cutting various public expenditure programmes, introducing a new North Sea oil tax and increasing employees' National Insurance contributions. And, significantly, despite the rapid rate of monetary growth, the Government argued that financial conditions were tight, as shown by the strength of sterling. So MLR was cut by two points to 14 per cent. The first version of monetarism, of which the primary objective was to keep sterling M3 within the stated target range, was therefore modified within eighteen months of the 1979 election.

The Decisive Phase: 1981

It was in 1981 that the extent of the change of emphasis was confirmed. By contrast with Keynesian theory and the practice of Governments up to the mid-1970s, a restrictive policy was maintained despite the clear evidence of recession and the continuing sharp rise in unemployment. In particular, in the March 1981 Budget there was no increase in income tax thresholds or allowances even to take account of inflation, which amounted to a big rise in the personal tax burden. When this was announced there was strong criticism not only from the Opposition parties but also from the so-called 'wet' critics of the strategy within the Cabinet and on the Conservative backbenches. Just before the Budget the all-party Treasury and Civil Service Committee of the Commons said that it had not seen 'any firm evidence of factors leading to a sustained level of growth in the medium term which would significantly reduce unemployment'.

Yet on the face of it the 1981 Budget represented a more flexible interpretation of the Medium-Term Financial Strategy. The planned level of public-sector borrowing for 1981–2 was revised upwards to £10.5 billion compared with £7.5 billion in the original strategy a year earlier, although the increase was less than it would have been without the rise in the tax burden. The measure was designed to take account of the impact of the recession and was in line with ministerial statements in 1980 that there would be a phased or stepped reduction in public-sector borrowing, unchanged as a percentage of total national income or output in recession years but falling when the economy was growing. The Treasury Committee noted in its report on the 1981 Budget that the measures amounted to 'a tightening of the fiscal stance in 1981–2 compared with an unchanged policy position. This tightening comes at a time when the economy is already in deep recession.'

The Government's intention was not, however, to make policy more restrictive but rather to change the balance between the fiscal and monetary elements in order to make room for some easing of the financial position of companies by means of a reduction in interest rates. And MLR was duly cut by a further two points to 12 per cent. Monetary policy was also interpreted more flexibly. A large increase in sterling M3 in 1980—1 was accommodated, and the Government argued that this monetary measure alone was not a good guide to decisions about short-term interest rates. These should also take account of changes in other monetary aggregates and in the sterling exchange rate. The Treasury Committee concluded that 'in its tentativeness, time horizon, setting of targets relative to expected inflation, conditionality, and accommodation of temporary increases, the Medium-Term Financial Strategy has been substantially modified.'

In retrospect, the 1981 Budget was a turning point, though in part unintentionally. Public-sector borrowing in 1981—2 undershot the original target by about £2 billion, making fiscal policy look tighter than planned. Unemployment also rose even faster than expected — up a further 645,000 during 1980 to 2.78 million. The main direct response was an expansion of special employment measures and subsidies which took more than 250,000 people off the unemployment register in 1981.

Mrs Thatcher later made a virtue of the unpopularity of the 1981 Budget. During the run-up to the 1983 election she repeatedly claimed that the tough measures of 1981 had made possible the later cuts in taxation and in interest rates. The maintenance of the broad direction of the Medium-Term Financial Strategy turned out to be more important than the increasing flexibility of its interpretation. But, as discussed in the next chapter, the modifications did raise questions about the chain of causation claimed by Treasury Ministers.

The undershoot of public-sector borrowing and the faster than expected slow-down in the inflation rate allowed greater room for manoeuvre from late 1981 onwards. The result of the autumn public expenditure review was to raise the proposed planning total for 1982—3 from £110 billion to £115 billion, measured in the cash terms then adopted as the means of control. There was also a further devaluing of the significance of sterling M3 despite, or perhaps because of, its continuing overshoot of the target range.

The Treasury Committee noted in its December 1981

report that as there was now doubt about the underlying strategy, it should be restated. It was clear that interest rate decisions were being determined as much by fluctuations in the exchange rate as by domestic monetary movements. This applied especially from the second half of 1981 onwards, when the pound fell sharply, partly in response to a weakening in world oil prices. A further modification was the abandonment, after mid-1980, of the Government's hands-off view of pay. While there was no general norm or limit, a clear assumption was embodied in cash limits in the public sector, coupled with much more exhortation in the private.

The Pre-Election Phase

The final phase of Conservative economic policy ran from early 1982 until after the June 1983 election. The keynote was flexibility. The Medium-Term Financial Strategy was formally modified in the March 1982 Budget. For the first time the ranges for monetary growth openly covered several aggregates, and sterling M3 was no longer the sole measure of money being targeted. The exchange rate was also given explicit emphasis. The target range was raised, as was the projected level of public-sector borrowing. Overall, fiscal policy was little changed as an increase in employees' National Insurance contributions was offset by a cut in the employers' National Insurance surcharge, while income tax thresholds and allowances were raised by slightly more than necessary to match inflation. An apparent decline in public-sector borrowing to below the target for 1982—3 led to the announcement, in November 1982, of a further cut in the employers' surcharge. But the pick-up in the economy remained slow, and unemployment continued to increase.

Sir Geoffrey Howe was able to announce some modest overall tax relief in his final Budget as Chancellor in March 1983. Income tax thresholds and allowances were raised by 14 per cent, or more than double the amount necessary to match the previous year's inflation, and the employers' surcharge was further reduced. Although the benefits were spread widely, the total impact of the Budget stopped well short of a pre-election give-away, and analysts pointed to a number of major questions about rises in future levels of public spending and borrowing.

The Record Assessed

This narrative of policy has concentrated on the Government's actions rather than on its effects on what Denis Healey liked to call the 'real economy' of output and unemployment, over which the Conservatives have said they have no control. Any assessment of the record since 1979 must inevitably be subjective, but the following points and accompanying tables, which provide a commentary on both financial and 'real' aspects, are intended to highlight its main features.

Monetary Policy

Sterling M3, the broadly defined money supply, rose more rapidly than permitted under the official target range from 1979 to 1982, though the narrower monetary aggregates at times grew more slowly. Sterling M3 was again overshooting the upper level of the target in the two or three months before the June 1983 election.

TABLE 1   *Monetary targets (% growth)*

	1979–80	1980–1	1981–2	1982–3	1983–4
1979 Budget[a]	7–11				
1980 strategy[a]		7–11	6–10	5–9	4–8
1981 strategy[a]			6–10	5–9	4–8
1982 strategy[b]				8–12	7–11
1983 strategy[b]					7–11
Actual rise in sterling M3	12[c]	19	13	9[d]	—

Notes: a These ranges apply to sterling M3 only; *b* these ranges applied to M1 (the narrowly defined money supply, cash and bank accounts) and the broader aggregate PSL2 (private-sector liquidity, including building society deposits) as well as to sterling M3; *c* eight months to mid-February 1980 at an annual rate; *d* twelve months to February 1983.
Source: Official statistics and Treasury Committee report on the 1983 Budget.

Public-Sector Borrowing

The total has fallen as a percentage of national income (or Gross Domestic Product — GDP), as proposed in the strategy, but the decline has not been as marked as was intended when the Medium-Term Financial Strategy was first announced in March 1980. There was a bulge in 1980—1 when, as a result of the recession, borrowing rose sharply as a percentage of GDP. The target level of borrowing for future years has been revised upwards. Nevertheless, by 1982—3 the level of borrowing was the lowest relative to GDP since the early 1970s, and the deficit has been reduced more than in almost any other industrialized country.

TABLE 2   *Public-sector borrowing plans (% of GDP)*

	1980—1	1981—2	1982—3	1983—4
1980 strategy	3.75	3.00	2.25	1.50
1981 strategy	5.70	4.25	3.25	2.00
1982 strategy		4.25	3.50	2.75
1983 strategy		3.50	3.30	2.75

Source: Official statistics.

Public Expenditure

The original aim of the Conservatives in Opposition was to reduce public spending in real terms to the level of 1977—8. After the sharp jump in expenditure in 1978—9 and 1979—80, the target was revised at the time of the March 1980 Budget, when the volume of expenditure was projected instead to decline by 4 per cent between 1979—80 and 1983—4, with a drop in its proportion of GDP from 42 per cent to under 40 per cent over the period. In the event, public expenditure rose steadily, reaching 44.5 per cent of GDP in 1981—2, in part because of the recession, before falling back to about 44 per cent in 1982—3. Public expenditure in cost terms (similar to volume though adjusting for changes in relative prices) in 1982—3 was 9.25 per cent higher than in 1977—8 and 4.25 per cent higher than in 1979—80. But, according to Treasury estimates, the 1982—3 level was more than 5 per cent less than the total planned for that year by the Labour Government in its final expenditure White Paper in January 1979.

Taxation

Instead of the promised fall in taxes, the overall tax burden rose from just under 34 per cent of GDP in 1978—9 to nearly 40 per cent in 1982—3. During the 1983 election the Conservatives concentrated on the reduction in the basic rate of income tax from 33 to 30 per cent and the raising of personal income tax allowances by 5 per cent in real terms between 1978—9 and 1983—4 (though if the year of comparison had been 1982—3, the change in allowances would have been 3.5 per cent less than the rise in inflation in the period). These figures ignore the ending of the 25 per cent reduced-rate band of income tax and the steady rise in employee National Insurance contributions, a form of income tax in all but name.

TABLE 3   *The impact of tax changes: income tax and National Insurance contributions as a percentage of gross earnings (including child benefit where relevant)*

Percentage of average earnings	1978—9	1979—80	1980—1	1981—2	1982—3	1983—4
Single person						
75%	29.04	27.57	28.84	30.63	31.40	31.00
Average	31.65	29.80	30.81	32.30	33.20	33.00
200%	33.80	30.95	32.12	34.66	34.70	34.00
500%	52.60	43.10	44.50	46.70	46.30	45.20
Married couple with two children						
75%	20.80	32.05	22.49	24.40	24.90	24.20
Average	25.24	24.65	25.84	27.60	28.10	27.70
200%	29.93	27.91	29.77	31.37	31.50	30.70
500%	49.70	41.20	42.70	44.90	44.40	43.20

Source: Various parliamentary answers.

The proportion of gross income paid in income tax and National Insurance contributions by a single person on average earnings rose from 31.6 per cent to 33 per cent between 1978—9 and 1983—4. For a married couple with two children the share has risen from 25.2 per cent to 27.7 per cent. And the increase in the share has been even larger if rises in indirect taxes and local authority rates are also taken into account.

Moreover, the sharpest relative increases in the proportion of income paid in taxes have been for those on below-average earnings. Only a relatively few at the top end of the income scale have retained any benefit from the 1979 income tax cuts; for instance, the proportion of gross income paid in income tax and National Insurance by a single person on five times average earnings dropped from 52.6 per cent in 1978—9 to 45.2 per cent in 1983—4.

Inflation
The twelve-month rate of growth of retail prices was 10.3 per cent in May 1979 (and fractionally below 10 per cent in the last figures to be announced before the election). The rate rose to a peak of 21.9 per cent in May 1980 before falling back to single figures in April 1982 and declining to 3.7 per cent in May 1983, the lowest level for fifteen years. This compared with a twelve-month rate of increase in consumer prices in the major seven industrialized countries of about 5 per cent in the spring of 1983, ranging from just over 2 per cent in Japan, approximately 3.5 per cent in the USA and West Germany, to 9.25 per cent in France and nearly 16 per cent in Italy.

Earnings
The twelve-month rate of growth of average earnings for all industries and services accelerated from 13.4 per cent to 22.2 per cent between the second quarters of 1979 and 1980 before falling back to 8.7 per cent by the beginning of 1983.

Living Standards
Real personal disposable income is normally regarded as the best yardstick for average living standards, since it takes

account of changes in gross earnings, prices, taxes and social security benefits. It rose by nearly 3 per cent on average between the first half of 1979 and the second half of 1980, reflecting the impact of the acceleration in earnings growth and the appreciation of sterling. But real personal disposable income then fell back as the recession deepened, so that by early 1983 it was at about the same level as in spring 1979. But there were differences in the position of those in work, whose real take-home pay rose during the period, and of that of the growing number of unemployed, whose living standards fell.

Output

Gross Domestic Product fell by 5.5 per cent between the first half of 1979 and the low point of the recession in the first half of 1981 before recovering by 2.5 per cent by the end of 1982 and early 1983. Consequently, over the 1979–83 period as a whole GDP was more than 3 per cent down. But this masked large variations between sectors. North Sea oil and gas output rose by 72 per cent between 1979 and 1982. By contrast, manufacturing production fell by 15.75 per cent over the period. Much of the rise in output in 1982–3 was the result of North Sea operations, and manufacturing production only started to pick up noticeably in the first half of 1983.

Consumer Spending

In contrast to the squeeze on manufacturing production, consumer spending rose by 3.5 per cent in real terms between the first half of 1979 and the end of 1982 and early 1983. At a time when real disposable income was little changed overall, this increase reflected a reduction in the level of personal savings, a result of the fall in the inflation rate and in interest rates in 1982–3. There was a mini-consumer boom during the second half of 1982, which stretched into 1983. The volume of expenditure rose by 3 per cent between the first quarters of 1982 and 1983, with spending on durables up more than 21 per cent in real terms. However, this increase was met in part by a sharp reduction in stocks and by a nearly 10 per cent rise in imports of consumer goods, since domestic production of consumer items rose by only 0.25 per cent.

External Trade
The UK had a record surplus on the current account of its balance of payments for much of the period, rising to £6 billion in 1981 before falling back to nearer balance in early 1983. The counterpart was a large deficit on capital account as financial institutions increased their investments abroad after the end of exchange controls. Towards the end of the period a rise in the surplus in the oil trade partly offset a sharp deterioration in the balance in non-oil trade. By early 1983 there was the first deficit in trade in manufactured goods since the Industrial Revolution, two centuries ago. Britain's share of world trade continued to decline in the early 1980s, though more slowly than during most of the 1970s. And there was a further sharp increase in the share of the domestic market taken by imports. Both developments reflected the decline in competitiveness produced by the appreciation of the sterling exchange rate and the rapid growth in labour costs.

Unemployment
There have been a number of changes in the method of calculating unemployment figures. In particular, in summer 1982 there was a shift from recording those registered as unemployed to a new method of including those claiming unemployment and related benefits. On the new claimants' basis, the UK total rose from 1.22 million in May 1979 to 3.05 million in May 1983, equivalent to 12.8 per cent of the labour force. However, the latter total also reflected a change in April 1983, whereby men aged 60 and over no longer had to sign on at unemployment benefit offices in order to secure National Insurance credits. This removed 103,000 from the unemployed total. On a like-for-like basis there was an increase of 1.93 million between the 1979 and 1983 elections. If the figures had been calculated on the former registration basis, they might have been about 200,000 higher, which would have produced a total of 3.35 million after account had been taken of

the recent changes affecting men over 60.

In addition, the Government's various special employment measures — a wide variety of schemes, ranging from temporary job subsidies to the encouragement of early retirement — were helping between about 600,000 and 650,000 people in the spring of 1983. The impact on the unemployment total was to reduce it by 350,000. Furthermore, there may have been a large pool of hidden unemployment, explained in part by aspects of the National Insurance rules which excluded many women from benefit, and large numbers of people may have been discouraged from seeking work. These groups may have added another 400,000 to 450,000 to the total. On the other hand, a number of 'work-shy' people may not have been genuinely seeking jobs. Nevertheless, these estimates explain why many politicians and economists argued that the 'true' unemployment total had risen to over 4 million by the middle of 1983.

Employment
The striking feature of the 1979—83 period was the sharp downturn in employment. During previous ups-and-downs of the economy in the 1960s and 1970s employment had generally fluctuated by no more than between 300,000 and 400,000 either way. However, between June 1979 and December 1982 the total number of people in employment in the UK fell by 2.32 million to 20.7 million. There was a particularly sharp drop in manufacturing industry, where employment fell from 7.06 million to 5.48 million over the period. And, unlike in previous post-war recessions, employment in service industries also declined, from 13.24 million to 12.82 million. The number of redundancies notified to the Department of Employment (only part of the total) rose from 173,000 in 1978 to a peak of 532,000 in 1981, before falling back to just under 400,000 in 1982.

Productivity
The pronounced drop in employment during the recession contributed to a large improvement in recorded productivity, as measured by output per person employed. For the whole economy productivity rose by 3 per cent between 1979 and

the end of 1982, at a time when total output fell by over 3 per cent. The contrast was much more marked in manufacturing industry, where output per person rose by just over 7 per cent over the period.

The Benefits and Costs

These statistics do not add up to an inspiring record. On most counts of welfare and well-being, the Thatcher administration's record in its first term was worse than that of any previous post-war Government in Britain. Yet was all the suffering necessary to make long-overdue changes to the economy? And had 'the foundations of recovery been firmly laid', in the words of the Conservative's June 1983 election manifesto? Inflation had, of course, been reduced to the lowest rate for fifteen years. This was a real achievement, though one produced in part by accident, thanks to the much greater appreciation of sterling than had been expected (as discussed in more detail in the following chapter). Beyond that, is there any basis for believing that by mid-1983 the British economy was in fundamentally better shape than it had been during the previous twenty years?

The debate has turned primarily on the productivity figures. The Government has argued that the sharp rise in output per head indicates a major break away from previous trends, as improved working practices have been introduced and overmanning has been reduced. Even such a normally cautious man as Sir Geoffrey Howe has talked of 'a dramatic improvement in productivity'. The overall figures do indeed appear to suggest a big improvement. Between the end of 1980 and mid-1982 output per head in manufacturing rose at an annual rate of 7.5 per cent, compared with an average increase of 2.25 per cent a year during the 1970s. However, this marked improvement followed a 6.75 per cent drop in output per head during 1980. There were also fluctuations in the number of hours worked. If the figures are adjusted to changes per person-hour, the increase becomes smaller.

In some respects the pattern was similar to the usual one in a recession. In the first phase output generally falls faster than employment, since companies are slow to declare redundancies because they are uncertain about the scale of the downturn. Hence published productivity falls. In the later phase output stops falling but companies continue to reduce the size of their labour forces and, at any rate, do not recruit when the recovery starts. In the 1979–83 period this pattern was reinforced by the size of the drop in manufacturing output, which was even larger than in the early 1930s.

When the figures are adjusted for the impact of the recession the improvement looks less spectacular. John Muellbauer of Nuffield College, Oxford, and Lionel Mendis of the London School of Economics have undertaken research (as set out in the *Financial Times*, 20 April 1983) which shows that there was a breakthrough but that it was short-lived. It began in 1980 but petered out by mid-1981. Their conclusion, based on an adjustment to the published figures for short-term fluctuations in the utilization of labour, is that the main cause was 'the drastic shedding of plant, labour and management which on the average tended to be less productive than the surviving parts of British manufacturing industry'. This was a once-and-for-all shake-out reflecting the special circumstances of the recession, when employers took advantage of the conditions to close down marginal plant and to reduce their workforces.

The research indicates that the improvement in the published productivity figures from mid-1981 to late 1982 was largely the result of a cyclical increase in the utilization of labour as activity picked up. This finding is borne out by the slower growth in output per head in the second half of 1982. Muellbauer and Mendis argue that the evidence denies a more lasting Thatcher effect on the rate of productivity growth. Indeed, they maintain that the growth of output per head is unlikely to exceed that of the 1970s unless there is a substantial recovery in new investment.

This conclusion suggests that there has not been a permanent alteration in productivity performance in Britain since 1979. Where does this leave the much heralded new era of industrial relations, the enhanced role of the manager and the reduction in the power of workers and trade unions to resist the introduction of new working practices and technology? After all, Ministers have constantly pointed to large-scale productivity gains at BL and British Steel, while leading private-sector companies have indicated the big improvements secured during the recession. The pattern has been patchy. The growth of output per head has been well above previous trend rates in, for example, metal manufacturing, electrical and instrument engineering, motor vehicles and the food and drink sectors. These industries should be much better placed than they were before the recession.

The improvement in particular sectors does not necessarily alter the overall conclusion that the big apparent jump in output per head in the early 1980s was mainly the result of a once-and-for-all shock rather than the start of a better trend. Yet there may be scope for a better performance; overmanning has clearly been reduced in many companies, and trade union behaviour, if not underlying attitudes, has changed at BL, if not in Fleet Street. Sir Douglas Wass, the Permanent Secretary of the Treasury over the period, noted in a farewell interview in *The Times* on 31 March 1983, 'What has emerged in shop-floor behaviour through fear and anxiety is much greater than I think could have been secured by more co-operative methods. That is a surprise to me. There is a potential for productivity growth on a scale we have not had in this country.'

That potential has yet to be fully realized in practice. Its impact will anyway be dependent on other factors, such as the rate of growth of labour costs and the exchange rate. Indeed, according to the usual measures of relative unit labour costs, the competitive position of British manufacturing industry in mid-1983 was still considerably worse than in the late 1970s despite an improvement since 1981 as a result of the fall in the exchange rate and the much slower growth of manufacturing earnings.

If the Thatcher economic miracle was still far from established at the time of the 1983 election, the costs were all too apparent. Not only had total unemployment risen by about 2 million between 1979 and 1983, but also the number of long-term unemployed (those without a job for over year) had jumped to 1.14 million by spring 1983. The impact had also been greater on weaker groups and in certain regions. By late 1982 half the long-term unemployed were aged under 24 or over 55. The rate of unemployment was over 20 per cent in Northern Ireland and in many manufacturing centres in northern England, Scotland and Wales. Moreover, in the formerly prosperous West Midlands the total had risen by roughly three times between 1979 and 1983.

High unemployment also cost the UK a great deal in a direct financial way. A major House of Lords inquiry into the subject estimated that in the summer of 1982 the annual fiscal cost to the Exchequer in lost tax revenue and extra expenditure was £5,000 per person unemployed per year. At that time this was equivalent to over £15 billion.

There were considerable social costs in terms of poor health and increased crime, let alone the damage to individual self-respect. The rise in unemployment and the recession also exacerbated poverty and inequality. The number of people receiving supplementary benefit rose by over two-thirds between 1979 and 1982. Inequality in the distribution of wages also increased. These changes were reinforced by Government policy — the rise in the personal tax burden, the changing pattern of public expenditure and cutbacks in the real value of certain social security benefits (discussed in more detail in later chapters).

At the end of four years in office the Thatcher administration still had almost everything to prove about its economic policies. The costs were all too plain; any benefits were still tentative and uncertain.

5

Economic Policy:
the Alternatives and Prospects

If neo-Keynesian demand management was the necessary condition of economic growth, we would all still be living in caves and wearing woad.

Nigel Lawson
Speech to the Institute for Fiscal Studies
March 1981

There are no examples in British history, except possibly in the early 1820s, of cyclical recoveries taking place at a moment when the authorities were actually exerting downward pressure on prices, other than through incomes policy.

Professor Robin Matthews and J. R. Sargent
Contemporary Problems of Economic Policy, *1983*

The relationship between the monetary aggregates and prices has, in the event, turned out to be not as simple as the Government originally thought.

Treasury and Civil Service Committee of the Commons
December 1982

The Debate

Towards the end of 1981 an unprecedented event occurred. No fewer than 364 university economists produced a statement expressing strong disagreement with the economic policies of the Thatcher administration. As significant as the contents was the list of signatories, which included seventy-six professors of economics, four former chief economic advisers to the Government (Lord Roberthall, Sir Alec Cairncross, Sir Bryan Hopkin and Sir Fred Atkinson) plus the Nobel prize-winner Professor James Meade. In short, the statement represented a revolt by Britain's post-war economics establishment against Thatcherism. The signatories declared:

(a) there is no basis in economic theory or supporting evidence for the Government's belief that by deflating demand they will bring inflation permanently under control and thereby induce an automatic recovery in output and employment;

(b) present policies will deepen the depression, erode the industrial base of our economy and threaten its social and political stability;

(c) there are alternative policies; and

(d) the time has come to reject monetarist policies and consider urgently which alternative offers the best hope of sustained economic recovery.

Critics pointed out that the statement was negative and did not specify any alternatives. Moreover, there was heavy bias towards Cambridge, the heartland of Keynesianism. Of sixty teaching economists at Cambridge, fifty-four signed, but there was a much smaller proportion from Oxford and the London School of Economics and none at all from the strongly monetarist Liverpool faculty and the City University's founding Banking and Finance Unit. Lord (Ralph) Harris, the Director of the Institute of Economic Affairs, who had been ennobled by Mrs Thatcher, noted that with a few honourable exceptions the list of the most prominent signatories read like 'a charge sheet of those responsible for Britain's relative economic decline since the war'.

The impact of the statement was enhanced by the intense public controversy unleashed only a few days earlier by the March 1981 Budget, by which taxes had been raised in the face of the deepest recession for fifty years. Moreover, at the beginning of March the all-party Treasury and Civil Service Committee of the Commons produced the result of a major inquiry into monetary policy, which expressed considerable scepticism about the Government's arguments. In particular, the committee noted that it had 'not been convinced by the evidence of a direct causal relationship from growth in the money supply to inflation'. And some senior Tories were also very critical. After his dismissal from the Cabinet in September 1981 Sir Ian Gilmour remarked that monetarism had become 'the uncontrollable in pursuit of the indefinable'.

The Government persisted with its strategy, albeit in a modified form. The continuing debate over the merits of the strategy and over the results raises several questions. First, was the basic strategy right? Second, what mistakes were made, and were workable alternatives available? Finally, what are the economic prospects for the second term?

Inflation and Recession: Ways and Means

At one level the strategy has succeeded in its primary aim, since in the twelve months to May 1983 the rate of retail price inflation was reduced to 3.7 per cent, the lowest level for fifteen years. Leaving aside for the moment the question of whether this was just a temporary dip, there is considerable dispute about how the reduction had been achieved. In 1979–80 Treasury Ministers stressed the direct relationship between a lowering of the rate of growth of the supply of money in the economy and a reduction in the rate of price inflation. Yet a significant reduction in the rate of growth of prices has been achieved despite the consistently more rapid rate of increase of most of the monetary measures. These have remained above the upper limit of permitted target ranges. The Treasury committee pointed out in December 1982 that 'since the Medium-Term Financial Strategy was introduced in 1980, changes in the price level have not been closely related to changes in the monetary aggregates, even allowing for variations in time lags.'

Some critics have said that this demonstrates the futility of monetarism. Lord Kaldor, for instance, has argued in a series of speeches in the House of Lords and elsewhere (collected in Kaldor, 1983) that no monetary aggregate has any practical meaning as an indicator of financial conditions and that the record has shown that no Government can control the supply of money. The Conservative Government's efforts to do so have led to changes in the behaviour of banks and the public and have therefore had little effect on expectations and on inflation. According to this view, all the authorities have done is to affect the cost of borrowing and hence influence the demand for money, not its supply. The impact of a tight monetary policy is thus felt indirectly through its effect on real output and unemployment — that is, by generating a big enough slump. Prices and wages are not, according to Lord Kaldor, flexible in response to market pressures, and inflation is influenced primarily by rises in the costs of raw materials, fuel and labour rather than by excess demand. The rate of inflation has been reduced by old-fashioned deflation and high interest rates, which have helped to push up the pound and to squeeze industry, thereby frightening wage bargainers into accepting low pay rises.

In response, the Government has argued that its basic approach has been valid, despite modifications. The discrepancy between the performance of sterling M3, the main monetary measure, and the rate of growth of prices and of total national income and expenditure has been blamed on structural changes and special factors.

The Treasury has argued that the change in the ratio of the money supply to national income, which is known as the velocity of circulation of money, has reflected changes in savings behaviour, the expanded role of banks as financial intermediaries and the removal of exchange controls and the so-called 'corset controls' on banking activities. Yet the change in the ratio was puzzling in relation to past experience.

The pressures on company liquidity led to distress borrowing by industry. And, coupled with the rise in public-sector borrowing as a result of the recession, this pushed up the rate of growth of sterling M3. In particular, the banks became the main intermediaries in financing the large cash needs of industry in the absence of a market for raising funds for long-term fixed-interest loans such as debentures. Companies were forced to raise their overdrafts. The monetary figures were also boosted from 1981 onwards by the entry of the High Street banks into the market for house mortgages on a large scale. There were further complications as a result of the series of public-sector pay disputes, notably in the Civil Service in 1981, which delayed tax receipts and seriously distorted the figures for several months.

These explanations were convincing up to a point, but they did not help the implementation of a policy which in 1979–80 had been presented in simple terms in relation to one monetary variable, sterling M3. The confusion and complications over monetary behaviour in the period undermined any direct impact which the announcement of successively lower monetary targets might have had on expectations and attitudes, especially in the labour market. Managers and trade union leaders did not suddenly start to follow each month's money supply figures. The Government's response, especially after March 1982, was to assert what it claimed had always been implicit – namely, that policy was based on a range of monetary indicators, including the exchange rate.

However, some of the most zealous academic and City monetarists argued that the Government had been following the wrong monetary indicator and had, in effect, not been monetarist enough. Some in this group argued for an immediate and a much more severe squeeze on the growth of the money supply than the gradualist approach favoured by the Government. Policy, they suggested, should be steered in relation to a narrow definition of money rather than a broad aggregate such as sterling M3, and stricter control should be applied by focusing on the 'monetary base' of the banking system. But this could in turn have led to further instability in the monetary system; short-term interest rates might have fluctuated much more and been at a higher level than otherwise. This was presented as a modern version of the inescapable discipline imposed by the gold standard – nasty at first but beneficial (at any rate for those with jobs) over the longer term. This comparison did not widely commend the case.

The Treasury and the Bank of England anyway preferred some form of broad aggregate or a range of monetary measures, in part because an aggregate such as sterling M3 was thought both to be more appropriate over the medium term and to correspond more closely to other aspects of policy such as public-sector borrowing and bank lending to the private sector.

Interest in the narrower aggregates developed in the autumn of 1980, following the row about the bulge in sterling M3 after the end of the 'corset controls'. Mrs Thatcher took up the idea, especially after a visit to Switzerland in August 1980, when she met some prominent Swiss-American economists who were strong advocates of such an approach and were critical of the Bank of England's alleged laxity. Professor Alan Walters, her personal economic adviser in Downing Street, also supported this view, but Treasury and Bank of England caution eventually prevailed, particularly since by late 1980 a monetary upheaval seemed less important than the immediate problems of the recession and the exchange rate.

There was increasing concern about the pressures on output and jobs as a result of the rise in the pound. Policy focused more on the actual impact of the strategy on the economy than solely on the erratic short-term behaviour of a single monetary aggregate. The ultimate objectives of policy, prices and output had to be taken into account as well as the intermediate targets. Only the most ardent monetarists dissented from the comment of Ministers that despite the overshoot in the growth of sterling M3 the economy was clearly showing all the evidence of a monetary squeeze. This was reflected in the pressures on the company sector as well as the falling inflation rate after mid-1980. As one very senior adviser remarked, all that Ministers had to do in August 1980 was to look outside their windows to see the frost on the ground.

The squeeze was the result of the sharp rise in the sterling exchange rate, coupled with the earlier rapid growth in labour costs. The competitive position of British manufacturing industry, as measured by its relative labour costs, had deteriorated by late 1980 by between 35 and 45 per cent compared with its long-term level. This swift and unforeseen change accounted for much of the pressure on manufacturing industry, leading to a wave of redundancies and closures. Britain's exports became more expensive in foreign markets as the pound rose, forcing producers to slash profit margins if their companies were to retain a foothold abroad. Simultaneously, imports became cheaper in Britain. The strong pound contributed to the reduction in the inflation rate, both directly by cutting the cost of imported goods and raw materials and indirectly by obliging domestic producers to hold down their prices if they were to compete with foreign goods. This was reflected, for example, in the negligible rises during 1980–1 in the prices of both domestic household goods and clothing and footwear, sectors that were exposed particularly starkly to international competition.

There has been considerable disagreement about the reasons for the rise in the sterling exchange rate. Many elaborate calculations have been done to estimate the relative impact of various factors. There were probably several influences which cannot be separately quantified. They include the rise in North Sea oil production to near self-sufficiency by 1980, the impact of the Iranian revolution and subsequent events on oil prices (both factors underlining sterling's status as a petro-currency), the effect on international confidence of the arrival of a 'sound money' Government in May 1979 (the 'Thatcher factor') and, possibly most significant, the impact of the sharp rise in UK interest rates in June and November 1979.

Conservative Ministers had always wanted a reasonably strong pound in order to put pressure on industry to hold down its costs and to become more efficient. In a speech in September 1981 Professor Terry Burns, the chief economic adviser to the Government, noted:

It was expected that the exchange rate would move ahead of the deceleration of wages and prices simply because financial markets adjust ahead of the labour and goods markets. It was also anticipated that there might be some over-shooting of this exchange rate position because of the need for higher interest rates [to launch the process of reducing monetary growth].

The rise in the pound and its impact on industry were, however, much more pronounced than expected. The appreciation was, at each stage, greater than that forecast by Treasury economists and difficult to explain by reference to monetary behaviour alone.

The exchange rate was clearly the main mechanism by which the policy was translated into a lower inflation rate, and sterling M3 ceased to be the overriding constraint and determinant of short-term interest rates. By late 1981 the Medium-Term Financial Strategy was no longer really monetarist even in the sense that a range of monetary aggregates were the main guiding lights of policy. For instance, references to the money supply in ministerial speeches became much less frequent in 1982–3.

The revised Medium-Term Financial Strategy was somewhat confusing. The monetary aggregates still had a place as an indicator of financial conditions, but a more qualified one. The Financial Statement and Budget Report (the Red Book) produced in March 1983 noted that 'the interpretation of monetary conditions will continue to take account of all the available evidence, including the exchange rate, structural changes in financial markets, savings behaviour, and the level and structure of interest rates.' It was difficult for people in the City, let alone managers and trade unionists, to know what this might mean in practice. The Treasury Committee of the Commons remarked in its report in December 1982 that 'given the unsteady nature of the velocity of circulation of money...it is unclear what the existing monetary targets imply for the future paths of either prices or real activity.'

The problem was that the operational guidelines were only half-stated. Admittedly, the commitment to fiscal policy was clear, and the stress on reducing the scale of public-sector borrowing was maintained. But the significance of the exchange rate was less explicit. Policy was determined more by the rate of change of the pound, in either direction, and action was taken to check too rapid an adjustment. But there was also a desire to avoid identifying an exchange-rate target for fear that it could not be sustained in the face of the instability of international capital markets, especially for a petro-currency like sterling. This was also the main reason why the sterling exchange rate was not formally linked to the main Continental currencies within the European Monetary System. Yet many observers believed that for much of the time the Government was trying to keep the exchange rate within an unstated and movable range.

The question is whether the more flexible, and ambiguous, interpretation of the strategy may have weakened the impact of the counter-inflation policy by removing an important constraint. Not so far, is the most probable answer. Whatever was happening to sterling M3, the 1981 Budget showed that the Government meant business. Its refusal to adopt a Keynesian approach to soaring unemployment or to reflate demand, as would have happened in the past, was a clear demonstration of its will and intentions.

This approach was maintained until the June 1983 election, though the uncertainty was never wholly resolved. Over a year before the election John Fforde of the Bank of England raised this question (set out later in Fforde, 1983). He wondered whether it was necessary to provide a clear medium-term direction in addition to the modified and qualified monetary targets — for instance, by setting out a path for national income (money Gross Domestic Product). This idea, advocated in particular by Samuel Brittan of the *Financial Times*, would enable 'a greater emphasis to be placed on the favourable development of demand and output that could be accommodated...if, for example, unit labour costs grew sufficiently slowly for the stance of policy to be made less restrictive'. Up to mid-1983 Treasury Ministers and officials had included figures for the path of money GDP in the strategy but had regarded them as further evidence rather than as operational guidelines.

The debate has turned on the balance between discretion and rules in the conduct of economic policy. The early Conservative approach was based on a desire to establish clear rules for the conduct of policy, reducing the scope for the exercise of discretion, which might dilute the thrust of the counter-inflation strategy. The later practice was more pragmatic, recognizing the problems of applying a simplified version of monetary policy and shifting the balance of the strategy while maintaining its direction. John Fforde, himself a participant on the side of discretion in the policy debates of 1980—1, concluded that 'except in some grave emergency, or in the initial phase of a novel strategy, the abandonment of judgement in favour of some simple, rigid, quantitative rule about the money supply does not reliably deliver acceptable results.' These lessons took a long time to learn.

Were there Alternatives?

This analysis has so far concentrated on the Medium-Term Financial Strategy in its own terms rather than in relation to the ultimate objectives of prices, output and employment. Would alternative approaches have produced better results? And what mistakes were made?

The Government's view has been almost oriental in its fatalism: no other policy would reduce inflation, and anyway the loss of jobs has been the inescapable result of past errors and international pressures. When he was Chancellor of the Exchequer Sir Geoffrey Howe frequently said that his emphasis on the priority of reducing inflation had been endorsed by his fellow finance Ministers and by international financial organizations.

Admittedly, there would almost certainly have been a severe recession and a sharp rise in unemployment in the UK with or without the Thatcher administration, partly because of world influences such as the recession induced by the second oil-price shock and the large increase throughout the industrialized world in competition from the newly industrializing countries, particularly those in the Far East. The rows over steel quotas and shipbuilding subsidies have highlighted the worldwide extent of the problems of these sectors. In addition, the UK has probably been less well able to cope with these shocks than have other leading industrialized countries. The ability of the British economy to adapt had been undermined by rigidities in the structure of its industry and in its labour market. Consequently, some of the closures and redundancies of the 1979—83 period may have reflected long-delayed but inevitable decisions to increase efficiency which had previously been deferred. However, this has only been part of the story. Fiscal policy has been much tighter in the UK than in other major industrialized countries. Table 4 is from the December 1982 *Economic Outlook* of the Organization for Economic Co-operation and Development (OECD), the Paris-based secretariat of the twenty-four leading industrial countries. It shows the change in Budget deficits as a percentage of national income, or Gross Domestic Product, for the seven major countries from 1979 to 1982. A plus means a move towards restriction (through public expenditure cuts or tax increases); a minus indicates expansion. The second column adjusts for changes in the level of economic activity, that is, the automatic impact of the recession in reducing tax revenues and boosting payments to the unemployed, which pushes up deficits. The third column shows increased interest payments on public debt as a result of higher interest rates and increased indebtedness. The last column, the apparent 'ex ante' change, indicates the alteration in the budget deficit as a consequence of the Government's own decisions.

TABLE 4   *Changes in budgetary policy 1979—82: percentages of Gross Domestic Product*

	Actual change	*Effect of changes in economic activity*	*Effect of increased interest*	*Apparent 'ex ante' change*
UK	+1.1	-4.4	-0.5	+6.0
Japan	+1.5	-0.7	-1.2	+3.4
Canada	-4.4	-5.7	-1.3	+2.6
West Germany	-1.4	-2.8	-0.7	+2.1
France	-2.2	-2.5	-0.9	+1.2
Italy	-2.9	-2.3	-1.8	+1.2
US	-4.3	-3.5	-0.6	-0.2
Average of above	-2.3	-3.0	-0.8	+1.5

Notes: + = move towards surplus (restriction; - = move towards deficit (expansion).
Source: OECD, *Economic Outlook*, December 1982.

Table 4 shows that after adjusting for the recession and higher interest payments, the British Government tightened its fiscal policy, via a reduction of its Budget deficit, by an amount equivalent to 6 per cent of GDP. This was four times the average change for the seven countries taken as a whole. The UK has thus been the least Keynesian of all major industrial countries.

The increase in unemployment in the UK has also been much larger than that overseas. Using standard international measures, the UK unemployment rate rose by over 140 per cent between 1979 and early 1983. Over the same period the total in the big seven industrialized countries rose by just over 80 per cent. These figures have been analysed to establish how much of the above-average rise in the UK total can be attributed to the policies followed by the Thatcher administration as opposed to other influences. As discussed above, there have probably been structural weaknesses in the British economy which might anyway have resulted in a faster rise in unemployment in the UK than overseas.

With all the necessary qualifications, economists have estimated that between two-fifths and a half of the rise in unemployment can broadly be attributed to Government policy. Both monetarists and Keynesians have reached similar conclusions. Dr Cliff Pratten (1982) calculated that in 1978 UK unemployment was 93 per cent of the combined total for West Germany, the Netherlands and Belgium, but by late 1981 the comparable proportion was 120 per cent. If UK unemployment had risen in line with these three countries, it would have been over 730,000 higher than in 1978, compared with an actual rise of 1.35 million. This leaves a 'Thatcher factor' of just over 600,000.

Other economists have suggested that Government policy may have had a somewhat more profound effect. A draft report prepared by advisers to the Treasury Committee of the Commons estimated that only up to a half of the rise in unemployment since 1979 could be attributed to the effects of the worldwide recession. Much of the remainder could be blamed on the Government's determination to use monetary policy to defeat inflation by pushing the exchange rate up excessively and restricting output. The report was never completed because of the calling of the June 1983 election, but its publication in draft form during the campaign provoked a row. Sir Geoffrey Howe argued that, apart from the world recession, other influences were at work, such as the pay explosion of 1978—9 and Britain's long-standing non-competitiveness, restrictive practices and over-manning in industry. In any event, by the time of the June 1983 election possibly between 750,000 and 900,000 of the rise in unemployment figures could be blamed on the Thatcher administration. But these estimates were really only informed guesses, since an alternative policy might also have raised unemployment faster in the UK than overseas. But the figures counter some of the blander comments of Ministers.

The main alternative approaches rested on a belief that Governments could do something directly to cut unemployment. They consisted mainly of a mixture of reflation and incomes policy, though with many varieties of scale and title. Would a massive expansion of demand in 1981 — through, say, tax cuts and higher public spending — have absorbed the unused capacity in the economy, or would its main long-term result have been a higher inflation rate? The answer has naturally turned on rival theories of how the economy works and on the scale of the action proposed. Three issues are involved. First, is the UK's problem a lack of supply rather than insufficient demand? Second, would reflation mean inflation? And, third, would an expansion in the Budget deficit raise interest rates, thus choking off recovery?

The evidence on all three points is controversial. First, there has been a contrast between the 1930s and the 1980s. Whereas fifty years ago there was a drop in total national income in money terms, a genuine deflation, in recent years national income, as measured by money Gross Domestic Product, has continued to grow. A drop in real (or inflation-adjusted) GDP has been accompanied by inflation, underlining the inflexibility of wages and prices. In the Conservatives' view, there has been not so much a shortage of demand as an inadequate supply response, illustrated by the combination of rising domestic demand, falling manufacturing output and growing imports in 1982. According to the Government, the problem has been low productivity and outdated and inefficient plant, so that there is a much smaller gap between potential and actual output than is commonly assumed. Hence any expansion of demand might quickly hit supply constraints, though this was less plausible in the depths of the recession in 1981.

Secondly, there has been a fierce debate about how far a large expansion of demand would worsen inflation. Any sizeable package would probably undermine the confidence of financial markets and depress the sterling exchange rate, whether or not exchange controls were reintroduced. This would in turn push up domestic costs, contributing to upward pressures on wages. In 1979–80 these pressures would have been additional to strong inflationary pressures that were already in the pipeline, though this would have been less true later on. Any Government elected in 1979 might have had to take a restrictive stance in the face of the rise in public expenditure, the breakdown of the Labour Government's incomes policy and the sharp rise in oil prices.

A central question is whether the inflationary pressures resulting from a reflationary policy could have been contained by an incomes policy. It is extremely doubtful whether a workable new policy restraining the size of money wage increases could have been constructed and made to stick in the 1979–81 period, following the 'winter of discontent'. The disadvantage of such policies had become apparent in 1978–9. Any deal with the trade unions along traditional lines would probably have required concessions on industrial relations law and job subsidies, which might have undermined the drive to improve industrial performance. The 17-year-old on/off series of incomes policies of both Conservative and Labour Governments seemed to have run into the sands by the late 1970s. Events since then, notably changes in the attitude of the trade unions, have underlined the difficulty of relaunching even a modified form of such a policy.

A connected issue is whether it is possible to live with inflation. The evidence of the past twenty years is that a high rate of inflation, and the related phenomenon of sharply changing relative prices, have produced serious disturbances to the efficient allocation of resources in the economy, as well as to the distribution of incomes. It appears to be impossible for the UK to accommodate a high but stable rate of inflation. The result in the 1960s and 1970s was a steady acceleration in the long-term rate of inflation, as the labour and financial markets were constantly adjusting rather than stabilizing around a new equilibrium level. These factors have also made it difficult to aim for, and impossible precisely to achieve, a balance between levels of employment and inflation. Monetarists would anyway point to the so-called natural rate of unemployment (as determined by the structure of the labour market) below which the total cannot be pushed without generating accelerating inflation. While this natural rate may have risen during the 1970s, it was presumably well below the actual rate reached in the early 1980s.

The third question is how far an expansionary policy would have 'crowded out' the private sector by pushing up interest rates and thus limiting business expansion and investment. Much of the argument turns on self-fulfilling, and possibly self-defeating, views about the impact of confidence factors on financial markets. The empirical evidence is ambiguous. There has been no close correlation between levels of short-term interest rates and public-sector borrowing and the money supply. Much has depended on what has been happening to interest rates overseas and to the exchange rate. There may therefore be scope for some flexibility in the level of public borrowing — of, say, £2 billion to £3 billion either way — without a major impact on interest rates. But this does not mean that an increase of £5 billion or more would have no effect on financial markets. The supply of public-sector financial assets, notably gilt-edged stocks, would have to be raised to finance the borrowing, and this would push up interest rates. The experience of the USA, with its spiralling Federal Budget deficit under the Reagan administration, has suggested that a sufficiently high level of borrowing does affect interest rates. But there is room for manoeuvre, and for judgement, within these extremes.

Overall, large-scale reflation was not, and is not, a feasible alternative. The result is likely to be instability, with no assurance of soundly based jobs and growth. Packages of the type and scale advanced by the Labour Party and the Trades

Union Congress in 1982—3 were carefully worked out, but they did not overcome the doubts outlined above. Action to raise public-sector borrowing from £8 billion to £14 billion, as proposed by Labour, with only a flimsy incomes policy, was more likely to provoke an immediate crisis of confidence and higher inflation than to create sustainable non-inflationary growth.

This does not, however, mean that the Government's refrain of 'There is no alternative' has been right and that all the suffering has been unavoidable. A middle way may exist between the Thatcher approach and full-scale reflation. It is possible to talk enticingly about 'modest' or 'moderate' reflation, almost splitting the difference between the Conservative and Labour proposals, as the SDP/Liberal Alliance has at times appeared to do. Such a proposal sounds appealing but it is open to the charge that it will do little for jobs while blunting the thrust of the counter-inflation strategy. However, there may be a mix of policies which can contain inflation while minimizing the impact on output and jobs. The Government may not be able to produce full employment any longer, but its actions can still have some effect on levels of activity and unemployment.

Mistakes in the Strategy

The possibility of modifying the strategy is suggested by the identifiable errors made by the Thatcher administration since 1979. They amount mainly to a lack of feel in economic management — that sixth sense, or capacity to react to problems, which Denis Healey at times possessed. First, the Government failed to take sufficient account of the significant deterioration in the domestic and external environment when it came into office in May 1979. Secondly, it took a long time to respond to the severities of the recession and to the sharp rise in the pound. Both mistakes exacerbated the recession.

The first charge is that the Government boosted inflation, and thereby helped to aggravate the 1979—80 upsurge in labour costs, as a result of the decision in the June 1979

Budget to raise VAT to 15 per cent and to force up public-sector prices. The Government did not take sufficient notice either of the acceleration in the inflation rate that was already in the pipeline or of the possible impact of the upheaval in oil prices that was becoming apparent before the June 1979 Budget. The increase in public-sector prices would have been reduced if the basic rate of income tax had not been cut from 33 to 30 per cent, which would have averted the full rise in VAT to 15 per cent. Moreover, less ambitious immediate targets might have been set for the elimination of nationalized industry deficits, thus limiting the rise in their prices.

The contrary view is that if the higher rates of income tax were to be cut to boost the incentives of managers, then the basic rate had to be reduced. But the benefits of the lower basic rate do not seem to have been widely appreciated by comparison with the rise in prices. Treasury Ministers have also argued that under any Government a tough Budget would have been necessary to deal with the rise in public expenditure. This would probably have involved a sharp rise in VAT and other indirect taxes. All that a less ambitious Budget might have achieved therefore would have been 2 to 3 per cent less on an inflation rate which was already accelerating up to the mid-teens and above. Still, even that might have been significant if coupled with a tougher counter-inflation policy.

A related criticism concerns the Government's attitude to wages. The Conservatives' commitment, during the 1979 election, to accepting the awards of the Clegg Commission was undoubtedly damaging economically, both because it affected the climate for wage bargaining and because it added £1.5 billion to the public-sector wage bill in 1979–80 and about £2 billion in 1980–1. However, having made the commitment, it would have been politically very difficult for the Government to go back on its pledge just after the election. It persisted with a hands-off approach to the level of pay settlements during 1979–80, merely pointing to the monetary target and to cash limits. This left a vacuum. Therefore when the Budget measures helped to raise the forecast inflation rate at the end of 1979 to around 18 per cent, against just over 10 per cent in May, trade unions immediately raised the level of their wage claims even further.

The problem was that the Government's desire to cut income tax conflicted with its counter-inflation objective both directly, via the VAT decision, and indirectly because of the risks taken over public-sector borrowing. A more sensible course, especially for a newly elected Government, might have been to use to the full the opportunity to blame the previous Labour administration for the dreadful state of the Treasury 'books' which it had inherited, soaring public expenditure and so on. These, together with the increasingly gloomy world economic scene, might have justified a decision to defer tax cuts in order to concentrate on countering the upsurge in inflation. At the same time, a more explicit view might have been taken on pay, especially in the public sector, even though any formal type of incomes policy was out of the question. With hindsight it is possible to argue that a sharp increase in public-sector wages and in nationalized industry prices was inevitable and that it was better to get the bulge in inflation out of the system as quickly as possible. But there was a cost, higher wages and lost competitiveness, which aggravated the recession.

The second charge is that the Government's monetary policy hoped to push the sterling exchange rate up too far. The criticism is essentially that the Government's monetarism was too simple-minded and too narrowly focused. The concentration on sterling M3 in 1979–80 prevented the Government from taking sufficient account of possible, and actual, peculiarities in its behaviour and of international influences such as the growing demand for the pound. Admittedly, the Government responded in the summer and autumn of 1979 by accelerating the end of outward exchange controls. This produced a substantial outflow of capital, without which the rise in the exchange rate might have been larger. But this action was inadequate, and during 1980–1 the Government was slow to respond to clear evidence that the rise in unemployment was far worse than expected and that the appreciation of sterling was partly to blame. The Government was initially trapped by its adherence to the sterling M3 target, although this measure was giving misleading signals of a loose stance when policy was clearly tight. Even broadly monetarist economists such as Professor Alan Budd of the London Business School have blamed the Government for the severity of the recession because of its refusal to budge from its strategy.

A better approach might have been to present the strategy in more general terms, in relation to either total national income (that is, money Gross Domestic Product) or much broader financial guidelines rather than to one erratic monetary aggregate. The policy might then have been more robust and would have allowed the Government to lower interest rates when the full extent of the upward pressure on the exchange rate became clear in early 1980. It might also have permitted official intervention in the foreign exchange markets in 1980–1 to take the froth off the appreciation of sterling. The pound would undoubtedly have risen sharply in 1979–81 because of sterling's status as a petro-currency, because of the strength of the UK's current account position and because of its generally tough counter-inflation stance. But the damage done by the final sharp spurt in the pound in late 1980 and early 1981 might have been avoided in part if policy had been more broadly based. The strategy might also have been better able to withstand the monetary upheavals of the period.

These modifications might not, however, have permitted a significantly different fiscal policy, even though in 1981–2 it was unintentionally tighter than planned. Public-sector borrowing could have been up to £2 billion higher than otherwise planned to take more accurate account of the recession. But, as argued above, a substantially higher level of borrowing might have pushed up interest rates to choke off any private-sector recovery. Even within these constraints producers could have been helped by a transfer from still relatively well-off consumers. This could have been achieved by raising taxes from those in work, whose living standards had been boosted by the rise in the pound. That was what happened in a back-door way via the increase in employee National Insurance contributions, which could have permitted earlier help for industry. A start to the phased reduction in the employers' National Insurance surcharge, an immediate boost to cash flow, could have been made in 1980 rather than in spring 1982. Moreover, once the severity of the recession had become clear, there could have been scope for bringing forward some much needed public-sector capital projects.

Similarly, the various special measures to subsidize employment (and to reduce the published unemployment total) could have been brought in earlier. In particular, the youth training scheme was due to come into operation only in autumn 1983, after two years of planning and consultation, although unemployment among school leavers began to rise sharply in 1980.

Action to help industry and the unemployed in these ways might have taken some of the edge off the shake-out of the 1979—80 period. After all, it is doubtful whether such measures would have undermined the drive to improve industrial efficiency and to reduce inflation.

Prospects for the Second Term

Some of these options were still valid in mid-1983, while others had become interesting historical speculations. But what are the prospects for the strategy in the second Conservative term? The party's election manifesto was notably short on detailed plans for the economy. It did, however, state: 'In the next Parliament, we shall endeavour to bring inflation lower still. Our ultimate goal should be a society with stable prices.' The manifesto also pledged that 'the further improvement in allowances and lower rates of income tax remain a high priority, together with measures to reduce the poverty and unemployment traps.'

The early remarks of Nigel Lawson as Chancellor of the Exchequer, notably in the Commons on 29 June 1983, did little to fill out the picture. He referred merely to the intention of keeping the underlying trend of inflation downwards. The Medium-Term Financial Strategy, he said, provided 'the essential framework of financial discipline'; 'the heart of the strategy is continued downward pressure over the years on both monetary growth and public-sector borrowing as a proportion of total output. Monetary and fiscal policy have to go hand in hand.' He laid particular stress on 'firm control of public expenditure, otherwise there will be no room for tax cuts throughout the lifetime of this Parliament'. The aim, he said, was to keep expenditure in constant prices (or real terms) roughly level; as the economy grew, the total should fall as a proportion of Gross Domestic Product.

These comments naturally raised a number of questions about the implementation of the strategy. The first test came in early July, when there were indications of a significant overshoot of public spending above planned levels. The response referred almost solely to the fiscal rather than the monetary implications, though only two days earlier further confirmation had been provided that the money supply was also over its target range. The monetary target remained important as a general warning signal and indicator of City confidence rather than as a precise operational guideline. The key target appears to have become fiscal – public spending and borrowing – with the exchange rate kept clearly in view.

Over the longer term did the pledge to stabilize prices signify a target of zero inflation? Was there to be a return to the nineteenth-century world of the Forsytes, who confidently invested in undated 2.5 per cent Consols with no fear of loss of value? No doubt in her more passionately Victorian moments – perhaps when reading Kipling – Mrs Thatcher would like to see an absolutely stable price level, but this is in no sense a formal target. Indeed, when (as in mid-1983) the UK rate of price inflation had already been reduced to low single figures, an intense further squeeze would have been needed to push the rate down to zero, in part because in an open economy such as Britain, with a high proportion of imports, the price level is heavily affected by international factors. It would require either a steadily appreciating currency or a reduction in domestic costs to produce absolute stability. This was not a likely objective, since the costs on the way could be enormous.

There anyway appears to be no simple trade-off between inflation and unemployment. Consequently, the ingenious calculations of some economists and politicians proving that it is possible to generate x hundred thousand more jobs at the cost of y per cent more inflation are largely computer artefacts. It may be possible to calculate retrospectively the unemployment cost of a specified reduction in the inflation rate, but this is essentially a comparison of two sets of figures without a clearly identifiable causal link. Both the labour and the financial market are likely to over-react to any attempt to fine-tune such a balance. Up to the late 1970s it was never possible to say that inflation had been contained at, say, 8 to 10 per cent and that priority could now be accorded to reducing unemployment. Inflation continued to smoulder.

There may be more room for manoeuvre in policy when the inflation rate is lower than when it is higher. A choice may exist between a further considerable squeeze and the continuation of the gradualist approach which, it is hoped, will hold the inflation rate down to around, or slightly below, the international average and will permit some growth in output. The latter approach is implicit in the assumption in the Financial Statement and Budget Report of March 1983 that national income or money GDP is expected to grow at an average rate of 8 per cent a year in the period to 1985–6. But this would not permit any relaxation of fiscal policy.

The view of most economic forecasters is that life, at any rate for those in work, should improve during the mid-1980s, but not spectacularly, and certainly not sufficiently to make a large dent in unemployment. The Bank of England noted in its *Quarterly Bulletin* for June 1983 that the recovery seemed unlikely to be very strong. The growth in consumer spending was likely to taper off; export prospects were dull; the impact of the rebuilding of industry's stocks was likely to be temporary; and imports were rising. At the same time, the rate of profitability of investment remained very low, and companies continued to report sufficient capacity to meet expected demand.

A boom was expected by neither Keynesians nor moneta-rists. After a projected 2.5 per cent growth in total output in 1983, Keynesian economists such as the National Institute of Economic and Social Research and stockbrokers Simon and Coates were in mid-1983 projecting a slow-down in expansion to 1.25 or 1.5 per cent in 1984. This would mean a continuing steady rise in the level of unemployment. The broadly monetarist London Business School was slightly more optimistic. In July 1983 it forecast a rise in total output of over 2.5 per cent in 1984, though it projected a slight slowing down thereafter. However, this would be sufficient only to stop unemployment from rising further in 1984 and would lead to a decline of perhaps 100,000 a year in later years. These mid-1983 forecasts projected that the twelve-month rate of retail price inflation would rise from its artificial low point of 3.7 per cent in May 1983 to around 6 per cent by the end of 1983 and to perhaps 7 per cent plus in 1984.

These forecasts were naturally subject to several qualifications. They were dependent on some modest growth in world output and on no significant upsurge in inflation. They were also constrained by continuing uncertainties about the impact of the high level of US interest rates in view of the continuing large Federal Budget deficit. This was the major single external cloud that hung over the UK's prospects. There were related worries about the serious debt problems of less developed countries, especially those in Latin America. The forecasts were also generally dependent on the absence of sharp fluctuations in the sterling exchange rate, which would either push up the inflation rate or hit exports. In short, successful monetarism, like successful Keynesianism, could not be built in one country.

Domestically, there was the dilemma of how far modest growth in total output, sufficient to check the rise in unemployment — say, 2.5 per cent a year — could be combined with an inflation rate of about 5 per cent per year, as assumed in the March 1983 version of the Medium-Term Financial Strategy. Keynesians argued that 1983 was likely to be an unusual year of low inflation and relatively high growth, at least by recent standards. According to this view, inflation might start to pick up again if the economic recovery was sustained. World expansion would push up commodity and oil prices, while a domestic upturn would produce demands for higher wages, following the suppression of pay rises because of fear of unemployment during the recession. The Keynesians therefore suggested that in the absence of an incomes policy and specific measures to hold down prices, growth in total output of 2.5 per cent a year could not be combined with lower inflation on a sustained basis.

If a broadly monetarist approach is maintained, is there a Catch-22 that rules out sustained growth of output as long as a low inflation rate remains the goal? That view was implicit in the pessimistic statement issued by the 364 academic economists in March 1981. Ministers have argued that this represents a false choice. They have pointed out that output has grown, albeit slowly, since 1981 despite a tight fiscal policy and no reflation. Consequently, in their view, financial discipline can be compatible with non-inflationary growth. The sceptics have said that the limited recovery in activity in the 1981–3 period reflected the once-for-all impact of the slow-down in the inflation rate and the end of industry's run-down of stocks. But they have questioned whether this would be enough to sustain growth. In any event, the Conservatives' hopes for their second term clearly rest on continued recovery. During the 1983 election campaign Nigel Lawson, then still Energy Secretary, offered his hunch, based on many years as a financial journalist and politician, that unemployment would stop rising in 1984. But this hunch has not been transformed into a formal forecast.

Public Spending and Tax Cuts

These estimates are also of crucial significance for the Government's hopes of cutting taxation. Without sustained growth of output, public borrowing would not fall as a proportion of Gross Domestic Product, and taxes could not be cut at the same time as public-sector borrowing was being held in check. The narrowing of the room for manoeuvre, on the Government's own assumptions, was underlined by the leaked Treasury documents prepared in September 1982 for the Cabinet's discussion of long-term public expenditure trends. The debate was aborted because of the row about an accompanying Think Tank paper about possible options for containing public expenditure, especially in the context of the welfare state. The documents reveal the dilemma facing the Conservatives in their second term.

Public spending and taxes were projected on the basis of existing policies and commitments in mid-1982, after adjusting for inflation. The projections were little changed by mid-1983. There were two 'scenarios'. One, very similar to the Medium-Term Financial Strategy, assumed a 2.5 per cent rate of economic growth and a 5 per cent average rate of inflation. The second scenario assumed a 0.75 per cent average rate of growth of output until 1985–6 and then 0.5 per cent a year until 1990, with a 10 per cent average inflation rate in the mid- and late 1980s.

The key to the scenarios was public spending. Table 5 includes projections from the report of an inter-departmental group of officials that was prepared for the Cabinet's discussion. This shows that under both the higher- and the lower-growth scenarios public expenditure would grow in real terms. Under the higher-growth projection public expenditure (including debt interest) would rise by just over 12.5 per cent between 1982–3 and 1990–1; under the lower-growth projection the rise would be just over 11.5 per cent.

TABLE 5   *Public expenditure for the rest of the 1980s:*
percentage change between 1982–3 and 1990–1 in real terms

	Higher-growth scenario	Lower-growth scenario
Total (including debt interest)	+12.6	+11.6
Defence*	+39.7	+39.7
Industry, energy, trade, employment †	−1.0	+7.9
Housing	+20.9	+89.9
Education, science and the arts	−2.0	−3.9
Health and personal social services	+24.4	+17.5
Social security	+7.1	+2.5

Notes: * Increase of 26.1 per cent if defence costs are assumed not to rise faster than inflation generally; † excluding grants to nationalized industries.
Source: Report of inter-departmental group of officials to Cabinet, September 1982.

The differences in the expected rates of growth of expenditure can be explained largely by the varying impact of the two growth projections upon the relative rate of change of public-sector costs. The latter were assumed to increase faster if the economy grew more rapidly. There were also complicated offsetting factors; higher growth was assumed to lead to more road-building, while continued slow growth was taken to imply higher spending on industry, employment and housing.

Under both scenarios public expenditure would clearly grow more rapidly than would be desired by the Government. The projected increases are to be compared with the stated intention of holding public expenditure unchanged in real terms and the implied projection in the February 1983 White Paper of a 1.7 per cent rise in real terms between 1982–3 and 1985–6 (slightly higher if debt interest is excluded). This gap is clearly significant for hopes of tax cuts.

Critics have argued that the assumptions of the interdepartmental report were unnecessarily pessimistic. In particular, it has been suggested (notably by David Blake in *The Times*, 8 November 1982) that perhaps a quarter of the projected increase could not be justified because of the assumption of a 2 per cent faster rate of increase in the cost of defence equipment than in prices generally. Yet Treasury policy has been not to allow such adjustment for relative price movements. Moreover, the assumed rise of nearly 90 per cent in expenditure on housing under the lower-growth scenario looked implausible. It was based on the view that some increase in gross capital expenditure was necessary to improve and replace decaying houses. And if the economy grew more slowly and interest rates were high, private-sector house-building would probably be low, leaving a gap to be filled by the state. This projection appeared to conflict with the steady fall in housing expenditure between 1979 and 1983.

The Treasury's critics pointed out that expenditure on the other major social programmes was not projected to rise especially rapidly, though this forecast accorded with a minimalist view of the standards of service. Consequently, the overall position was, and is, not as gloomy as that painted in the report. None the less, even if some of the Treasury's specific assumptions were too pessimistic, others might be too optimistic — such as the projection under the lower-growth scenario that adult unemployment would be only 3 million in 1990–1. Similarly, there would be strong pressures for increases in the real value of social benefits and for a faster growth in National Health Service resources.

In any event, on the given assumptions, public spending would rise from 44 per cent of Gross Domestic Product in 1982–3 to 46.8 per cent by the end of the decade under the lower-growth view and would fall to 39.3 per cent under the higher-growth projection. The share of taxes in GDP would fall slightly on the latter projection, though the decline in the relative proportion of public spending would be sufficient to cut public-sector borrowing to just over 2 per cent of GDP by the end of the 1980s. This would be about the same, in percentage terms, as the target for 1985–6 set out in the Medium-Term Financial Strategy. It would not, however, allow for any easing of the personal tax burden in real terms or for a cut in business taxes.

Under the lower-growth scenario, public-sector borrowing would be 7 per cent of GDP by the end of the 1980s — more than double its level in 1982–3. If borrowing had to be cut back to 2 per cent of GDP without reductions in public spending, taxes would have to be raised by £15 billion (at 1982 prices). This would be equivalent to either an increase in the basic rate of income tax from 30p to 45p in the pound or a rise in VAT from 15 to 25 per cent.

The Treasury paper concluded that the projections demonstrated

the difficulty of financing the levels of public expenditure implied by the continuation of current policies. If the economy grows very slowly [as in the low-growth scenario] the consequences for taxation and/or borrowing are very serious. The economy would need to grow steadily and strongly [as in the higher-growth projection] to permit the sort of expenditure levels envisaged.

The Treasury said it was doubtful whether this growth could be achieved without further Government action to improve work incentives and to stimulate business profitability through tax cuts.

> But if taxes were cut, borrowing could not be restricted to 2 per cent of GDP, and the inflation and interest rate assumptions would begin to look implausible.

Sir Geoffrey Howe concluded, in an accompanying note, that the rates of tax implied by the lower-growth scenario would 'plainly be quite unacceptable'. The higher-growth projections would also not allow for sufficient reductions in business and personal taxation to encourage the private sector to expand: 'The way forward to better economic performance can therefore only be through reducing expenditure.' The record of the past two decades, he claimed, showed 'all too clearly the danger of formulating or accepting policy commitments on the assumption of continuing economic growth which in the event has not been achieved'. The evidence bears out Sir Geoffrey's warning against over-optimism, though in September 1982 the Treasury may have painted too gloomy a picture of the medium-term outlook in order to obtain short-term restraint. However, events that occurred between the preparation of the paper for Cabinet discussion and mid-1983 underlined the upward pressures on expenditure and suggested that the Treasury's caution might be justified. The announcement by Nigel Lawson in early July 1983 of a £500 million general squeeze on cash-limited programmes, in order to offset an overrun on demand-determined expenditure, was an indicator of the continued Treasury desire to hold down spending as well as the difficulty of achieving control. The result was likely to be a general squeeze on services.

Non-monetarists have argued that the Thatcher administration has been caught in a trap by its insistence on a further reduction in the scale of public-sector borrowing despite the continued high level of unemployment. In their view, there might be scope both for higher public expenditure and for some tax cuts if this restraint were relaxed. However, an analysis by Gavyn Davies and David Piachaud, two prominent Labour Party economists (in Glennerster, 1983), suggested that the room for manoeuvre might be less than sometimes supposed. They projected that on the basis of a 2.5 per cent average rate of growth of output during the 1980s, public spending on goods and services might be allowed to rise by 4 per cent a year in real terms. Private consumption might grow at 2 per cent a year in real terms, though most of this would be absorbed by a reduction in unemployment and by Labour's promised improvement in social benefits. This would leave the real living standards of people with jobs virtually static over the period. If output grew more slowly, the margin would be even smaller.

Davies and Piachaud concluded that Labour's promises of increased services and far larger transfer payments (such as social security benefits) were not compatible. So there are no free lunches for either monetarists or Keynesians. The problem is that the pressures for higher public spending will make the attainment of both the public borrowing targets in the Medium-Term Financial Strategy and cuts in taxation difficult, if not impossible.

Not surprisingly, therefore, in September 1982 Sir Geoffrey invited his Cabinet colleagues to make no further public commitments which would add significantly to expenditure beyond 1985–6 and to avoid repeating further pledges which would otherwise have expired. (In its vagueness the Conservative election manifesto followed this injunction to the letter.) Sir Geoffrey concluded on the characteristic note that the Cabinet should 'consider further how these difficult issues might best be presented to our supporters in Parliament and to the country at large'.

An Assessment of the Record and the Prospects

The last two chapters have discussed the record of the Thatcher administration – how the strategy has operated, possible alternative approaches and the prospects for the second term. The economic record up to mid-1983 has been indifferent, even allowing for the difficult economic and external circumstances. Some change of direction was necessary in the late 1970s, as the Wilson and Callaghan administrations at least tacitly recognized. Governments could no longer guarantee full employment; priority had to be given to the containment of inflation; and a shake-up of British industry, in order to make it more competitive, was inescapable. The Thatcher administration has been right to recognize these points and to stick to them. The alternative — large-scale reflation and the informal or explicit protection of industry — would not have worked and would only have deferred inevitable and painful adjustment. The Thatcher administration's failures have lain in the implementation of these objectives and in the social policies dictated by these economic measures.

Some rise in unemployment during the early 1980s was probably inevitable in view of the underlying problems and the world recession. Yet that is not a sufficient or satisfactory explanation of what has happened. The Thatcher administration's initial naive monetarism and lack of flair in economic management have exacerbated the problems. The Government failed to respond early enough, or on a sufficiently large scale, to the difficulties posed by the rise in the pound and the faster than expected rise in unemployment. Some of the social and economic problems could have been eased without impairing the drive to contain inflation and to improve competitiveness.

Nor is it clear that all the suffering has produced any deep-seated gains. After a once-for-all jump in output per head in 1980—1, there has been no sustained productivity miracle. And any evidence of a revival of enterprise is highly debatable (this issue is discussed in a later chapter). Similarly, the alleged new mood of realism in industrial relations and in management may still be no more than a temporary response to the deepest recession for fifty years. Firm evidence of a fundamental improvement in the supply response of British industry has still to be provided.

The economic prospects for the mid-1980s are admittedly somewhat better than in the first Thatcher term. Output should continue to grow patchily during 1983—4, with the inflation rate remaining in mid-single figures. But at best this may be sufficient only to lead to a stabilization of unemployment. there remain considerable inherent contradictions between some of the Government's economic goals — for example, between the desire to cut taxes and to maintain acceptable standards of public services. Both are dependent on sustained economic recovery.

Difficult economic decisions were probably inevitable in the early 1980s, but the Thatcher administration has yet to show that it can successfully manage, let alone reverse, Britain's long-term economic decline.

6

The Public Sector

The Government intends to reduce total public expenditure progressively in volume terms over the next four years, to a level in 1983–4 about 4 per cent lower than in 1979–80.

The Government's Expenditure Plans
March 1980

We were surprised to note the consistent and significant rise in expenditure for the period to date; when expressed in cost terms it has risen by 6.2 per cent over the last four years. Present plans imply a continuation of this trend with a rise of nearly two percentage points expected over the three years to 1985–6. This trend is all the more remarkable when the popular view — reinforced by the presentation in the White Paper — is that spending has been cut.

Treasury and Civil Service Committee of the Commons
March 1983

Why has Public Spending Over-Run Targets?

Public expenditure has been the Thatcher administration's abiding headache. It has been at the top of the short (but deeply distressing) list of Mrs Thatcher's acknowledged failures. The Conservatives came to power claiming that 'public expenditure was at the heart of Britain's present economic difficulties' (Expenditure White Paper, November 1979). But instead of the planned decline, the total has risen steadily. This has limited the scope for cuts in taxation and, indeed, was responsible for the rise in the personal tax burden in the 1980–2 period. Yet since 1979 there has been a constant chorus of complaints about 'savage' cuts in the welfare state.

This apparent paradox of rising public expenditure and simultaneous, and widespread, protest has highlighted the ambiguous character of Thatcherism — its far-reaching rhetoric and cautious practice. Fundamental questions have been raised about how far the Treasury and Whitehall (far from synonymous) control public expenditure, about the constitutional relationship between central Government and local authorities and about popular expectations about what services should be provided by the state.

The record appears straightforward, though it has in reality been more complicated. Public expenditure in cost terms (that is, after adjusting for inflation) rose by 4.5 per cent between 1978–9 and 1982–3 (or nearly 6.25 per cent if debt interest payments are included). This was 8.75 per cent (9.75 per cent including debt interest) higher than the level for 1982–3 proposed in the March 1980 Public Expenditure White Paper (as set out in table 6). However, at least the Conservatives have been able to point out that the 1982–3 figure was more than 5 per cent less than proposed for that year by the Callaghan administration in its final White Paper. Public expenditure has also risen as a proportion of Gross Domestic Product, from 41 per cent in 1978–9 to 44 per cent in 1982–3 — and not for want of trying by the Treasury. There has been a whole series of 'cuts' exercises (often more than one during a year), but overall the result of these reviews has been the elimination of proposals for additional expenditure rather than a reduction in the total.

There are several explanations. Table 7 shows the change in various categories of expenditure between 1978–9 and 1982–3. The pattern has been a sharp increase in some programmes, which has offset large declines in other areas. The main increases have been in defence, law and order, agricultural support, employment and social security. The largest reductions have been in overseas aid, net payments to the EEC and housing. So there has been no unstoppable public-sector juggernaut rolling forward in every area of Government.

TABLE 6   Public Expenditure: the changing plans, in cost terms at constant prices (1978–9 = 100)

	1978–9	1979–80	1980–1	1981–2	1982–3	1983–4	1984–5	1985–6
				Total expenditure (including debt interest)				
March 1980	100	99.6	99.6	98.7	96.5	95.8		
March 1981	100	101.5	105.6	105.3	103.6	100.7		
March 1982	100	101.0	103.6	106.3	107.3	105.7	105.3	
February 1983	100	101.0	103.3	105.7	106.1	107.0	107.4	107.9

Source: Memorandum by Mr Terry Ward, specialist adviser to the Treasury and Civil Service Committee of the Commons, February 1983.

TABLE 7 *Public expenditure*

	Percentage change in real (cost) terms, 1980—1 prices, 1978—9 to 1982—3	Cash figures for 1982—3 (£ million)
Defence	+16.7	14,411
Overseas aid	−19.5	959
Net payments to EEC institutions	−53.1	580
Other overseas services	−6.5	663
Agriculture, fisheries, food, forestry	+33.3	1,784
Industry, employment, energy, trade	+17.1	5,854
Transport	+7.6	4,340
Housing	−56;2	2,579
Other environmental services	−7.7	3,433
Law, order, protective services	+27.7	4,284
Education and science	−1.2	12,628
Arts and libraries	−3.4	579
Health and personal social services	+13.4	13,879
Social security	+19.9	32,473
Other public services	+4.6	1,670
Common services	+17.5	1,652
Scotland	+3.2	6,263
Wales	−2.4	2,379
Northern Ireland	+1.3	3,568

Source: Figures are based on Public Expenditure White Paper, February 1983.

The increase in some programmes was planned and was the direct result of political choice. The 1979 Conservative election manifesto had proposed increasing expenditure on defence and law and order. Similarly, the biggest reductions since 1978—9 have reflected the Government's political priorities — cutbacks in housing subsidies and capital investment and the pruning back of the overseas aid programme, in contrast to what happened under Labour, when defence expenditure fell in real terms, but the housing and overseas aid programmes grew rapidly. However, an increase in both the defence and the law and order budgets had been assumed when the Thatcher administration projected a fall in total spending.

The record of the past decade suggests that political views have affected the distribution of expenditure. This runs counter to the fashionable thesis that expenditure on particular programmes is likely to rise regardless of who is in power, that it is determined by the demands of pressure groups and by the skilful tactics of bureaucrats eager to defend and to augment their empires. Sir Leo Pliatzky, a former senior Treasury official and veteran of most of the spending battles of the 1960s and 1970s, has argued (Pliatzky, 1982) that trends in expenditure over the past ten years can probably best be explained in terms of the differing philosophies of the two main parties, in conjunction with the brute force of events. Sir Leo concluded:

> Experience shows, of course, that there is a natural tendency for plans to go wrong, and that the multiplicity of government objectives makes it extremely difficult to achieve all of them. Some of the difficulties were predictable from the outset: the commitment to increases in particular programmes, which meant that the Government would have to run fast just to stand still; the improbability of a turnround in the financing of nationalized industries on the scale proposed; the uncertainty of those savings which required the co-operation of local authorities; and the tendency of spending Ministers to want to spend once the pressure of events became more potent than the Brownie points awarded for cutting their programmes. But on top of these factors it was the slump, gathering momentum rapidly as the year [1980] progressed, which had not been anticipated in the 1980 Budget and which wrecked the expenditure plans.

The deeper than expected recession was clearly very important. As Peter Mountfield, a Treasury official, told the Treasury and Civil Service Committee of the Commons in February 1983, 'Ministers have decided to add to public expenditure, not to cut it back, and this is their response to recession, but they clearly are not minded to increase expenditure on a large-scale in a contra-cyclical way.' It is difficult to relate expenditure programmes precisely to the impact of the recession, but the broad categories of spending that have been affected particularly are unemployment and associated supplementary and housing benefits, employment and training schemes, support for various heavy industries (steel, shipbuilding and so on) and Government lending to nationalized industries. All these programmes have risen during the recession and, indeed, could not be directly limited by the Government, since they were determined more by factors outside its control.

The combined total of these programmes rose from £5.4 billion in 1978–9 to £9.56 billion in 1982–3 in real terms (in constant 1981–2 prices). However, although the March 1980 plans had assumed a small rise in unemployment during the early 1980s, total expenditure on these programmes combined had been projected to fall by about £1.2 billion over the period, and an especially sharp improvement in the position of nationalized industries was projected. The gap between the original 1980 plans for these programmes in 1982–3 and the out-turn was therefore £5.3–£5.5 billion. This more than accounted for the rise in total expenditure of £4.4 billion during the period, so that spending on other programmes fell slightly. However, the original intention had been that total expenditure should fall by a substantial amount. After deducting the recession-related programmes, there was still a gap in 1982–3 of £3 billion or £4 billion between the 1980 plans and the out-turn.

The gap can be explained in part by a small overshoot on the favoured programmes. Once the green light had been given, the service chiefs and those responsible for law and order exploited the opportunity to the full. Spending on these two programmes in 1982–3 was higher even than that proposed in March 1980. In the case of defence this was also partly to do with the unforeseen and expensive emergency of the Falklands war in 1982, but after adjusting for both the recession and these favoured programmes, there was a gap of probably over £3 billion. Spending on a wide range of non-recession-related programmes, such as health, education and transport, was slightly higher in 1982—3 than had originally been planned.

This gap between plan and out-turn, together with the generally higher than desired level of expenditure, did not necessarily imply any major breakdown of control — at least not in central government, though there were problems with local authorities. Instead the outcome may have been a reflection of the earlier over-optimistic assumptions. However, many of the proposals worked out by the Conservatives during their Shadow expenditure review in Opposition were implemented. The total would probably have been much higher without this preparatory work. But some Conservative critics have argued that, for all this work, it took two years for the Treasury to get a proper grip on spending, especially public-sector pay, and that John Biffen, the Chief Secretary to the Treasury from May 1979 to January 1981, was too easy-going in his bilateral discussions with spending Ministers.

Moreover, given the inherent upward pressures on expenditure on social security and the health service, the real question may be not why did public expenditure overshoot, but how did the Government manage to contain the rise in the face of the deepest recession for fifty years? For example, international figures compiled by the Organization for Economic Co-operation and Development show that public expenditure (after excluding transfer payments such as social security benefits) rose less in real terms in 1981 and 1982 in the UK than in any of the other big seven industrialized countries.

The measures needed to accommodate the recession and higher defence and law and order expenditure involved a tight squeeze on other programmes. If these former programmes are excluded, the rest of public spending declined by 3.75 per cent in real terms between 1978—9 and 1982—3. For example, in 1982—3 expenditure on housing, other environmental services and education was 16.75 per cent lower in real terms than in 1978—9. Most of these programmes had grown steadily, even rapidly, in real terms during the 1960s and early 1970s. While the check to their growth had generally come under the Wilson and Callaghan administrations, the first clear decline in spending occurred after 1979, which explains the protests.

Options in 1979 and the Path of Execution

There were no easy options in May 1979. As Joel Barnett, that most wily and successful of Chief Secretaries to the Treasury, has pointed out (J. Barnett, 1982), the Wilson and Callaghan administrations had removed much of the obvious fat. Their succession of 'cuts exercises' had already squeezed out a lot through the familiar equal-misery approach, involving a fixed percentage off each programme. Similarly, many of the 'painless' reductions had been made. These included purely financial transactions, like the refinancing of shipbuilding and export credits which involved a transfer to the banks, and the trimming back of unrealistic capital investment plans.

The going was always likely to be tougher for the Thatcher administration. Unfortunately, despite the private preparatory work, the Conservative election manifesto was short on suggestions about how the public sector should be cut back. It referred to the elimination of 'expensive socialist programmes' and to 'a reduction of waste, bureaucracy and over-government'. The snag was that the Healey–Barnett regime at the Treasury had anyway not been keen on 'expensive socialist programmes', and Labour's tight cash limits had already tried to reduce waste. About the only specific examples given in the 1979 Conservative manifesto were an end to the nationalization of building land, a reduction in government intervention in industry and a search for economies in the running of the tax and social security system. But this would not have added up to much even if it could all have been achieved and would certainly have been dwarfed by extra defence and law and order spending.

The first problem for the Conservatives, as for any other Government, was that a high proportion of public expenditure was already committed. This was not only a question of time lags but also a reflection of the sizeable percentage which was said to be uncuttable. Apart from the favoured programmes of defence and law and order, there were the demand-determined services, notably social security. These are programmes under which people have a legal entitlement to a payment or a service, so that Whitehall cannot place a cash limit on the total amount of expenditure. An unemployed man for instance, cannot be denied benefit in February because the forecast cash for the financial year to the end of March has run out. On the National Health Service the Conservatives had committed themselves in 1979 not to reduce spending. Indeed, a rise of 1–1.5 per cent a year in real terms was officially seen as necessary to maintain services at existing standards because of demographic changes, such as the rising proportion of old people in the population, and because of changes in medical technology.

These factors clearly limited the scope for cutting back unless major Government functions were to be redefined. But there was no obvious sign of political will or of popular pressure to question the post-Beveridge legacy of the role of the public sector — the universal provision by the state of education, welfare and social services. So the Conservative approach between 1979 and 1983 was based on an attempt to limit the growth in resources devoted to these commitments by making cuts substantially in the one area, housing, where these constraints did not apply. The main means of limiting the growth in spending has been to narrow the scope of some of the entitlements (for example, by altering the method of indexing benefits), by increasing charges and by encouraging the expansion of private provision. The question is whether the overall impact of these changes has been so to restrict available resources as to undermine the practice, as opposed to the theory, of universal provision.

New Approaches to Planning Expenditure,
Manpower and Efficiency

The other principal Conservative approach has been a drive to improve efficiency and to squeeze administrative costs, including wages. This has been effected partly via a change in the method of planning public expenditure and partly through a series of specific initiatives — for example, the establishment of a target for the reduction in Civil Service manpower, the Rayner scrutinies and the MINIS studies launched at the Department of the Environment.

First, planning. During the 1960s and 1970s annual surveys were undertaken of the resources to be made available for public expenditure for several years ahead. The plans were expressed in constant prices in volume terms, that is, the price ruling at some date before the survey started. When the Cabinet had decided on the appropriate level of expenditure for three or four years ahead (generally involving a lower total in the later rather than the earlier years), the figures were automatically translated into cash estimates, which were necessary for approval by Parliament. This involved adjusting to whatever changes had occurred both in the general level of inflation and in the relative increase in prices of the relevant programme. Individual departments had little incentive to contain price and cost changes, and the results of nationally agreed wage increases were accommodated. The system broke down in the mid-1970s under the impact of the big rise both in the general rate of inflation and in the relative level of public-sector costs.

The outcome was the imposition, from 1976 onwards, of cash limits on the money available, according to predetermined inflation assumptions for the immediate year ahead on top of the continuing medium-term planning in constant prices. However, this still allowed for changes in relative prices — for example, the faster rise in the cost of defence equipment than in prices generally — to be accommodated between one annual survey and the next. Consequently, from 1981 onwards the Treasury introduced a new system of cash planning, which was introduced with the personal backing of the Prime Minister and against the opposition of many spending departments. The new system involved expressing the plan for several years ahead in terms of expected cash outlays, after making specific assumptions about the future rate of inflation. In effect, this was to make the medium-term constraint on expenditure explicitly financial — and to relate it to taxes and borrowing — rather than to link it with the more notional concept of the volume of resources.

The implication of the new system is that, unlike the former practice, the cash provision will not be altered automatically in later years because of changes in the expected rate of inflation. This has increased potential problems for individual departments and programme managers in planning ahead, given uncertainty about future price changes. A related problem is that the cash figures have left it unclear what the volume of resources available for a particular programme will be — how many hospital beds and so on. However, departments have been given greater freedom to determine the distribution of resources within their overall cash allocations as a result of the increased use of block budgets. This has allowed a department to allocate a specific sum of money for its whole programme rather than obliging it to provide a predetermined, detailed breakdown between specific projects. The idea was pioneered for defence and has subsequently been applied to the Scottish, Welsh and Northern Irish programmes.

The evidence so far suggests that the system has worked reasonably well — at least from the Treasury's point of view — partly because the first two years after its introduction coincided with a falling rate of inflation. Hence, despite apparently tight inflation assumptions and associated cash limits, programme managers have been able to enjoy some flexibility, for in 1981–2 and 1982–3 spending was 1.8 and 2.2 per cent respectively below the upper end of central Government cash limits. The problem has been that cash limits have covered only about three-fifths of the total. Demand-determined services, such as social security, have been outside the limits, and they have in general grown more rapidly than expected because of the rise in unemployment.

Second, Civil Service numbers. The Government has attempted to supplement its overall financial controls with the more direct instrument of a target for Civil Service manpower. The total number of civil servants had been reduced by the Callaghan administration from 748,000 in 1976 to 732,000 in 1979. After an initial freeze on recruitment, a target was set to reduce the number by about 100,000, to 630,000, by April 1984. This looked like being achieved with a reduction of 80,000 to 650,000 by April 1983, the smallest total since the mid-1960s. The Government has claimed that the whole exercise should produce annual savings of over £600 million a year in the Civil Service pay bill, but the process has provoked allegations that the reduction has been achieved in part by the transfer of operations from the public to the private sector through contracting out. However, a report on manpower reductions made to the Treasury and Civil Service Committee of the Commons took account of the costs involved in contracting out building maintenance work and cleaning in its estimate of net savings. In 1981–2 the number of staff was reduced by 23,240 to produce net savings of £144.4 million in a full year. Moreover, in direct fulfilment of the 1979 manifesto, the number of Civil Service staff per 10,000 taxpayers was reduced from twenty-four to twenty-one between 1978–9 and 1980–1. The Government has also claimed that the relative cost of administering social security benefits dropped by 6 per cent between 1978–9 and 1981–2.

Third, efficiency. In line with the 1979 manifesto, there has been a concerted drive to improve efficiency in Whitehall, both for its own sake and in order to contribute to the overall savings in public expenditure. Best-known have been the studies conducted by the special unit under Sir Derek (later Lord) Rayner. He operated as the Prime Minister's personal adviser on efficiency, and his unit, based in the heart of Government, worked in co-operation with departments in carrying out reviews. Both particular operations and general problems, such as the use of administrative forms, were reviewed to see if they could be tackled better. Between 1979 and 1982 there were 135 scrutinies and six general inter-departmental reviews, which produced actual and potential annual savings of at least £300 million, in addition to once-for-all economies of £37 million.

The aim of the Rayner scrutinies has been to secure lasting improvements. The figures indicate that their impact, while widespread, has not been enormous in total — more a delicate duster than a new broom. One example was the scrutiny of

Government statistics which, within fifteen months, was said to have reduced the burden of inquiries on industry and other organizations by 10 per cent and to have produced savings of £10 million (690 staff) a year. However, there have been costs in terms of reduced services for the public. For instance, the review of statistical services reduced the information available about the business scene by, *inter alia*, ending the regular survey of export prospects.

The Rayner scrutinies have also been criticized for being too narrowly focused. A report in April 1983 from the Foreign Affairs Committee of the Commons strongly attacked the Rayner reviews of the Overseas Development Administration's scientific and special units. The committee said the scrutinies were 'fundamentally flawed' because, while purporting to deal with efficiency, they largely ignored benefits and were concerned almost exclusively with costs. According to the committee, the scrutinies took virtually no account of wider questions such as international links.

A further approach to efficiency was MINIS, a management information system launched in the Department of the Environment in 1980 by Michael Heseltine, which reflected his view that the 'managerial ethos' should run through Government as well as through the private sector:

> By managerial ethos [he said] I mean the process of examining what we are doing, setting realistic targets, fitting them to the resources available, and monitoring performance — and then, very important, telling people what the results are so that we can go back to the beginning of the loop and improve from there.

As applied to the Department of the Environment, this involved establishing a detailed breakdown of the responsibilities of officials for particular functions. The resulting information was set out on massive charts in Michael Heseltine's office, alongside his favourite portrait, that of Lloyd George.

The advantage of MINIS over existing procedures used by departments was said to be that it was more systematic in its review of objectives, more precise in its definition of tasks and clearer in its presentation of results. And it was said to have contributed to the large-scale savings made by the Department of the Environment. There has been much debate about whether the technique could be transferred to other departments or whether it was a reflection of the enthusiasm of a particular Minister who was unusually interested in management as well as in conventional policymaking. A presentation of MINIS to the rest of the Cabinet in early 1982 met with a less than enthusiastic response. There has been scepticism about whether it is as deep-seated and radical a solution as has been claimed by Mr Heseltine. Ministry of Defence officials reckoned that they were already doing what MINIS sought to achieve, though, ironically, shortly after Michael Heseltine moved over to become Defence Secretary in January 1983 he instituted an even larger-scale MINIS review.

After examining the record of MINIS, Andrew Likierman, a London Business School lecturer, concluded that 'the chances of widespread adoption must be slight, bearing in mind the strength of opposition or merely indifference. Only if there is a major central initiative is the system likely to be adopted on a much more widespread basis' (Likierman, 1982).

One important result of MINIS, the Rayner scrutinies and a major inquiry by the Treasury and Civil Service Committee was the announcement in September 1982 of the Financial Management Initiative. This stated that departments should produce plans defining both their objectives, with means of assessing performance, and the responsibility for maintaining the best use of resources, as well as providing the necessary information to exercise this role.

Public-Sector Pay

These efforts to tighten the planning system and to improve efficiency have achieved some results. But at times they have appeared to be dwarfed by major problem areas which have upset the fine calculations of the Treasury — notably public-sector pay, local authorities and nationalized industries.

The Thatcher administration started off with the view that, having set cash limits for the increase in money available for a particular programme, employers and trade unions should bargain within this constraint. There would be only a general allowance for inflation but no specific wage assumption; there were to be no pay policy and no norms. It would be up to negotiators to balance out jobs and pay rises. This turned out to be a hopelessly naive approach, which ignored the strength of centralized bargaining and of public-sector unions, not only within the Civil Service but also within local authorities and nationalized industries.

Consequently, two years were wasted in a series of bloody and fruitless battles before the beginning of a new approach was worked out. The initial problem was that the cash limits were implausible because of the Government's commitment to honour the awards made by the Clegg Commission on Pay Comparability. These sharply inflated public-sector pay bills in 1979–80, in some cases by 15 to 25 per cent. These figures bore no relation to the theoretically tight cash limits or to the even tighter monetary target. A particular difficulty arose over the pay settlement for 1980–1 for the non-industrial Civil Service. The Government wanted to impose cash-limit increases of 14 per cent, but the Civil Service Pay Research Unit recommended a rise of 18.75 per cent. The result was a messy compromise, in which manpower reductions and deferral of the date of implementation allowed the recommended increase to be paid in full. The Treasury committee was critical of this method of 'end-loading', which sharply increased the base for the following year's settlement.

This affair and other embarrassments associated with public-sector pay led to a change in the Government's approach towards a more declaratory style. As Peter Middleton, a senior Treasury official (and from April 1983 Permanent Secretary), told the Treasury Committee in July 1980, 'It is impossible for the Government not to have some sort of public-sector pay policy.' During the summer of 1980 Ministers stressed the importance of lower pay rises in the next round and urged that pay increases should be held as closely as possible to the cash limit. A specific assumption with respect to increases in total pay costs was made (6 per cent) rather than just to an overall figure for both pay and non-pay elements. The staging and deferral of increases was ended; the Civil Service Pay Research Unit was suspended; and the whole policy was seen as shifting closer to an explicit incomes policy, at least for the public sector.

The problems were brought to a head in the lengthy and bitter Civil Service pay dispute of 1981. Nine separate unions formed a united front and took selective action that focused on the national computer centre. The strikes were eventually called off with a settlement of a little over the Government's previous offer and the establishment of an independent inquiry under Sir John Megaw, a retired judge. Its report, in July 1982, suggested a shift from the former comparability approach whereby pay levels were fixed in relation to equivalent jobs in the private sector. Instead the Megaw inquiry preferred a system of job evaluation, with a more detailed analysis of relative accountability and responsibility. This gave greater weight to prevailing market forces by taking into account 'evidence on recruitment and retention of staff within and outside the Civil Service'. The conclusions were broadly accepted by the Government but were strongly criticized by most of the unions, though after the 1981 dispute they were in a much weaker overall position.

In the two years up to the 1983 election the Government was increasingly explicit about its assumptions on pay increases for public services (that is, excluding nationalized industries). The Treasury insisted that any excess should be accommodated within the total cash limit — an aim which was easier to achieve when the rate of inflation was falling. However, disagreements about how pay should be fixed in the public sector continued and were exacerbated by the lengthy dispute in the National Health Service in 1982, which underlined the confusion over the status of the various review bodies. It was significant that in announcing in July 1983 the establishment of a new review body for nurses and other NHS professionals, the Government reserved the right to exclude any group which 'resorts to industrial action'.

The result was an atmosphere of bitterness. While the Government was increasingly able to contain the growth of public-sector wages within its financial targets, this was at the cost of considerable resentment and accusations of unfairness as traditional procedures, pay reviews and arbitration were overridden. The previous system of comparability had many disadvantages, but the Thatcher administration's approach both took over two years to offer a plausible replacement and operated in a manner designed to make the creation of a new consensus more difficult.

The Local Authorities

The Government's relations with local authorities were even worse. The Treasury and the Department of the Environment had two main priorities: first, to ensure that local government expenditure was contained within the overall targets for public spending; second, to hold down increases in local rates in accordance with the Government's counter-inflation policy. Both aims brought central government into direct collision with local authorities (mainly, but not entirely, Labour-controlled ones). The argument of Ministers was that the 'old implicit consensus' about relations between central and local government had broken down. According to this view, up to the mid-1970s local authorities of whatever political complexion had broadly accepted the right of central government to set limits on total spending. Hence when local councils were considering spending above the desired level, central government had a duty to intervene, especially as it financed on average three-fifths of current expenditure via the Rate Support Grant.

The question at issue has been not just whether central Government should have an interest in local spending because of its wider economic implications but the extent to which Whitehall should seek to set binding targets. The difference between this and previous practice has been characterized by Professors G. W. Jones and J. D. Stewart (1983) as seeking no longer to influence the total but to control the particular. The conflict has been between centralization and local autonomy.

The Thatcher administration has undoubtedly intervened

in a much more detailed way than previous Governments, partly as a result of a new method of control, the block grant. Under the former practice grants were allocated on the basis of past spending, so that authorities which spent more automatically received an equivalent increase in central government grant. The new system is intended to relate the grant more closely to standard spending levels by what are known as 'grant-related expenditures'. These are stated benchmarks based on the principles of equalizing differences in local rateable values and of assessing expenditure needs. This has not stopped councils from deciding their own levels of expenditure or rates, but the system discourages over-spending, in that when a council's spending has risen above the benchmark level, the Government has progressively reduced the rate of grant, which has forced councils to raise rates if they have wanted to maintain expenditure.

The Government has, in addition, set separate targets for reductions in expenditure which have differed from the stated benchmarks, so some councils have faced conflicting targets. Not surprisingly, this system at first provoked confusion and criticism and provided no solution. Some local authorities, particular Labour-controlled ones in inner-city areas, continued to increase expenditure well above the Whitehall targets and therefore to levy big rate rises. Consequently, further legislation was brought in to abolish supplementary rates and to allow the Department of the Environment to adjust the block grant paid to individual local authorities in order to encourage reductions in spending. The Government has also introduced a series of other measures to restrict authorities, such as tighter regulations concerning the operation of direct labour organizations and more extensive outside auditing of local authorities.

The results have been unsatisfactory, both for many local authorities and for many ratepayers. The Government's critics have said there has been no real problem of local overspending, that any difficulties have been the result of excessively tight financial targets and of a sharp reduction in Whitehall's Rate Support Grant contribution, which has put more of a burden on the ratepayer. Professors Jones and Stewart (1983) have argued that local government expenditure has fallen since the mid-1970s as a proportion of total public spending, but this has been principally because of a very large fall in capital investment, especially new housebuilding. Local authority current expenditure has continued to rise, both absolutely and relative to total public spending — from 21.8 per cent in 1978—9 to 22.7 per cent in 1982—3 — despite a 4.8 per cent reduction in staff numbers in England and Wales between 1979 and 1982.

Central government was aiming for a much lower level of expenditure, however. In cash terms current expenditure of councils in England and Wales was between 5.7 and 8 per cent above target levels between 1979 and 1983. But councils were underspending below target levels on capital investment by sizeable, if not quite as large, amounts. The pattern varied considerably between authorities, which anyway had individual targets in 1982—3. Some Labour-controlled metropolitan authorities and London borough councils were spending well over their targets and suffered a substantial reduction in grant. As a result, many householders in inner-city areas faced substantially higher rate increases even than the near doubling in the average domestic rate bill in England between 1979—80 and the proposed figure for 1983—4.

The Government's series of expedients to deal with local authority expenditure has failed both to control spending and to produce an acceptable constitutional balance between the centre and the rights of local authorities and ratepayers. There has been more central intervention, yet ratepayers in many cities have understandably felt oppressed (and let down by central government) when faced with 30 or 40 per cent annual increases in rate demands, which have sometimes been imposed by councils elected by only 35 per cent of those voting and under a fifth of the total electorate.

There has been no shortage of suggestions for the reform of local government finance. Much ministerial and official time has been spent on agonizing over possible reforms, such as local sales and incomes taxes and poll taxes. A Green Paper on the subject in December 1981 showed how difficult all the alternatives to domestic rates were; a complicated, though modest, package of reforms prepared by a ministerial committee was rejected as inadequate by Mrs Thatcher and the full Cabinet in early 1983. The Conservative manifesto in June 1983 promised action 'to curb excessive and irresponsible rate increases by high-spending councils and to provide a general scheme for limitation of rate increases for all authorities to be used if necessary'. This pledge followed Scottish legislation, which allowed for central orders (to be confirmed by Parliament) limiting the level of rate increases, a major encroachment on local autonomy. In addition, the Conservatives promised to abolish their particular bogies, the metropolitan counties and the Greater London Council. Yet none of these proposals offered any long-term answer to the problem of how to balance national economic priorities, local democracy and the role of central government as a major provider of local funds.

The Nationalized Industries

Nationalized industries have also presented problems for the Treasury's drive to contain public expenditure. The industries' total external financing needs form part of public expenditure. They consist of grants of all kinds and borrowing both from the Government and from financial markets. This money is used mainly to finance capital investment. The external financing figure is fixed after account has been taken of an industry's ability to generate its own funds from retained profits. These in turn are extremely sensitive to fluctuations in trading conditions and in the rate of inflation. Consequently, the figures are difficult to predict precisely. For instance, for 1982–3 the external financing requirement of £2.2 billion was the difference between total capital needs of £6.4 billion and internal resources of £4.2 billion.

Over the past decade there have been large differences between projections of external financing needs and the out-turn. For 1981–2 there was a gap of around £1 billion between the original forecast and the outcome. This was the result of increases in the external financing limits of the National Coal Board, the British National Oil Corporation, the British Gas Corporation, British Telecommunications, the Post Office and British Airways. Four industries (the

National Coal Board, British Rail, the British Transport Docks Board and British Steel) exceeded their stated limits. Capital investment was roughly at the expected level, but internal resources fell about £1 billion short, particularly in those industries most affected by the recession. However, in 1982–3 the position was very different, as external financing needs were roughly £500 million less than forecast at the beginning of the financial year. Internally generated funds from trading were again less than expected because of the recession. But the industries had reacted to the deterioration in the demand outlook for their products by cutting back capital investment, which was more than £1.25 billion less than expected.

These figures highlight the unpredictability of the nation-alized industry component of total public expenditure, which is at best only indirectly under Treasury control. Indeed, many other countries exclude public corporations from their definitions of their Budget or public-sector deficits. The outcome has been that largely (though not entirely) because of the recession, the improvement in nationalized industry finances has been slower than expected. Even after an adjustment for price changes, the external financing needs of these industries in 1982–3 were over £1.75 billion more than projected in the March 1980 Budget. (The implications of the financial and other problems affecting the relations between central government and nationalized industries are discussed in chapter 8.)

Record and Prospects: the Think Tank Options

The overall picture is of a Government coming to power determined to contain public expenditure but with its hopes frustrated. This has been to a considerable extent because of the deeper than expected recession but also because Ministers had not worked out in advance what sort of public sector they wanted or how to run it. The shambles over public-sector pay policy from 1979 to 1981, the continuing rows with local authorities and the promises to raise expendi-ture on defence and law and order would all have made it difficult to fulfil the general aim even without such a severe recession. But despite all the ideas for detailed cuts worked out in Opposition, the Thatcher administration has never had a coherent strategy for shifting the frontiers of the public sector. Indeed, when Ministers were presented by the Think Tank with alternative ways of significantly reducing expenditure in September 1982, they recoiled in horror and had the paper withdrawn.

The Thatcher administration has probably had the worst of all worlds in declaring its hostility to many public-sector activities yet only chipping away at part of the edifice. Up to the 1983 election the chipping was more extensive than many observers and politicians had expected in 1979. Yet the basic, though somewhat battered, framework created by the Attlee Government remained — the National Health Service, social security, the education system, support for industry and employment, etc. Ironically, that may have been one of the Government's main problems. If the core responsibilities are still to be borne and if the aim is also to hold down total expenditure, it may be impossible to maintain current standards of expected service.

Moreover, capital investment has probably been cut back as far as — and possibly further than — is necessary to maintain and renew existing standards of building and infrastructure. Total central and local Government spending on fixed assets fell by more than 25 per cent in real terms between 1978–9 and 1982–3 (see table 8), following a sharp drop during the late 1970s. Capital spending has also consistently fallen well below planned levels — so much so, indeed, that in November 1982 the Government sought to encourage both nationalized industries and local authorities to spend their capital allocations. The record of the past decade, both before and after the 1979 election, has been of cuts in capital investment to accommodate higher current spending.

The Thatcher administration's macroeconomic dilemma over how to contain public expenditure in the course of the next few years if taxation is to be cut was discussed in the previous chapter. The report of an inter-departmental group of officials for the Cabinet in September 1982 projected a steady increase in expenditure under existing policies. The

TABLE 8   *Public-sector fixed investment in real (cost) terms at constant 1981—2 prices (£ million)*

	1978—9	1979—80	1980—1	1981—2	1982—3	% change since 1978—9
Central and local government spending on fixed assets	7,959	7,983	7,267	6,200	5,909	−25.7
Nationalized industries	5,748	5,894	5,820	5,631	5,660	−1.5
Total	13,707	13,877	13,087	11,831	11,569	−15.6
Percentage change from previous year	—	+1.2	−5.6	−9.5	−2.2	—

Source: Treasury and Civil Service Committee of the Commons report on the Government's expenditure plans, February 1983.

implication was that over the medium to long term some existing major commitments would have to go if total public spending were to be held broadly unchanged in real terms from 1983 onwards. The 'unacceptable' Think Tank analysis produced for the Cabinet (as disclosed by the *Economist*) outlined four major areas for possible savings: defence, social security, the National Health Service and education.

Defence
The inter-departmental report had assumed that Britain's commitment to NATO for a 3 per cent annual real growth in expenditure would be extended beyond the present formal expiry date of 1985—6 to 1988—9. The Think Tank suggested that beyond the mid-1980s defence's share of total public spending should be frozen.

Social Security
Big savings could be produced if all social security payments no longer rose fully in line with price rises, according to the Think Tank. The inter-departmental projections assumed price protection of all benefits, no change in eligibility for benefits and a 1 per cent growth in the real value of existing benefits under the higher-growth scenario.

The National Health Service
The Think Tank report suggested as an option the introduction of private health insurance, eventually saving between £3 billion and £4 billion a year from a total budget of £32.5 billion in 1982—3. There might have to be a compulsory minimum of private insurance for everyone. In the interim, charges could be introduced for visits to the doctor and could be raised further for prescriptions. The inter-departmental projections had assumed, under the low-growth scenario, a growth rate which would 'barely maintain present standards'.

Education
The ending of state funding for all institutions of higher education was suggested by the Think Tank. Instead fees could be set at market rates, and state scholarships could be made available, along with student loans. The possibility of education vouchers for primary and secondary schools was considered, though this would not have produced any savings in expenditure. The inter-departmental report was based on existing levels of provision, though it noted the pressures for improvements in standards.

The widespread outcry, not least from within the Cabinet, at some of these suggestions, coupled with the pressures of an election year, led to a series of ministerial commitments which appeared to rule out the more radical solutions. In particular, the present broad pattern of financing the National Health Service was to be maintained, while proposals for student loans on a large scale were shunted aside. Similarly, the 1983 election manifesto specifically promised to give price protection to pensions and certain related long-term benefits, though Ministers declined to offer a similar pledge for other benefits.

These commitments have narrowed the scope for any substantial cutback in expenditure below the increases projected in the Cabinet paper of September 1982, even allowing for excessively high estimates for spending on some programmes (as discussed in the previous chapter). Nevertheless, defence and social security will almost certainly be the budgets most argued about during the second Thatcher term, not least because they account for over 41 per cent of total expenditure. Spending in other areas, such as housing and education, has already been held down to a level at which major savings could now be made only with the sacrifice of major functions. And expenditure on economic programmes such as industry and employment may fall substantially only when unemployment drops.

Mrs Thatcher's desire for tax cuts may, however, lead to a revival of the Think Tank options. There is no evidence that the ideas were all as 'unacceptable' to her as they were to many of her Cabinet colleagues. And definitions of acceptability could change after a big election victory. The debate about the longer-term financial implications of current expenditure commitments will not go away. Even by July 1983 senior Ministers were talking of the need for a major review of the welfare state.

In any event, there is likely to be a continuing squeeze on the money available for the NHS and other services. This may be coupled with discussion of the extent to which extra resources should be devoted to previously favoured programmes like defence, while some of the non-pledged benefits may be only partially protected against inflation. Further large-scale privatization could make some difference during the later 1980s, but it is unlikely to be very significant, given the projected reduction in Whitehall support for these industries.

The outcome may be no more than the placing of limitations on the future rate of growth of total expenditure in real terms rather than an absolute cut or even stability. That would none the less be a remarkable event compared with past trends and probable needs. It could, however, mean a reduction in the standards of provision in some areas — notably health and education. Even if some adjustment of existing expenditure commitments is probably inevitable, Mrs Thatcher's Finchley instincts may mislead her if she attempts to make lower income tax a priority rather than the maintenance of standards in public services. Indeed, within two months of the June 1983 election Mrs Thatcher recognized the constraints when she said that it would be 'very difficult' to cut personal taxation in real terms in the spring 1984 Budget.

7

The Welfare State

The National Health Service is safe with us. As I said in the House of Commons on December 1st last, 'the principle that adequate health care should be provided for all regardless of ability to pay must be the function of any arrangements for financing the NHS.' We stand by that.

Mrs Margaret Thatcher
Speech to Conservative Party Conference, Brighton
8 October 1982

The development of private facilities draws on other sources of finance and increases total health-care provision in this country and, in so doing, helps to bridge the gap between the demand for health care and its supply. The independent sector can relieve pressures on hard-pressed NHS services.

Department of Health and Social Security
Note to chairmen of regional health authorities
February 1983

The objective of the Family Policy Group is to identify, and to seek ways of counteracting, those factors which tend to undermine, or even prohibit, the exercise of personal responsibility and a sense of individual self-respect.

Central Policy Review Staff (Think Tank)
Note to Ministers
September 1982

The Thatcher administration's general approach to the welfare state has been determined primarily by the constant pressure to hold down public expenditure. Even within the social security budget, where expenditure has risen sharply because of the recession, total spending has been reduced by more than £2 billion below what it would otherwise have been as a result of changes in the method of inflation-proofing some benefits. In all other social programmes expenditure since 1979 has been less than planned for the early 1980s by the Callaghan administration and has grown more slowly than in the late 1970s — apart from the National Health Service, where there has been little overall difference.

A squeeze on social expenditure has been accompanied by various measures to encourage the private provision of services such as hospital pay-beds, assisted places in schools and private insurance schemes. These have been quite separate from the moves to expand the contracting out to the private sector of work, such as catering, cleaning and building maintenance, in services which have continued to be provided by the state. The two have tended to be confused under the catch-all label of 'privatization', but they are distinct concepts.

The Conservatives' manifesto in 1979 was short on specific commitments as far as the welfare state was concerned, merely including some generalized pledges to make better use of available resources, cut back on bureaucracy and maintain spending on the NHS. Admittedly, there had previously been discussion of proposals to increase private provision and to extend the use of charges throughout the social services, stimulated by the work of the Institute of Economic Affairs, but the presentation and implementation of these ideas in the first two years of the Thatcher administration appeared piecemeal. The continuing financial pressures have given the drive towards privatization and contracting out a new momentum since 1981, typified by the quotation from the Department of Health and Social Security note at the beginning of this chapter.

This philosophy was summed up in an important lecture given by Sir Geoffrey Howe in July 1982 (Howe, 1983). He said:

There are powerful reasons why we must be ready to consider how far private provision and individual choice can supplement, or in some cases possibly replace, the role of Government in health, social security and education. Most of these reasons are economic.

He noted that 'the need to reform our system of social provision would be pressing on public spending grounds alone', but he also stressed other reasons, such as the desirability of devolving power and responsibility to the lowest tier, notably by extending the use of charges and by increasing private-sector involvement.

The way forward must embrace a constant readiness to review our commitments and to consider market mechanisms as a means of promoting greater cost-consciousness and of extending choice. We must meet the increasingly frustrated demands of society in a fair and efficient way.

What emerged was a three-pronged approach, as set out in January 1983 in a Bow Group lecture by Norman Fowler, the Social Services Secretary. His aims were, first, that the proper starting point for the consideration of social policy was the economy; second, that the Government should get the best possible value for the amount of money that the taxpayer provides; and, third, that not everything should or can be done by the state. Despite the assurances of Mr Fowler and others about their commitment to the NHS, critics have suggested that this approach has been leading in practice to an increasingly threadbare, safety-net standard of provision. While there has been no overt challenge to the post-Beveridge consensus — the provision of free and comprehensive state services — there has been a change of emphasis and of priorities. As Professor David Donnison remarked after his experience as chairman of the Supplementary Benefit Commission (Donnison, 1982), 'The new team had shed the burden of "social conscience".'

Social Security

Total expenditure on social security rose sharply in real terms between 1978—9 and 1982—3, largely because of a big increase in the number of people receiving benefits. For example, over the period the number of retirement pensioners increased from 8.53 million to 9.07 million; the average number receiving unemployment benefit jumped from 570,000 to 1.2 million; the number receiving the short-term supplementary allowance increased from 925,000 to 1.81 million (again largely reflecting the rise in unemployment); and the number of people obtaining rate rebates leapt from 3.05 million to 4.92 million.

In addition, there were some improvements in the real value of benefits, though on a smaller scale than under the Wilson and Callaghan administrations. The real value of pensions increased by about 7 per cent between the Novembers of 1978 and 1982, but this was partly because of the 2.7 percentage point over-estimation of inflation in 1982. The change in 1983 in the method of uprating, to a historic rather than a forecast basis, reduced the size of the real increase.

The real value of some other benefits — attendance and mobility allowances, family income supplement and the one-parent benefit — were all raised between 1979 and 1982, but the real value of other important benefits was reduced as a result of certain Government decisions.

First, the freezing of child benefit from April 1979 to November 1980 and the change from weekly to monthly payment (saving £250 million). Over the first Thatcher term as a whole child benefit lagged about four percentage points behind the rise in prices, though the increase to £6.50 a week in November 1983 would slightly more than restore its earlier real value.

Second, the abandonment of the linking of long-term benefits to the movement of either earnings or prices, whichever had risen most. Instead the link has been to prices (saving about £500 million a year by 1982—3).

Third, the abolition of the earnings-related supplement

and the fixing of the rise in unemployment and sickness benefit at five percentage points less than the increase in inflation. The latter was justified on the grounds that it was in preparation for the taxation of unemployment benefit from July 1982. But the 5 per cent abatement was not due to be restored until November 1983. Total savings were at least £500 million a year in 1982–3.

Fourth, the recovery in 1981 of the one percentage point over-provision in uprating of benefits in 1980 as a result of an over-estimation of the inflation rate then in the official forecast (saving £200 million).

Together with other smaller changes, the total savings have been officially estimated at around £2 billion a year by 1982–3, which is equivalent to 2p off the basic rate of income tax.

These measures were justified by the Government on the grounds that any attempt to control the overall level of public spending must include the social security budget because of its size. Ministers also argued that other countries, such as France, West Germany and the Netherlands, had also been cutting back on the real value of social security uprating. The Government could fairly point out that between 1975 and 1979 the Wilson and Callaghan administrations had several times broken the link between earnings and benefits and that price protection was sufficient, especially given the growing number of pensioners. The change of the method of uprating benefits in 1983 led to an immediate loss, as the inflation rate was rising between the new historic date and the old forecast one. This was around two percentage points, but the loss was less than the over-provision the previous November, when the inflation rate was falling faster than expected.

The prospect is for a continuing rise in total expenditure, though the number of beneficiaries should increase more slowly during the late 1980s than in the late 1970s and early 1980s. The February 1983 expenditure White Paper envisaged a further increase of 200,000 in the number of retirement pensioners between 1982–3 and 1985–6, near-stability in the number receiving unemployment benefit, a small increase in demand for the supplementary allowance, a further rise in demand for housing and a continuing steady fall in the number receiving child benefit. This was expected to decline from 600,000 to 12.3 million, reflecting demographic changes, though the trend could be reversed in the later 1980s. Other influences are likely to be the growing maturity of the new pension scheme and the increase in the proportion qualifying for certain benefits (such as sickness and contributory benefits payable to married women). The inter-departmental report to the Cabinet assumed that the real value of all benefits would be maintained, with a small real growth of 1 per cent a year under the higher-growth scenario. To achieve any savings in social security, therefore, there would have to be changes either in entitlements or in the real value of benefits. The Conservative leadership committed itself during the 1983 election campaign only to compensation for price increases for retirement pensions and related bene-fits, which covered about 57 per cent of the social security budget, but Ministers specifically refused to make a similar promise in relation either to unemployment and sickness benefit or to short- and long-term supplementary allowance.

Any reductions in the real value of unemployment and related benefits would turn as much on the desirability or otherwise of widening the gap between the incomes of those in and out of work as on the potential public expenditure savings. This is the 'why work?' argument: the alleged dis-incentive effects of the overlap between money received from benefits and what can be obtained from work. The issue raises two separate but related questions. First, how large is the overlap? And, second, does it matter?

Economists such as Professor Patrick Minford of Liverpool University (Minford, 1983) have maintained that, taking all benefits together, as high a proportion as 15 per cent of the unemployed may be nearly as well off, or even better off, receiving benefits rather than working. The Institute for Fiscal Studies has argued that only 2 per cent of the long-term unemployed (those out of work for over a year) are better off without jobs. Its view is that the whole direction of Government policy has been towards reducing the benefits of the unemployed (taxing them and abolishing earnings-related benefit), while their incomes fall anyway the longer they are without a job. According to a Child Poverty Action Group analysis (Bull and Wilding, 1983), 'the gap between average net incomes in work and incomes out of work has widened in the case of most benefits.' The Department of Health and Social Security's own sample surveys of the unemployed have suggested that in the early 1980s a lower proportion of unemployed people have been better off without a job than the 6 to 9 per cent range shown by the 1978 survey. Any disincentive effects are probably small, at any rate in regions of high unemployment, even though in parts of south-east England some men with families may be discouraged from seeking low-paid and possibly unpleasant work by the current level of benefits.

In any event, it is far from clear, even if some people are slightly better off out of work, that this establishes the case for cutting the real value of benefit for all. The question is in part whether there is any advantage in forcing a few people into low-paid jobs and leaving those who anyway cannot get jobs worse off than they are at present. The issue is also one of political principle. Sir Ian Gilmour has not been alone in arguing (Gilmour, 1983) that 'the unemployed are the innocent casualties of the battle against inflation, and the least well off people in the country are having to bear the brunt of the Government's policies.'

Yet there is a real dilemma about how to finance not only the unemployed but also the old and the young. The new state pension scheme will have a rising cost from the 1990s onwards, while the number of retirement pensioners (at present retirement ages) will increase as a percentage of the total population. Consequently, those in work will have to support a growing financial burden to pay for social security benefits, whatever happens to the number of unemployed. The potential tax increases towards the end of the century are so large that Mrs Thatcher and other Ministers started a review of the issue shortly after the 1983 election. Among the possible options are a move to an insurance principle, thus sharply increasing contribution rates, and/or shifting more to the private and voluntary sectors. There is anyway pressure for further development of private pension schemes to provide larger benefits for people who change jobs.

The overall problem was summed up by John Kay of the Institute for Fiscal Studies in a paper written for a group of economists organized by the Bank of England. He noted that we have been able to enjoy the present level of taxation 'by selling promises that our children will pay more generous pensions than we are willing to pay our parents'. This is a genuine problem, by comparison with which cutting the real value of benefit for the unemployed is unlikely either to represent short-term social justice or to make long-term economic sense.

The National Health Service

The Thatcher administration could justifiably claim to have maintained expenditure on the health service not only in real terms — with an annual average growth rate of over 3 per cent — but also in relation to various output indicators. The number of nurses and midwives rose by 45,000 to 396,000 between 1978 and 1982; the number of doctors and dentists rose by 4,000 to 40,000; while the number of ancillary workers dropped by 2,000 to 170,000. But despite Conservative promises to prune bureaucracy, and despite the abolition of the middle-area tier of organization, the number of administrative and clerical workers rose by 8,000 to 108,000 (all figures for England). Official statistics show that between 1978 and 1981 the number of in-patients treated rose at an annual rate of 3 per cent a year, the only decline being for mentally ill and mentally handicapped patients. This largely reflected the shorter stay of patients in hospital.

The overall figures appear to point to a continuity of policy, but there have been important changes. For a start, the Department of Health and Social Security has stated publicly that total current expenditure on hospitals and the community health service has to rise by about 0.7 per cent a year in real terms if existing provision per head in each of the main age groups is to remain constant. This is because of the increased number of very elderly people. The latest calculations suggest that this figure may have underestimated the impact of the very old, and for demographic reasons the annual rise in resources may have to be nearer 1 per cent a year. In addition, the Department has calculated that 'an increase in real current expenditure of about 0.5 per cent a year is required as a contribution to the costs of medical advance to finance inescapable innovation without enforcing offsetting reductions in standards elsewhere.' After allowing for these factors and for the increase in charges, the rise in real resources for improvements in NHS standards since 1979 has been at most 1.5 per cent per year.

From 1981–2 onwards local health authorities have been required to provide some resources for the development of services through efficiency gains — with a target of 0.5 per cent a year. This move followed evidence that from 1979 to 1981 average costs for acute and maternity cases had been reduced significantly, partly through a shorter length of stay in hospital. Yet some of the initial savings have been achieved not just through greater efficiency but also as a result of cutting back on maintenance and deferring new projects. The Government has reinforced this efficiency drive with measures to strengthen accountability and with the introduction of manpower targets for each staff group, totalling cuts of 0.75 to 1 per cent by March 1984. Ministers have also started to undertake reviews with each regional health authority; Rayner-type scrutinies have been introduced; and performance indicators have been extended.

There have been two further complications. First, health authorities have had to finance higher than planned wage increases out of their existing budgets — for example, to cover some of the cost of the eventual settlement of the 1982 dispute — so putting a squeeze on other services. Second, there have been attempts to redistribute resources between regions on a more equal basis. The net effect of these moves has been to squeeze the resources available to many health authorities. There have been reports of unused hospital beds as a result of lack of money, as well as threats to prestige projects; these complaints have to be set against the increase in overall resources and the rise in the number of patients being treated, as noted above.

These pressures could become much greater during the

rest of the 1980s. The Government's published plans imply a slower growth in NHS spending in real terms in the mid-1980s than between 1978—9 and 1982—3. And shortly after the June 1983 election the Department of Health and Social Security announced that the real resources available for hospital and the community health service would rise by just 0.5 per cent a year for the rest of the 1980s. However, the inter-departmental report of officials for the Cabinet in September 1982 noted:

> If current policies were broadly maintained, with no improvement in levels of efficiency, the annual increase in provision necessary at least to meet the pressures exerted by demographic change and medical advance might be of the order of 1 to 1.5 per cent between 1982—3 and 1990—1. There are, however, many areas of health care where there is pressing need for more resources; for example, to improve standards in the worst mental handicap and other long-stay hospitals, to make hip operations, transplants, dialysis, etc., more widely available and to introduce minimum standards for maternity care. Expenditure would need to rise at 2 to 3 per cent a year to make significant progress in all these areas.

After noting the Government's commitment to securing improvements in efficiency, the officials said that it seemed

> doubtful (though not inconceivable) that a cumulative improvement of 0.5 per cent a year could continue throughout the decade. The growth of the private sector may take a little of the pressure off NHS acute services. There could also be some small increase in income through charges.

Consequently, the report suggested that the minimum net real growth in resources of 0.5 per cent a year under the low economic growth scenario, with a further 0.5 per cent a year efficiency savings, would 'barely maintain present standards'. And that was the view of cautious civil servants even before the upward revision contingent on the impact of demographic changes. But this rate of growth in resources and continued efficiency savings are precisely what have been assumed by the Thatcher administration — with the probability, and the fact, of a tighter cash limits squeeze in addition.

The inter-departmental report was clearly less enthusiastic about the possible contribution from alternative sources of finance and from the private sector than Ministers have been. The impact of sources of revenue other than taxation was limited during the early 1980s. Income from prescription charges, from private patients, from overseas visitors and from personal social services rose from £345 million in 1978–9 to £750 million in 1982–3 (in cash terms and in England only) and was predicted to grow more slowly thereafter. This was equivalent to a rise from 4.4 to 5.1 per cent of gross health expenditure. For NHS charges alone the rise was from 2.2 to 3.1 per cent of gross spending on health, a useful contribution but not significant overall.

Moreover, there are probably limits to the potential growth in charges after the rise in the basic prescription per item from 20p in 1979 to £1.40 in April 1983. Admittedly, retirement pensioners, children under 11, those on low incomes and some others are exempt, so that well over half the people who present prescriptions pay no charge at all. It would be difficult to change this eligibility, and Mrs Thatcher has ruled out charges for staying in hospitals and for visits to doctors. On the other side, there has been continuous wrangling between the Government and the main drug companies over allegations that the latter have been making excessive profits. Critics have argued that savings of over £150 million a year could be made if generic substitutes were used in place of branded drugs.

The most radical proposal has been to change over to a system of compulsory health insurance, as suggested by the Think Tank paper of September 1982. This would have the advantage of fully protecting the population and of financing private and charitable hospitals. However, costs would be difficult to control (in the absence of general cash limits). On the Continent, where there are such insurance schemes, health costs have risen faster than in the UK. Moreover, the public sector would still have to provide the services which the private or charitable sectors could not, or would not, provide. After commissioning a working party to study the possibility, the Government concluded that overseas systems of compulsory health insurance were unsuitable for Britain.

The contribution of private medicine is therefore likely to be at the margin of schemes to relieve the NHS of some of the costs of hospital care, though the Thatcher administration has taken certain initiatives in this area. From 1982–3 income tax relief on employer-employee medical insurance schemes has been restored for those with earnings of up to £8,500 a year. And the Government has eased restrictions on the development of private medicine in partnership with the NHS — for example, by encouraging the joint use of high-technology equipment and resources. The number of people, including dependants, insured by the three main provident associations rose from 2.5 million in March 1979 to 4.2 million by the end of 1982. By early 1983 there were about 34,000 beds in private hospitals and nursing homes in England and almost 3,000 private beds in Health Service hospitals. This compared with the provision of 380,000 beds in 2,100 NHS hospitals. (However, more than 20,000 of the private beds were in small nursing homes catering for old people.) The Government has also encouraged voluntary effort, citing the private and charitable contributions to the future of the Tadworth Court hospital for small children in Surrey. But there are fewer examples in less fashionable areas.

The Department of Health and Social Security has sought to stimulate the contracting out of work within NHS hospitals in the hope of saving money. A circular has been issued asking health authorities to test the cost-effectiveness of their cleaning, catering and laundry services by putting them out to tender, both to commercial contractors and in-house. The advantage for the authorities is that any savings made from cheaper provision of these services can be channelled into extra patient care. The NHS has been spending over £800 million on these services, of which only £17 million was paid to outside contractors in 1982. The Government believes that there is a big potential saving here, as with local authorities, and has given the example of the Defence Department, which made sizeable economies in contracting out its cleaning services.

Norman Fowler has claimed that savings of up to 20 per cent can be achieved in some NHS hospitals. The counter view of the trade unions (as reflected in Hastings and Levie, 1983) has been that over time the contracting out of services is more expensive than direct labour and the work more shoddy. Critics maintain that initial private tenders are put in at low prices, on a different basis from in-house bids, and then charges are increased and/or standards of service are lowered. There is probably some room for savings by contracting out, and opening up such services to tender should provide a desirable competitive discipline, but the benefits, as well as the dangers, are probably fewer than the enthusiasts and the critics will acknowledge.

Overall, the contribution that either private medicine or contracting out would make to containing the growth of public expenditure in the NHS is likely to be limited. This is to leave aside the question of whether the encouragement of private medicine will entail the diversion of talented medical staff away from the NHS. There are no easy ways of balancing the need to increase real resources by at least 1.5 per cent (and probably over 2 per cent) a year to provide an acceptable standard of service with the Treasury's desire to limit the growth in spending to a lower rate. Efficiency savings, contracting out, charges and the growth of private medicine will not be sufficient together to bridge the gap.

The dilemma for Conservative Health Ministers is that they are having to run faster and faster to stand still, while hoping to give the impression of going forward. But Mr Fowler and his team are no Fred Astaires or Gene Kellys. They will have both to squeeze at the margin and to defend existing planned expenditure allocations if they are even to begin to prevent the NHS from slipping back. The NHS is not going to be dismantled, but there is more likely to be a deterioration in the standard of service than an improvement.

Education

The irony of the Thatcher administration's educational record is that its proudest claim — the reduction in the average number of children per teacher to the lowest ever level — is founded partly on the fact that local authorities have spent more than proposed by central government. Education policy has been determined by the interaction of three strands: the falling school-age population, the pressures to reduce expenditure and the general desire to maintain, and if possible to improve, standards. The complicating factor has been the restriction on what Whitehall can do. Shortly after he became Education Secretary in September 1981, Sir Keith Joseph was heard to wonder, characteristically, where the levers were — what did he have to pull to bring about a change? The constraint is that local authorities account for about three-quarters of the programme (spending mainly on schools but also on institutions of further and higher education and excluding universities, student grants and science). The Department of Education and Science can influence such spending via the Rate Support Grant but cannot determine it. The power of the Secretary of State is strictly circumscribed.

The central theme of the period since 1979 has been the falling school-age population — down from 10 million in Great Britain as a whole in 1978–9 to roughly 9.1 million in 1982–3. On the basis of projections of a fall of roughly this scale, the Government planned to reduce current expenditure on school meals, milk and transport, as well as to cut the number of teachers and to close some schools. It would anyway have been impossible to reduce expenditure in real terms exactly in parallel with the number of pupils because of the geographical distribution of schools and the uneven pattern of decline. The size of schools and the number of specialist staff, especially in small towns and in rural areas, cannot be adjusted proportionately to the number of pupils. For this reason, and because of the Government's desire 'to maintain and improve the quality of education', it was assumed in 1979–80 that class sizes would be smaller and that the pupil/teacher ratio would decline.

The March 1980 expenditure White Paper projected a 6.9 per cent fall in expenditure on education in real terms between 1978–9 and 1982–3. On a slightly different basis, the outcome was a drop of only 1.2 per cent in real terms. The main reason was that local authorities maintained levels of spending. In 1981–2 current expenditure by councils was 6.5 per cent in cash terms above the target indicated by the Rate Support Grant settlement, while in 1982–3 the overshoot was 4.5 per cent. (In both cases expenditure on school meals and milk accounted for about a quarter of the excess.) The result of this spending above target was a somewhat larger number of teachers in 1982–3 than originally planned. Despite a slightly bigger than expected school population, the pupil/teacher ratio was therefore fractionally lower than previously predicted. If the authorities had kept to their targets, the ratio would not have fallen by nearly as much. In any event, despite the sharp drop in the number of pupils, the overall decline during the early 1980s has been only from about 18.8 to 18.3.

The contraction of the education service has posed considerable problems. The number of schools of all kinds in England fell by nearly 800 between 1979 and 1982 (out of a total of 29,800 in both public and private sectors). One result of the cutbacks has been an increase in the number of mixed-age classes in a significant minority of primary schools and a decline in spending on books in real terms. Moreover, the previous sharp rise in the proportion of 3- and 4-year-olds going to nursery schools was halted in 1981 and has begun to decline. These changes have been highlighted by evidence given to the Education, Science and Arts Committee of the Commons and in the reports of the Government's own Inspectorate. In 1981 the Senior Chief Inspector of Schools found reductions in the level of provision, compared with the previous year, in three-quarters of local education authorities, as well as widening gaps between areas. This has been in part the result of the relaxation of minimum statutory obligations — for instance, in the provision of school meals and milk — which has led to big differences in the quality of ancillary educational services.

Paradoxically, these disclosures about problems in some schools have been advanced by Sir Keith Joseph's decision to publish Inspectors' reports on individual schools as part of his general policy to provide more information about schools and to raise standards. In February 1981 the Government issued a guidance note to encourage local education authorities to provide primary school pupils with an education in the basic subjects, to ensure that all children are literate and numerate and to provide a 'core curriculum' in secondary schools, but there is a very limited amount which Whitehall can do except to exhort. The Government has also taken action to save the remaining maintained grammar schools, to strengthen parental choice and to establish an assisted places scheme, a version of the old direct grant system. Under this scheme 228 fully independent secondary schools in England and Wales have offered 5,000 places a year to pupils who could otherwise not afford to go to them. This is, however, a minor change in the balance between the private and public sectors.

Government expenditure on higher education has been reduced substantially in real terms. The number of academic posts has been projected to fall by one-sixth by 1984–5. This prediction has led to a series of rows – notably over cutbacks at universities well-known for technical and applied research work, such as Aston, Salford and Bradford. There has been a deterioration in staff/student ratios. However, local authority higher and further education institutions admitted more students than expected between 1980 and 1982, so that the overall number of students entering a full-time degree course rose during the early 1980s. Nevertheless, a lower percentage of 18- to 20-year-olds are in higher education in the UK than in many other industrialized countries, and the University Grant Committee's targets imply a fall. This policy can be defended on the grounds that there was an over-expansion in the growth of universities relative to Britain's economic base and public resources during the 1960s and 1970s and that some adjustment was necessary. The Conservative argument is that standards of degree work are higher in the UK than overseas. But the contraction appears to threaten the Robbins principle that higher education should be available to all who have the ability to pursue it.

Looking ahead, the Government's plans envisage a further squeeze on educational spending. The inter-departmental report for the Cabinet in September 1982 projected a further real decline over the rest of the decade. The expected demographic trends suggest that the reduction in the primary-school age group in the early 1980s will be followed by an upturn between the mid-1980s and 1991, while the 19-to-22 age group should peak in the early to mid-1980s and decline thereafter. There is expected to be a fall particularly in the secondary-school age group during the 1980s. However, the report assumed a decline in the percentage of 3- and 4-year-olds in state nursery schools from 40 per cent in 1980–1 to a little over 30 per cent by 1990–1 – in part reflecting the hope that voluntary play groups would fill some of the gap. And the report also envisaged that cutbacks in higher education would reduce the percentage of 18- to 20-year-olds enrolling from 13 per cent in 1980–1 to just over 11 per cent by 1990–1.

The report noted, however, that any reduction would be constrained by 'the constitutional difficulties in securing changes in local authority expenditure', 'the contractual position of staff and the extent to which employers are willing to accept redundancies' and 'the high proportion (65 per cent) of the programme which is spending on staff, salaries'. The officials concluded that pressures to maintain expenditure levels above those implied by the projections, to expand the curriculum and to extend participation beyond the compulsory 5-to-16 age group may be 'very great'.

So there is no obvious scope for cutting back on education spending without significantly undermining standards. Nor does the private sector provide any immediate answer; the number of pupils in independent schools as a percentage of the total in England increased fractionally, from 5.8 to 6.1 per cent, between 1979 and 1981. While politically, socially and culturally significant (where would novelists and film-makers be without public schools?), their contribution is small and is unlikely to increase rapidly. Various ideas have been suggested for changing the funding of higher education, but switching over to repayable student loans rather than grants would not be a money-saver in the short term and would pose immense practical and political difficulties. Proposals for education vouchers which could be used at schools of parents' choosing have been aired many times and considered by Sir Keith, but they would not save any money and might even be more expensive, while also being complicated. Other hare-brained schemes for abolishing the state's duty to provide primary and secondary education have been proposed, but Sir Keith seems to recognize that that battle was lost in the 1870s. As with the NHS, the likelihood is a further squeeze, possibly leading to a rise in pupil/teacher ratios, further cutbacks in higher education and a further reduction in the statutory obligations imposed on local authorities.

Housing

The largest change in the frontier between the public and the private sectors has occurred in housing. On coming to power, the Thatcher administration proposed a sharp fall in expenditure on both new housing and housing subsidies, prompting the Environment Committee of the Commons to note in 1980 that 'the present Government's strategy of reducing public expenditure thus relies principally on the achievement of the planned reduction in housing expenditure.' Unlike those in most other programmes, this reduction occurred. New public-sector house completions fell from 104,000 in 1979 (itself down from over 160,000 in the mid-1970s) to 49,200 in 1982, the lowest level since the 1920s. Over the same period council rents more than doubled in cash terms as subsidies from central government and from rate funds were cut by more than 50 per cent in real terms.

The Government's aim has been to introduce and to extend market forces, both by requiring the local authority sector to be self-financing and profit-making and by reducing the size of the public sector. This has been described as a minimalist view, according to which the private sector is regarded as the main provider of housing and the public sector as a safety-net. The balance between the two sectors has been tilted through pushing up council rents while maintaining the existing tax relief subsidies on mortgage interest. In addition, sitting council tenants have been given an incentive to buy through the 1980 Housing Act. Tenants of local authorities, new towns and non-charitable housing associations now have the right to buy their houses and flats at discounts of up to 50 per cent of the market price in some cases.

The results have been dramatic. About 500,000 houses and flats were sold between the 1979 and 1983 elections, out of an increase of 1 million in the number of owner-occupied properties over the period. Apart from the stimulus to the sale of council houses, other measures have been introduced to help first-time buyers, such as sales of land for starter homes and part-ownership and part-renting schemes. As a result, the percentage of owner-occupied households rose from just over 54 to nearly 59 per cent over the period in England and Wales, the largest change since 1945.

The social and political implications have been considerable. John Stanley, the Housing Minister in the first Thatcher administration, claimed in a speech in February 1983 that 'council estates, as they become areas of mixed rather than single tenure, are changing before our eyes — and for the better. They are becoming more varied, more individualistic, and more integrated with the surrounding area.' The most widely noticed distinguishing marks were the double-glazed windows and neo-Georgian front doors in houses which had been bought by their occupiers. These exemplified very much the world of Mrs Thatcher's values of independence and self-reliance.

The shift had its political rewards. According to a BBC/Gallup survey conducted on 8 and 9 June 1983 and analysed by Professor Ivor Crewe of Essex University in the *Guardian* on 13 June 1983, purchasers of council houses were strongly pro-Conservative. Of those who had bought their council houses, 56 per cent voted Tory and only 18 per cent Labour. Nor was this just a case of the Conservative working class buying its council houses. Of those who had voted Labour in 1979 and had then bought their council houses, 59 per cent switched to the Conservatives or the Alliance. Moreover, Labour did especially badly in new towns like Basildon, Northampton, Peterborough and Telford, where more than one-fifth of the housing stock in 1979 had already been, or was in the process of being, sold by the time of the 1983 election.

This was a painful lesson for Labour. Indeed, one of the first conclusions drawn by leaders such as Roy Hattersley and Peter Shore in the post-mortems after June 1983 was that Labour must recognize, and respond to, the desire of working people to own their homes. Many Labour councils had adopted an ambiguous and frequently a downright obstructionist attitude towards the sale of council houses and had been forced to sell by the Government. The case against large-scale sales is that only the best of the housing stock is sold; the result is the division of council estates, which makes it more difficult for local authorities to provide a high standard of housing for everyone.

The sale of council houses has not only been a skilful political move: it has also clearly reflected a widespread and understandable desire for home ownership. It has challenged the traditional paternalistic ideas of many local authorities, which have always championed renting, while offering a more significant redistribution of capital than any expedient proposed by Labour Governments. Those buying their homes will, over time, build up capital on a scale never previously envisaged by manual workers and their families. They will be able to pass this capital on to their children, who will often themselves own their own homes and thus have some spare capital, as many members of the middle classes already have. This will broaden the range of those in the community who own capital as opposed to just earning income.

The other side of the picture is the question of what happens to those families who cannot or do not want to buy their homes (an obvious example is single parents living in run-down flats in inner-city areas)? The danger of the emphasis on selling council houses is that it will widen social and economic divisions between the majority, consisting of the middle class and the 'new' affluent working class, and the minority, consisting of the low-paid and disadvantaged working class. The Thatcher administration's policies have been less convincing on this point, in that both public- and private-sector tenants have appeared to be second-class citizens by comparison with owner occupiers. The reduction in subsidies in council housing is justifiable to the extent that market pressures should have a greater influence and given that those in need are looked after by rebates and the new unified housing benefit. But there has been an imbalance compared with the favourable treatment of owner occupiers. The Government claims to have helped council tenants by giving them greater rights and security, while at the time of the 1983 elections there were proposals to allow tenants greater mobility between local authority areas.

The Department of the Environment has also tried to stimulate the private rented market — only 13 per cent of the total — but with little success. A shorthold system has been introduced to allow landlords the right to let for between one and five years with a guaranteed right of repossession. Similarly, assured tenancies with security of tenure have been created under which certain landlords, approved by the Environment Secretary, can build for rent at market levels outside the provisions of the Rent Act. Capital allowances have also been made available for the construction of houses and flats on these terms. This has encouraged some development by private builders, building societies and insurance companies, but in general financial institutions remain reluctant to return to the residential property market because of management problems and political uncertainty. The Environment Committee of the Commons noted in a report in 1982 that, taking account of the Government's actions, the current position 'neither gives most landlords an adequate return nor enables many tenants without hardship to pay rents on suitable secure accommodation'. Consequently, fundamental changes will be necessary if an adequate supply of decent and affordable accommodation is to be made available.

The key question is what has been happening to the quality of housing provided as well as its ownership? While the stability of Britain's population has removed the need for a large increase in the overall housing stock, there has still been a requirement to repair and replace existing houses as they age and decay. The *English House Conditions Survey*, published in December 1982, showed that the number of unfit homes remained relatively constant between 1976 and 1981 at between 1.1 and 1.2 million, with a substantial improvement in the northern region but a deterioration in London and the South-East. Over the same period the number of homes with high repair costs — over £7,000 at 1981 prices — increased, and the number in serious disrepair rose by about 200,000, or 22 per cent. The replacement of such houses has been held back by the cuts in public-sector house-building and by the fall in private house-building as well. In 1982 combined completions in the two sectors of around 171,000 were over 70,000 less than in 1979 and down from more than 300,000 in the late 1970s. However, from late 1981 onwards, starts did pick up sharply, especially in the private sector, as interest rates fell.

In the public sector there have been substantial receipts from sales of councils houses and land. In cash terms these rose from £383 million in 1978–9 to £1.87 billion in 1982–3. But local authorities have received only part of the benefit, and tighter Government controls have limited spending on new housing investment to even less than the lower allotted levels. In response both to concern about underspending on capital targets and to pressures from the construction industry, the Government took a series of measures during 1982 to relax controls. The aim was to give local councils greater assurance of future resources in planning investment programmes. Measures were also introduced to stimulate house improvement and to encourage local authorities to tackle the worst problems of poor housing in the inner cities through 'enveloping' schemes, under which whole streets of houses can be improved externally in a single operation. The number of houses renovated with the aid of Government grants and subsidies fell in 1981, but by 1982 it had risen, especially in the private sector, to above the 1979 level.

The inter-departmental report to the Cabinet assumed that the trends leading to the sharp fall in housing expenditure in the early 1980s were unlikely to continue beyond the present financial year [1982—3]. Further increases in the real level of rents would be largely offset by higher rent rebates [now part of the unified housing benefit], so that there would be little net gain to public expenditure. Some increase in gross capital expenditure is needed simply to maintain the habitability of much of the existing stock and to replace significant numbers of post-war dwellings built by industrial methods that are now becoming structurally unsound and in many cases are completely uneconomic to repair. The peak in sales will be this year; capital receipts therefore are expected to decline.

As noted in an earlier chapter, the report's projections of a sharp rise in housing expenditure may be exaggerated. But there is certainly no scope for a reduction without risking serious damage to the standard of housing provision not only in the remaining public-sector rented housing but also in parts of the private sector which will not be repaired without public money.

The Coming Squeeze

At first glance, the Thatcher administration's record has shown some continuities with what happened under the Wilson and Callaghan Governments after 1975—6. There has been a similar broad commitment, at least in public, to the state provision of the basic social services and also an overriding financial constraint which had not existed in the 1960s and early 1970s. The rows over 'de-indexing' social security benefits and raising council rents began under Labour. The lean years started before the 1979 election, but they have become leaner since.

The differences have been partly of degree, though increasingly of kind. The financial squeeze has been greater, notably in housing but also in education, social security and, probably much more from now on, in the National Health Service. The result has been that programme managers have found it more difficult, as time has passed, to maintain standards of provision. They have been able to do so only as a result of efficiency drives, which may be hard to sustain on a long-term basis, even though external reviews, manpower targets and contracting out may provide a helpful long-term financial discipline.

The impact of the squeeze so far has been unequal. Julian le Grand (in Glennerster, 1983) has analysed the distributional impact of social services as measured by the ratio of expenditure per person in the top fifth of the income range to that per person in the bottom fifth. On this basis, the only pro-poor services are council housing subsidies and rent allowances; primary and secondary education are roughly equal; bus subsidies, universities, tax subsidies to owner occupiers and rail subsidies strongly favour the better off. Yet the sharpest cutbacks have been in housing subsidies, while few of the services which particularly help the better off have been significantly squeezed. The main exception is the universities, which may explain why this has become such a sensitive issue. In contrast, mortgage interest relief has been maintained and was worth £2.15 billion in 1982—3.

Similarly, a Child Poverty Action Group analysis has suggested that the poor have suffered worst from Thatcherism. Ruth Lister and Paul Wilding noted (in Bull and Wilding, 1983) the stigmatization of failure (for example, in relation to the means-testing of school meal charges), the reduction of statutory responsibilities (school meals and milk and a narrowing of eligibility for supplementary benefit), the delegation of responsibility from central government to local authorities, the view of the public sector as a long-stop in provision and the extent of the cutbacks. The Government has also ignored the consequences of inequality, notably in its attitude to the report by Sir Douglas Black of the Royal College of Physicians. This revealed markedly higher rates of infant mortality among children of unskilled manual workers than among those of the professional classes. Such inequalities are reflected throughout life. Yet the Department of Health and Social Security did its best to limit discussion of the report by publishing initially only a limited number of copies and then giving no detailed response.

These inequalities seem unlikely to lessen. The Government's published public expenditure plans and the projections in the inter-departmental report of September 1982 may not be sufficient to maintain existing standards of service. Yet a real problem is posed by the issue of how to finance the rising cost of existing social security commitments and of the NHS in view of the growing number of very old people. As Mrs Thatcher has herself recognized, she will be a pensioner well before the likely date of the next general election.

But does the Government have any answer to these dilemmas? Its actions during its first term suggested no more than a piecemeal approach. But, according to the Labour Party, during the 1983 election there was a hidden strategy — the so-called 'secret manifesto'. There were certainly plenty of radical suggestions about the future of the welfare state in the series of official documents leaked during 1982—3 — the papers associated with the Think Tank row in September 1982, the Family Policy Group papers and the various documents which appeared in *Time Out* magazine during the 1983 campaign. In many cases they consisted merely of ideas being aired for discussion, but they did indicate a philosophy, instincts and prejudices that are characteristic of Thatcherism.

In particular, the papers prepared for the Family Policy Group of Ministers outlined a clear view of how society should develop, all pointing towards a reduction in the role of the state and a shift of responsibility to the individual. For example, in relation to the elderly the discussion was 'concerned with finding ways in which the elderly can be helped, particularly by their families, to live full and happy lives in the community with minimum dependence upon the state'. The papers also noted that 'One of the clearest signs of a society in which individuals are prepared and able to take care of themselves and their families is the existence of a vigorous voluntary sector.' Under the heading 'Encourage private provision of social needs', the summary of proposals for action listed the encouragement both of voluntary contributions to state and charitable services aimed at meeting social needs and the close involvement of the private business sector in the local community, the definition of a minimum safety-net for welfare needs and the consolidation and extended use of surrogate families (such as 'Homestart' and 'Adopt-a-Granny' schemes).

Many of the detailed ideas associated with this and other topics in the Family Policy Group's discussions were reasonable in themselves, and they might help to strengthen the family. The danger is that the overall thrust of the thinking is too narrow. It might limit opportunities by discouraging married women from working and by shifting responsibilities on to the family from a state which provided only safety-net support. The ideal no doubt reflects Mrs Thatcher's memories of her background in Grantham before the war, when the Roberts family included grandmother. This is a long way from the position of the poor single-parent family that needs state support to survive.

The other leaked papers revealed more radical proposals. The Think Tank's options implied a major shift to the private insurance principle in large parts of the social services. Similarly, in June 1982 a Cabinet committee known as MISC 14 (the Ministerial Steering Group on Government Strategy) discussed expenditure-cutting projects such as the privatization of national insurance and education. The former could in effect limit the role of the state to the payment of means-tested benefits. Obviously, this has provided powerful ammunition for the Government's critics, but to some extent it was, as Ministers subsequently claimed, simply one proposal among many in a discussion of all possible options. It is the style of some of Mrs Thatcher's colleagues and advisers to think the (previously) unthinkable.

Moreover, many of the ideas were unacceptable to a large number of Ministers and Conservative MPs. A major change in current methods of financing the NHS principally by taxation has several times been publicly rejected by Ministers. Gradualism is still the keynote. Yet the leaked documents did highlight a series of preferences which are likely to be reflected in future piecemeal decisions and could be revised on a large scale if there were a crisis of public spending.

There are, however, potential political dangers for the Government, since the majority of the public seems to be attached to the welfare state. According to a Gallup poll, the proportion favouring a cut in taxation, even if it meant a reduction in services such as the NHS, education and welfare, fell from about one-third to one-fifth between 1979 and 1983, while the proportion favouring an extension of services, even if it meant some increase in taxes, rose from one-third to half. A Gallup survey in July 1983 showed that around two-thirds of those questioned felt that too little was being spent by the Government on these services.

Similar results have been recorded by other polls. During the 1983 election campaign a Harris Research Centre survey for the *Observer* indicated that Labour policies with respect to the NHS were preferred to those of the Conservatives. The BBC/Gallup survey quoted earlier in this chapter also showed that the NHS had become a more important issue in voters' minds since the 1979 election. A direct mail survey in February 1983 of 1,700 'floating voters' in the north London constituency of Enfield North by Conservative MP Tim Eggar showed that 'looking after the elderly and sick' was rated second on a list of seventeen issues which most concerned people. It was behind unemployment but well ahead of cutting personal taxes.

The welfare state could prove to be one of the Thatcher administration's most difficult problems in its second term. Mrs Thatcher has yet to persuade the public of the need to challenge the post-Beveridge consensus on the social services.

8

The Enterprise Economy?

The poor performance of the British economy in recent years has not been due to a shortage of demand. We are suffering from a growing series of failures on the supply side of the economy. Many of these failures are themselves the result of actions and interventions by Government themselves — laws that stand in the way of change and stifle enterprise and, as important as anything, a structure of taxation that might have been designed to discourage innovation and punish success.

Sir Geoffrey Howe
First Budget Speech as Chancellor of the Exchequer
12 June 1979

Long and hard experience has demonstrated that no Government can eradicate the inherent defects of nationalization. The time has come to liberate ourselves from this burden — and then to liberate the industries themselves from this condition.

Nigel Lawson
Speech as Energy Secretary, Oxford
23 September 1982

The most challenging aspect of the Thatcher administration has been its attempt to create a thriving private enterprise economy. There has been an almost moral fervour about its desire to extol the entrepreneur, to roll back the state, to sell off public corporations and to change the whole climate in which business operates. The administration has been seeking a cultural change — the recreation of the conditions in which British commerce and industry were successful in the nineteenth century. And the attempt to boost enterprise has linked those who are divided on other issues — 'wets' and 'drys'.

Yet the record in the key areas of industrial policy and nationalized industries has often been incoherent. As with many other aspects of Government policy, Mrs Thatcher and her colleagues may have had a vision of the kind of society that they would like to construct — a cross between nineteenth-century Birmingham and contemporary Hong Kong, located in Esher. But this vision has not added up to a strategy. There has been forward thinking, normally when Sir Geoffrey Howe has been involved, though in practice policy has often been pursued in a gradualist and piecemeal fashion.

None the less, by the time of the 1983 general election the Conservatives claimed to have taken the following actions 'to create the climate for enterprise':

(1) controls over pay, prices, dividends, movements of capital in and out of the UK and hire-purchase lending had been ended;

(2) Office Development Permits and Industrial Development Certificates were no longer required as prerequisites for schemes, thus easing planning controls;

(3) enterprise zones had been created, offering businesses in some areas reduced taxation and ligher regulation, with duty-free trading zones known as 'freeports' on the way;

(4) reductions had been made in business taxation via changes in stock relief provisions and lower employers' National Insurance surcharge;

(5) a wider range of assistance was available for small businesses via the easing of employment and planning legislation, the reduction of taxes, especially Corporation Tax, and direct financial help through loan-guarantee and expansion schemes;

(6) specific aid for high technology was offered by Government support for training and innovation;

(7) there was a growing programme for privatizing nationalized industries and liberalizing further public-sector monopolies to increase the size of the free-market economy.

All these measures were in line with the theory that state ownership and regulation have limited consumer choice, have hampered innovation and the drive to efficiency, have resulted in higher prices, have encouraged the power of monopoly public-sector unions and have generally been a drain on the taxpayer.

Industrial Policy

The Thatcher administration started out with a determination not to intervene in industry (as discussed in chapter 2). The lame-duck industries were to be given strict target dates by which to become profitable; nationalized industries generally were to be dealt with at arm's length, according to clear guidelines; the National Enterprise Board's activities were to be wound down; and the private sector was to be allowed to get on with 'creating wealth'. Before the 1979 election Sir Keith Joseph denied having an industrial policy.

Life turned out to be different. Sir Keith had a policy forced upon him. Expenditure by the Department of Industry (excluding lending to nationalized industries) rose in cash terms from £1.09 billion in 1978–9 to £1.81 billion in 1982–3 (admittedly slightly down from the peak of nearly £2 billion in the previous year but still rising much more rapidly than the rate of inflation). After adding in direct government lending to nationalized industries as well as grants and subsidies, support for lame-duck groups (BL, the British Steel Corporation and British Shipbuilders) was £1.7 billion in 1980–1 but was projected to fall to under £750 million in 1983–4. The increase largely reflected the pressures of the recession, and the objective for 1983–4 may be difficult to achieve in view of the continuing problems of the world's shipbuilding and steel industries.

Yet there was still a need for an industrial policy. It was developed into a more positive framework when Patrick Jenkin became Industry Secretary in September 1981. His aim was not to run down his department but to switch the emphasis away from lame ducks to small businesses and high technology. Department of Industry support for innovation, science and technology (microelectronics, fibre optics, information technology and space) was increased almost fivefold between 1978–9 and 1983–4 to £250 million. This interventionism has been strongly backed by Mrs Thatcher, who has prided herself on being the first science graduate to become Prime Minister. Kenneth Baker, the Minister for Information Technology and super-salesman for innovation, has justified this spending (in Baker, 1982) by the need to open up university research to industry via 'awareness programmes' and assistance for companies in introducing robots and related manufacturing systems. There has been support for training in technology through the establishment of 150 Information Technology centres for unemployed youngsters and of microcomputers in every secondary school and a third of primary schools.

Apart from the problem industries, there have been cutbacks in other areas of industrial spending – in, for example, regional aid. The scope of the assisted areas was cut from 44 to 27 per cent of the population, while the differential between incentives for special development, development and intermediate areas was increased. Similarly, other assistance was trimmed back. The National Enterprise Board was directed to sell off its investments, and its responsibility for Rolls-Royce and BL was transferred to the Department of Industry, prompting the resignation of its board. The NEB was amalgamated with the National Research and Development Council to form the British Technology Group, with a more limited brief, notably to assist the transfer of inventions from the universities to industry.

There was little that the Government could do quickly to reduce the spending needs of the problem industries, which were anyway doing a great deal to try to regain competitiveness and lost about 250,000 jobs between 1979 and 1983. It was not easy for the Government to withdraw, and the alternatives of bankruptcy or total closure were never seen as politically acceptable. Indeed, there were strong pressures to maintain support, as was shown by the December 1982 decision to keep open the five integrated steel-making plants in the UK, including the loss-making

Ravenscraig works in central Scotland, in response to a successful campaign by George Younger, the Scottish Secretary, and his Ministers.

All this sounds rather like the familiar preference of all Governments for backing winners with taxpayers' money. However, Mr Baker has argued that the emphasis has been not on the state's owning equity in companies but instead on its using money catalytically, and he has cited the example of other countries where Governments often give support for technology on a much larger scale. It certainly makes more sense than indefinitely sustaining steel and shipbuilding capacity for which there is no foreseeable demand.

This activity has raised questions among some commentators about how committed the Government has been in practice to its free-market rhetoric. Professor P. D. Henderson of London University has argued (Henderson, 1983) that while notable steps have been taken towards a less regulated economy, such as the abolition of exchange controls and moves towards privatization, 'there are extensive areas in which long-established British dirigisme still rules undisturbed.' Professor Henderson has cited the continuing support for 'voluntary export restraint agreements with Japan, the clear protectionist bias in official purchasing policy (directing contracts to ICL and domestic arms suppliers) and the insistence on maintaining a restrictive interpretation of the Multi-Fibre Arrangement'. Similarly, the Government has prided itself on vigorous export promotion, and Ministers have acted as travelling salesmen heading teams of industrialists on visits to developing countries. In the context of energy these attitudes have been evident in official policy towards potential exports of North Sea gas, possible imports of coal and the development of UK nuclear power.

These policies can be regarded as the sensible recognition of a world in which other Governments subsidize, protect and intervene. 'We are not going to be the first to break the rules, but...' has been the usual ministerial refrain. Yet, as Professor Henderson has argued, in all this it has been hard to see Mrs Thatcher and her colleagues as 'influenced by doctrinal ideas of a liberal, market-oriented kind. On the contrary, the policies show little awareness of such ideas, still less a readiness to act on them.' He has identified two influences: first, the desire to defend and help out specific groups and interests within Britain that are faced with competition from abroad and, second, 'the age-old mercantilist conviction that every country stands to gain by adopting its own specifically tailored array of protectionist and promotional measures'.

Most Conservative backbenchers and supporters have been in favour of such intervention. This is not surprising, since the party has often been protectionist in the past. Every trade, industry and regional Question Time or debate in the Commons tends to be dominated by special pleading for local interests and industries. Indeed, not a single Tory MP expressed serious reservations when in late July 1983 Michael Heseltine announced the intention to buy a British anti-radar missile (ALARM) rather than a US-developed system (HARM), despite the higher cost, delays to its introduction and the doubts of some service chiefs. 'Buy British' won the day over the objections of the Chancellor and the Foreign Secretary.

The approach of Mrs Thatcher and many of her colleagues has been essentially nationalist and mercantilist. As with her general view of foreign policy, she believes in a strong assertion of British interests, though she adds the caveat that British goods must be of the right quality and price to compete internationally. The Thatcherite commitment is to private enterprise as opposed to the public sector, not to the operation of competitive markets as such. Indeed, she has resisted moves to end or to reduce subsidies for buyers of private housing through tax relief on mortgage interest payments. She pressed successfully for an increase in the upper limit of this relief in the 1983 Budget, against the opposition of the Treasury. It is ironic that while in 1980–1 Mrs Thatcher was among those urging tighter monetary control, which would inevitably have resulted in the greater volatility of interest rates, she intervened directly in early 1983 to criticize the banks when they raised interest rates in response to market pressures. Her approach has undoubtedly been populist – at least in terms of traditional Conservative support – but it has not been free-market.

The Nationalized Industries

The Thatcher administration developed an almost passionate aversion to nationalized industries, partly through frustration. As a result, by the time of the 1983 general election an ambitious programme for shifting the frontiers between the public and private sectors was being prepared. Virtually no industry was immune: everything was being questioned.

The surprising feature of the programme was that little of it had been appreciated in 1979. As discussed in an earlier chapter, a working party under Nicholas Ridley had produced a number of ideas for denationalization (as it was still generally known). But the party leaders had been cautious in the 1979 manifesto and had merely referred to selling back to the private sector the two industries nationalized under Labour (aerospace and shipbuilding) plus the National Freight Corporation. Indeed, the word 'privatization' was not even mentioned in Whitehall or in political discussion until the summer of 1979, after the election. Then, at the prodding of Sir Keith Joseph, the scope for denationalization began to be broadened.

The main economic Ministers favoured privatization on the grounds (discussed by Heald and Steel, 1982) that it would enhance economic freedom, especially that of the consumer; it would increase efficiency; it would ease the problem of public-sector pay; and it would reduce public-sector borrowing. As Sir Geoffrey Howe said in July 1981, 'The consumer is sovereign in the private sector. In the public sector he is dethroned by subsidy or monopoly.' Similarly, Sir Keith Joseph argued: 'Nationalized industries are immunized from the process of spontaneous change which competition and fear of bankruptcy imposes upon the private sector.'

The proposed sales of part or the whole of the Government's interest in various concerns were on a larger scale than previous denationalization moves (the return of the iron and steel industry to the private sector after the 1951 election and the sale of the Carlisle pubs and Thomas Cook under the Heath administration). But the disposals were mainly of businesses operating in a competitive environment and did not involve core monopoly public utilities such as gas, electricity or the postal service, so in a sense they could be regarded as the shedding of sizeable but essentially peripheral parts of the public sector. At this stage sales of public-sector assets — which totalled £1 billion in 1979–80 — were seen partly as a means of holding down the public-sector borrowing requirement. But this was largely a presentational device which did not really impress the financial markets. After all, disposing of shares in BP or advanced sales of oil was like selling the pictures off the wall; it was hardly a real step towards greater financial probity. However, by 1981 attention had turned to the heart of the public sector.

The initial Government approach had involved setting tight limits on external finance (that is, borrowing) and clear financial targets over the medium term. Otherwise it was to be hands off, and there was the usual stated intention to remove the industries from continual Whitehall interference. This did not happen. The problem has been partly the industries' much higher than expected public-sector borrowing needs (thus pushing up public spending), but there have also been increasing political strains between the industries and central government caused by the difficulties posed by the increase in prices charged by nationalized industries, which were much higher than the general rate of inflation (in part a result of Whitehall targets); the faster than average growth in earnings in public corporations; disputes over the level of investment; as well as the large deficits of some industries. At the same time some of the more successful industries were pleading for greater freedom to raise capital outside Treasury controls.

The complaints led to two parallel approaches from 1981: first, an attempt to put financial and constitutional relations between Whitehall and the industries on a better basis and, second, a drive to broaden the privatization programme. On the first point a whole series of studies looked at ways of introducing more flexibility into control over the industries' investment. The problem was defining what was or was not guaranteed by the Government. Would the financial markets accept that a fund-raising project for a nationalized industry did not really have Treasury backing? The final discipline of bankruptcy was absent, and hence fund raising by public corporations was akin to borrowing by central government and was competing with private-sector funds. Arguments about the alleged crowding out of private-sector investment by the public sector were sharply criticized in a major report by the Treasury Committee of the Commons. Moreover, some of the demarcation lines between what was regarded as inside and outside the public-sector borrowing requirement appeared arbitrary. The distinction depended principally on whether an organization was covered by the Companies Acts. The search turned to defining separate sources of revenue or investment projects, but these ideas, which were widely canvassed in the City, made little progress, especially following the collapse in September 1981 of plans for private funding of the gas-gathering pipeline in the North Sea.

Parallel to these efforts was the attempt to establish a better working relationship between the chairmen of nationalized industries and their sponsoring Ministers. The tensions had over the years come to resemble husband/mother-in-law clashes, as the partners criticized each other for fecklessness and meddling. Nationalized industry chairmen moaned about political interference (that is, decisions they did not like), while Ministers decried the privileged position of the industries. After the frictions of the 1979—81 period Mrs Thatcher attempted to break the impasse by commissioning a report from Sir Robin Ibbs of the Think Tank. This proposed a clearer framework of financial control and policy objectives for each industry, which would be laid down and monitored in close collaboration with Whitehall; a shift to a majority of non-executive directors on industry boards; and the setting up of business groups in each sponsoring department to assist with the preparation and monitoring of objectives. These suggestions infuriated the chairmen of the nationalized industries and some of the sponsoring departments, who argued that the industries were already supposed to be commercial businesses and that the change would undermine the authority of the boards' chairmen. The opponents largely won, except that arrangements for defining objectives were made, though with little noticeable effect by mid-1983.

Perhaps the most promising innovation has been the granting of powers to the Monopolies and Mergers Commission to investigate nationalized industries. At least part of the operation of each industry is likely to be examined every four years. The subsequent inquiries have included British Rail's London and South-East commuter services, the London Electricity Board showrooms, four public-sector bus undertakings and the National Coal Board. The reports have made trenchant points about efficiency, the motivation of managers and targets. At least these points have been exposed to outside scrutiny, even though they have not led directly to increased competition.

Many of the Government's hopes have in practice focused on changing the people running the industries. Mrs Thatcher and her senior Ministers did not disguise their impatience with some of the chairmen left over from the Labour era — notably Lord Ezra at the National Coal Board and Sir Peter Parker of British Rail. The belief that putting the right sort of chap in charge will help to improve performance has been shared by most Governments — and was also reflected in Mr Whitelaw's view of how to shake up the Metropolitan Police. The Tories' favourite industrialists have included Ian MacGregor, at British Steel and then the National Coal Board, and Sir John King (ennobled after the 1983 election) at British Airways. Mrs Thatcher has been reluctant to promote from inside a nationalized industry and has even brought in civil servants from Whitehall to run the Post Office and the Electricity Council. All this has reflected the view outlined by Sir Peter Carey, the Permanent Secretary of the Department of Industry throughout the period. In a farewell interview (*Financial Times*, 5 May 1983) Sir Peter argued that the key to better relations was finding the right person to do the chairman's job and paying him a sum equivalent to the salary that he would earn in the private sector. 'If you are getting someone to come in out of a sense of national loyalty, you do not get a relationship on a strictly commercial basis, and you need such a relationship when you are running a big commercial organization.'

The Thatcher administration backed Sir Michael Edwardes

in his tough stance at BL, but the relationship was not without its problems, as is clear from his revealing memoirs (Edwardes, 1983). He writes that the administration's priority, that of returning BL to the private sector, conflicted with his own view that recovery should come first — the political and the commercial time-scales were different. Sir Michael also disliked Government attempts to 'second-guess' the BL board. Friction developed, especially with Patrick Jenkin, Industry Secretary after September 1981, who had 'very little concept of, or even interest in, the strategic framework of the Government's relations with a high-calibre board of a state-owned company'. Sir Michael concluded from this experience that Government should not own industry except where absolutely necessary. ·

The same conclusion was reached by many of the sponsoring Ministers and was summed up by Nigel Lawson in September 1982, in a speech in Oxford. He said that 'industrial baronies' had been created which were not truly accountable to anyone and were satisfying no one. Mr Lawson argued that the conclusion was inescapable that 'no industry should remain under state ownership unless there is a positive and overwhelming case for it so doing. Inertia is not good enough. We simply cannot afford it.'

The intensified privatization drive since 1981 has had two interrelated aspects. First, there has been the continuing and expanded programme of sales of parts of the public sector; second, there has been the spread of competition into tightly regulated public-sector operations. The later phase of privatization has linked the two features through moves to sell off and inject private capital into the core public utilities. Table 9 (see pp. 176—7) lists the major moves which have occurred or are planned.

The disposals of assets have in the main been to traditional owners like pension funds and insurance companies. The Government's hopes of spreading direct property ownership have not been fulfilled, with the important exception of the sale of council houses. As a report of the Public Accounts Committee of the Commons pointed out in 1982, the number of shareholders in British Aerospace fell from 157,800 on flotation to 27,200 within a year; the number owning under

100 shares dropped from 40,000 to less than 3,300. The same trend was apparent in the case of Cable and Wireless and Amersham International. And, despite the Government's rhetoric, there were no sizeable employee shareholdings — the percentage holdings were tiny. In some respects the initial small shareholders had been smart to sell, for the first offers were heavily over-subscribed, and the share prices rose sharply in the first few months of dealing on the stock market.

The very success of the early offers and the large premiums over the original offer prices in the first dealings provoked the criticism that the assets were being sold off cheaply. The offers at a fixed price gave large profits to those who obtained shares, including the small shareholders, and made the underwriting of the offers look like a waste of fees on City banks and financial institutions. However, when the method was switched to sale by tender, with a variable price, in the case of Britoil (the production side of the British National Oil Corporation) there was a notable under-subscription, which meant that the institutions which had underwritten the offer were left with a sizeable initial loss, later to be recouped. According to the Public Accounts Committee, the cost of selling shares in BP, British Aerospace, Cable and Wireless, Amersham and Britoil was nearly £43 million, which went in fees and underwriting payments to merchant banks, stockbrokers, pension funds and insurance companies. Similarly, the sale of council houses and land has been good business for solicitors and estate agents.

The main exception has been the National Freight Corporation, the shares in which were bought out by its management with the help of bank finance. A significant minority of non-management employees also bought shares, despite the strong opposition of the Transport and General Workers' Union, which argued against the purchase on the grounds that the financial security of employee shareholders was doubtful, that the new firm would not be a workers' co-operative but would leave power in the hands of management and the banks, and that there would be an inevitable conflict of interest between shareholders and employees (see Hastings and Levie, 1983). The union's opposition did not, however, extend to taking disruptive action. Indeed, protests by unions

TABLE 9   *Privatization and liberalization since 1979*

Public-sector operation	Action taken
Transport	
British Rail	Sales of property, laundries, hovercraft and some hotels
Docks	Sales of shares in Associated British Ports
National Freight Corporation	Sale to consortiums of managers and employees
Coaches	Removal of licensing restrictions on long-distance coach routes
Road-construction design	Contracting out to private consultants
Energy	
Gas	Abolition of British Gas Corporation's monopoly of North Sea gas and sale to industry; direction to sell 50 per cent share in Wytch Farm oilfield in Dorset and oilfields; sale of showrooms delayed until legislation on safety is complete
Electricity	Sanction for generation by private companies as a main business, via national grid
Oil	Sale of shares in production side (Britoil) of British National Oil Corporation
Amersham	Sale of shares in former Radiochemical Centre
British Petroleum	Series of sales of Government shareholdings
Air	Sale of over half the shares in British Aerospace Conversion of British Airways to Companies Act status but sale delayed by financial restrictions
	Proposals to inject private capital into at least some British Airways Authority airports

TABLE 9   *continued*

Public-sector operation	Action taken
Communications	
British Telecom	Liberalization of supply, installation and maintenance to allow scope for competing suppliers and for the use of the network by independent groups (only one licence granted — to Mercury); proposals in 1983 to permit sale of shares
Post Office	Ending of monopoly for express mail and licences to permit document exchange
Cable broadcasting	Main investment to be by private sector; Bill in 1983—4
Cable and Wireless	Sale of nearly half Government shares
Other	
BL	Sale of Prestcold (refrigerators), agricultural tractors and forklift truck businesses; plan to sell off other subsidiaries, such as Jaguar
British Steel	Joint ventures (in rod and bar steel production with GKN); sale of Redpath, Dorman, Long engineering side
British Sugar	Sale of Government's 24 per cent shareholding
National Enterprise Board	(Renamed British Technology Group) Sale of interests in Ferranti, ICL, Fairey and other groups
Royal Ordnance factories	Legislation in 1983—4 session to convert to Companies Act status as prelude to introduction of private capital
Property Services Agency	Hiving off of jobs in architectural design, maintenance, transport and vehicle repair
British Shipbuilders	Hopes to introduce private capital into at least part of operations, probably naval shipyards
Rolls Royce	Hopes to transfer back to private ownership

have made little impact on the pace of disposal, though there have been threats from unions in British Gas and British Telecom over the plans for their industries.

Management objections have been more significant. Sir Denis Rooke, the chairman of British Gas, made no secret of his opposition to the proposed sale of some of the Corporation's assets, which he described in November 1981 as 'the piecemeal break-up of an economic structure which has a proven record of success'. Sir Denis was, as a result, reprimanded by Nigel Lawson, the Energy Secretary, but he successfully delayed the implementation of some of the proposals and survived to deal with someone who was, to him, a more congenial Minister, Peter Walker, who was appointed after the June 1983 election. In other cases too managements objected to the breaking up of what they regarded as integrated operations. But in general the boards have favoured privatization — not least as a means of escaping from Treasury control. Anyway the Government has appointed chairmen who support privatization.

The Government has claimed that the first batch of companies to be privatized have prospered — pointing to the sharp increases in profits reported by Cable and Wireless and Amersham International. But it is difficult to prove that in the short term these increases have had anything to do with being freed from Government controls, as opposed to general trading conditions. And, almost by definition, the Government has been able to sell off the more profitable and rapidly growing concerns first. The rate of disposals has been held up by the financial problems of some businesses and by the recession, both of which have affected the timing of the flotation of British Airways.

The related drive to increase competition and contract out to the private sector has been even more controversial, in particular because it has struck, and has been intended to strike, at the power of public-sector unions. There have been bitter rows in many local authorities over the contracting out of refuse collection, allegations of deteriorating services and clashes between unions and private contractors. The experience to date has been mixed (the NHS is discussed in chapter 7).

The hiving off of the Department of Transport's road-construction design and supervision work to fifteen firms of private consultants has raised costs. Gordon Downey, the Comptroller and Auditor General who audits government accounts on behalf of Parliament, reported in early 1982 that this decision would mean that about £4 million would be paid out in redundancy money to about 1,700 staff, even though many were re-employed by private consultants. Moreover, the consultants were being paid familiarization fees of up to £1.25 million. Officials pointed out that 'although there was no significant difference in the efficiency of performance, it costs more to employ consulting engineers than viable sub-units [within the Department of Transport].' The official estimate was that the extra cost would be £4.7 million in 1981−2, with a similar excess in the following year and probably less in later years. The justification was that the extra costs would be outweighed by the advantages of strengthening private consultants. The Department of Transport seems to have learned part of the lesson by backing away from the disposal of the heavy goods vehicle testing centres.

Clearer gains have come from the introduction of competition into long-distance coach routes. The 1980 Transport Act removed licensing and fares control from express coach services, excursions and tours. Provided the safety regulations are met, any operator can run a long-distance service. Controls were also relaxed on local stage carriage services and on car-sharing schemes. The immediate result in October 1980 was a large-scale development of express coach services and a reduction in fares on many routes. The consumer has clearly benefited in terms of lower charges, better services (including films during journeys) and comfort. British Rail has also been forced to compete via Saver routes and Supersaver fares. There has also been intensified competition between public- and private-sector operators. One of the main beneficiaries has been National Express, a subsidiary of the nationalized National Bus Company, which now carries many more passengers and which accounts for nearly three-fifths of long-distance services. However, NBC has clashed with the Government over its plans to inject private capital into coach activities. NBC argues that it is an integrated company and that there should be cross-subsidization between profitable operations and what it regards as socially necessary services. There has also been an increase in private commuter services, notably in the Medway towns, Berkshire and parts of Surrey, although with tight competition there have been casualties.

There has not, however, been a 'Laker of the coachways', as Norman Fowler, then Transport Secretary, envisaged when the Transport Act was passed in 1980. (This was, fortunately, well before the collapse of Sir Freddie Laker's airline.) The liberalization has been a clear plus to the consumer, not least in stimulating a response from the dominant nationalized transport services.

More complicated issues have been raised by plans to privatize the core public-sector utilities. The problem is that most are natural monopolies because of the nature of their supply or distribution processes. It is impossible to have competing sources of gas or electricity supply in any single town. The Government still believes that freeing the industries from state control will give their managements more independence to develop their businesses, though it recognizes that there will have to be continuing close regulation. This has, however, resulted in considerable confusion. The Government's first stage has been the introduction of competition wherever possible in these industries. The statutory public monopoly has been ended for express delivery services and document exchange, while the law has been changed to permit the private generation of electricity as a main business via the national grid system, by allowing private companies to supply gas to large industrial users and by permitting the licensing of an inter-city telephone network.

In general, these moves have involved the more profitable parts of the public monopolies and have concentrated on large industrial suppliers and customers rather than on the domestic consumer. Indeed, it has been recognized that for the foreseeable future the importance of private suppliers of electricity, gas and telecommunications will be strictly limited. The intention is mainly to keep the industries on their toes. But there is a danger that the sale of shares in these concerns will merely transfer a virtually complete monopoly from the public to the private sector, and there is an inherent conflict between freeing the industries sufficiently to make them attractive to outside investors and regulating them enough to reassure consumers that rural services, for example, will be maintained.

These questions have been central to the Bill to permit the sale of half the shares in British Telecom, which was debated at length before falling at the announcement of the June 1983 election and was reintroduced at the start of the new Parliament. The Bill aims at balancing the conflicting interests by introducing a new regulatory body (the Office of Telecommunications), which will issue a licence to British Telecom. This will lay down conditions so that British Telecom provides a universal telephone service, covering rural areas and including emergency provision. British Telecom will also be obliged to keep price increases for domestic rentals and local calls to a figure fixed below the rise in retail prices. However, as some Conservative MPs have pointed out, the change will be limited — British Telecom will still be in a dominant position. There will be only one national competitor and that solely for business services — the Mercury Consortium, formed by Cable and Wireless, BP and Barclays Merchant Bank. Critics, notably Richard Shepherd, the Tory MP for Aldridge Brownhills, have argued that competition should be more open and that the regulation of British Telecom should be tighter to prevent it from abusing its position to cross-subsidize between services. The Government has argued that an open and unregulated market would lead to an excessive concentration on the business market at the expense of the less profitable domestic market.

The issue of competition and regulation raised by the Telecommunications Bill are also relevant to the other utilities, such as gas and electricity, which the Government has also been considering privatizing. The worry is that these industries — and strong-willed chairmen like Sir Denis Rooke — will in practice remain in a near monopoly position in their sectors, and they may exercise a dominant influence over regulatory agencies. This linking of the attitudes of utility and regulatory body is known as 'agency capture' in the US — the closest parallel in the UK so far is the National Farmers' Union and the Ministry of Agriculture.

The privatization and liberalization programmes may turn out to be the most lasting achievements of the Thatcher administration. They highlight the differences of philosophy between the collectivist and the private enterprise view. The argument for the former (as advanced in, for example, Whitfield, 1983) is that public services are aimed at meeting social needs, not the demands of private profit; at fulfilling the demands of everyone, not just those who can afford it. Moreover, they can distribute resources between areas more fairly, are directly accountable to the public rather than just to shareholders, can achieve higher standards of employment and services than can the private sector and are often less wasteful than the private market.

The counter-view is that only competition and private enterprise spur organizations on to efficiency and to the satisfaction of the consumer. Professors Michael Beesley and Stephen Littlechild (1983) have argued that privatization should not be seen just as a means of selling shares, since the underlying aim should be to increase the role of market forces. Consequently, the disposal of assets should be supplemented by other measures to promote competition — the removal of artificial restrictions on entry and moves to make resources equally available to all entrants. They have argued that stricter competition policy is preferable to rates of return regulations, efficiency audits and related forms of government 'nannying'. Their conclusion is that the scope for privatization is greater than is commonly believed and that the greatest benefits to the consumer could come from privatizing the Central Electricity Generating Board (excluding the national grid), British Telecom, the National Coal Board, British Rail and the Post Office. In other industries, notably buses, airports and the local distribution of electricity and gas, the main benefits would come from restructuring them to form smaller units and from facilitating new entry.

The evidence of the past two decades is that the existing structure of nationalized industry/Whitehall relations is unsatisfactory. On the one hand, the industries and their unions are too powerful in relation to both consumers and taxpayers. On the other hand, Governments cannot resist intervening. So a policy of extending competition, contracting out services and decentralization has much merit, though each instance should be assessed separately. The danger is that the Thatcher administration has been so keen on selling everything in sight that it has confused transferring ownership to the private sector with increasing market forces through competition. The two are not the same. While there may be gains from putting public industries on a more commercial basis, the advantages of increasing competition are distinct and more important. There is also a crucial difference between public industries (whether manufacturing or utilities) and public services. There is a strong argument for making the former more responsive to market pressures, with appropriate subsidies where necessary. Social, health and education provision is, and should remain, a different matter.

Boosting Business

The Thatcher administration has introduced a wide range of measures to encourage the formation and expansion of small businesses — the heart of the entrepreneurial spirit, in the view of Mrs Thatcher. The emphasis has been on removing obstacles and providing incentives via over a hundred separate actions. The burdens of regulations, of employment law and of taxation have all been lightened. Most significant has been the creation of new schemes to encourage investment in, and by, small companies. For example, the Business Start-Up Scheme was launched in 1981 to encourage outside equity shareholdings in new trading companies by allowing the cost of such investments to rank (for the investor) as a deduction for income tax purposes. The initial response was disappointing, and the rules of the scheme were gradually relaxed so that the relief applied to investments of up to £40,000 in any one year. In the 1983 Budget the scheme was extended (and retitled the Business Expansion Scheme) to include investments in new concerns. A possible annual take-up of £75 million was envisaged.

Investment by such companies was also encouraged by the Loan Guarantee Scheme. Loans of up to £75,000 extended by the clearing banks were guaranteed by the Department of Industry in return for a risk premium. The scheme started with an overall limit of £50 million and was subsequently extended to £300 million. In 1983 it was announced that a further £300 million would be available for the following three years. By February 1983 some 8,860 guarantees had been issued, with a total loan value of £295 million. The Government claims that well over 20,000 new jobs have been created, though how many would have appeared without the scheme is open to question.

The most radical innovation has been Sir Geoffrey Howe's pet scheme for enterprise zones in rundown areas with economic problems. Businesses have been encouraged by a variety of tax reliefs and exemptions from laws and regulations. These have included simplified planning proposals, 100 per cent capital allowances for industrial and commercial building, complete exemption from Development Land Tax, 100 per cent derating of industrial and commercial property, exemption from industrial training board rules and levies, and a reduction in Government requests for statistical information. The first batch of eleven zones was followed by thirteen more, each covering a small inner-city area. A report by urban economists Roger Tym and Partners, published in April 1983, showed that in the first seventeen months of their life up to the end of 1982, 520 firms and over 4,500 jobs had been attracted to the zones.

The report said that the early impact of the zones had been significantly to increase the level of economic activity by encouraging local authorities and property owners to co-ordinate their activities. The main criticism has been that the zones have produced a shift of development and employment from neighbouring areas which have not had such a favoured status. This appears to have happened in several cases, judging by the complaints of property developers and agents. Indeed, the report showed that in the early months of the zones many of the firms attracted would probably have located in the same county, so that there may have been some offsetting reduction in development in areas around the zones. However, the report suggested that firms which might otherwise have operated outside the regions were concentrated in Corby, Swansea, Wakefield and the Isle of Dogs.

Overall, the importance of the zones seems marginal, while they have had distorting impacts on neighbouring areas and on market forces. The report specifically rejected the charge of the critics that the zones have led to unfair competition between firms inside and outside. But local authorities in the zones have engaged in considerable spending and promotion, akin to highly selective regional aid. John Blundell, an American academic specialist in this field, argued in the *Daily Telegraph* on 4 February 1983 that the establishment of the zones was like 'trying to fly a kite in the face of a hurricane. Enterprise cannot be neatly packaged into conveniently sized, tidy little blocks and then dropped into areas that politicians wish to favour.'

It is almost impossible to assess what the series of measures to help small business has achieved. The view of Ministers like Sir Geoffrey Howe is that there has been a much greater willingness to get new enterprises going. He has cited management buy-outs, the level of private-sector investment, the increase in VAT registration as an indicator of new company births, and the response to the Government's various initiatives. The evidence is mixed. Births of new companies of all kinds certainly substantially outnumbered deaths in 1981–2 by a margin of nearly 18,000, after a small drop in 1980, but the figures have to be treated with caution.

The recession appears to have had a double-edged impact, making life more difficult for small businesses but also encouraging, or forcing, the unemployed to start their own concerns. There have been many stories of people using their redundancy money to start their own small firms. But it has also been argued that there has been an employment culture — dependency on the public sector — resulting in a lack of entrepreneurial drive in some of the high-unemployment black spots of Scotland, Merseyside and the North-East.

The central question is whether there has been a cultural change, whether risk-taking and business life have become more attractive. Reports have circulated of businessmen returning to Britain following the cut in the top marginal rate of income tax, and there have been new entrepreneurs in the electronics and high-technology sectors. The archetype has been Sir Clive Sinclair, the head of the Sinclair mini-computer empire. The expansion of some of these newer businesses has been reflected both in the development of the unlisted securities market in London and in the growth of venture capital funds. There has been bullish talk of groups of high-technology companies concentrating in areas similar to Silicon Valley in California. The British examples have been sited along the M4 in Berkshire, around Cambridge and in central Scotland, and there are plans for the creation of science parks linked to universities in many cities.

Whether all this has added up to the rebirth of the entrepreneur is still an open question. The British executive has remained more attached than his US counterpart to job security — in part because of the problems of transferring pension rights and the high level of fringe benefits. So the flowering of the high-tech tycoons may signal only an oasis and not a change in the vegetation of the whole desert. After all, the number of jobs created will not be nearly enough to offset the enormous job losses in traditional manufacturing since 1979.

Industrial Relations

Like generals, most politicians prepare for the last war. Much of the discussion before the 1979 general election had been about how to avoid a confrontation between the Government and the trade unions similar to the protests against the Heath administration's Industrial Relations Act of 1971 and during the winter of 1973—4. Yet there has been no such confrontation. There have, admittedly, been bitter industrial disputes. The TUC has denounced the Government with every curse and insult in its locker. But there has been no dramatic 'who governs Britain?' battle. The unions have been the dog that did not bark.

The Conservative strategy has been a mixture of radical intent and cautious practice. There is little doubt that the aim of Conservative leaders such as Mrs Thatcher, Sir Geoffrey Howe and Norman Tebbit has been significantly to weaken the position of the unions. They regard them as monopolistic organizations which distort the operations of the labour market, slow down necessary change through restrictive practices and limit employment by pushing up wages.

The intention was made clear by a leaked Treasury memorandum, written in September 1981 for distribution to the Cabinet and entitled 'Action to Combat Unemployment and Improve the Working of the Labour Market', which noted that 'if the Government were to make the fragmentation of labour markets part of its general drive and publicity, it is possible that progress could be made.' The memorandum also talked of 'action to weaken the bargaining position of public-sector unions' and of the 'unique disruptive capability' of those unions.

The approach has in practice been step by step, in deliberate contrast to the policy of the early 1970s, when the Heath administration attempted to create a new framework of law with new institutions and new procedures. The Thatcher Government has introduced new legislation every two years. And despite their marked differences of personality and style, this approach was maintained even after Norman Tebbit took over from James Prior as Employment Secretary in September 1981. The Government was also careful to try to take public opinion along with it at each stage. The opinion polls suggested that the main changes had broad popular support, including among union members.

The following changes were introduced by the Employment Acts of 1980 and 1982, which

(1) restricted lawful picketing to the pickets' own place of work;
(2) provided compensation for people unreasonably excluded or expelled from a union in a closed shop (under the 1982 Act this was extended to some dismissals during the 1974–9 period);
(3) ensured that new closed shops must be approved by four-fifths of the workers in a secret ballot and made it unfair to dismiss a person in a closed shop because of a

conscientious objection (this was further strengthened by the 1982 Act to cover existing closed shops);

(4) restricted immunity for secondary action (sympathy strikes, blacking) to that taken by employees of a supplier or customer of the employer in dispute and aimed directly at the supply of goods or services between their own employer and the employer involved in the primary dispute;

(5) removed those provisions of the Employment Protection Act which affected small businesses by increasing the qualifying period for complaints of unfair dismissal from six months to a year, and to two years in the case of firms with fewer than twenty employees;

(6) made it unlawful to refuse to include firms in tender lists or to offer or award contracts to them on the grounds that they do not recognize unions;

(7) changed legal immunities from civil actions for trade unions in order to make them liable to an injunction or damages up to a specified limit where they are responsible for unlawful industrial action;

(8) restricted the definition of lawful trade disputes to include only those between workers and their own employers over pay, conditions of work and jobs, thus excluding disputes between a trade union and an employer whose workers are not in dispute;

(9) required companies with more than 250 employees to insert in their annual reports statements about what they have done to develop arrangements for consulting and for involving their employees.

The impact of the Acts has clearly been to shift the balance in favour of employers. But the legislation appears to have had a psychological rather than a practical effect. Studies of the 1980 Act have shown that employers have used the provisions against secondary pickets only in a handful of cases, and infringements have been more common. Yet the legislation has helped to strengthen management morale by showing that the Government supports 'the right to manage'.

Much more significant in changing attitudes has been the recession. The huge wave of redundancies and closures which started in 1980 undoubtedly led to a changed environment in many manufacturing businesses. Managements were able to win back control over production processes and to get rid of many restrictive practices. Union protests against redundancies were seen as largely self-defeating. And, not surprisingly, the surviving workers identified more with their companies and believed all the warnings about shortage of money and market problems. The result was a sharp drop in the number of strikes in the private sector, together with a general weakening of any militant drive. In many cases the predominant mood on the shop floor was seen as resignation and apathy. Yet unions have survived. The percentage of the smaller workforce in unions has dropped slightly, and the framework of shop stewards in plants has remained largely in place, principally because both workers and management have wanted it. There have been spectacular clashes – as at BL, where Sir Michael Edwardes and his management bypassed the shop stewards in a series of ballots in the early 1980s – but in many cases there have been no such confron- tations, and employers have negotiated new agreements with unions in the usual way.

The sharpest conflicts have been in the public sector, where the Government has won over – or at any rate has seen off – previously powerful unions. The first test came in the bitter and long-drawn-out steel strike of 1980, which significantly weakened the Iron and Steel Trades Confedera- tion in national bargaining, especially in the face of the consequent large-scale redundancies. The strike by the National Union of Railwaymen in 1982 was called off by delegates at the union's annual conference. Most startling has been the change in the mining industry. There was much talk about the power of the National Union of Mineworkers when, in February 1981, the National Coal Board and the Government retreated before strong union reaction to plans for pit closures. The Government agreed to increase the industry's external financing limit at a cost of £250 million. Yet this did not mark the beginning of a more militant phase at the NUM. Moreover, pits have continued to be closed down – but more quietly and more discreetly. In January and October 1982 the miners voted in ballots to accept pay offers and rejected calls for strike action from their executive. In March 1983 they acted in the same way on the issue of pit closures despite the overwhelming election to the presidency of the union of Arthur Scargill, who wanted to pursue a confrontational approach.

Similarly, after both the lengthy Civil Service dispute of 1981 and the National Health Service dispute of 1982, the unions emerged weakened, even though there was considerable public sympathy for the workers' case in the latter case.

Union leaders were left demoralized. Attempts to organize mass action and co-ordinated campaigns against redundancies generally failed. The emphasis shifted during 1982–3 to protests against plans to contract out to the private sector many ancillary services in hospitals and in central and local government. The unions regarded this as a deliberate attempt to fragment their power, since the private-sector contractors often had no unions or were weakly unionized.

The main question is whether there will be a return to the pre-1979 type of conflict if the economy picks up. Len Murray, the General Secretary of the TUC, warned in 1982: 'if and when there is an upturn in economic activity, and the balance tilts towards the workers, then do not be surprised if workers remember the scars inflicted on them in the current recession and are ready to inflict a few scars themselves.' Some commentators saw this happening in the spring of 1983, with the month-long strike at Ford's Halewood plant, a strike over a parity claim at Tilbury and a sit-in by Timex workers in Dundee over closure plans. Yet these disputes were exceptions, as was shown at BL's Cowley plant by the rank-and-file revolt against the strike over washing-up time.

Yet has anything changed permanently? The shake-out has altered attitudes in the sense that it has created a buyer's rather than a seller's market for labour. Many managers believe that unemployment has been the main check on wages and militancy. Other industrialists argue that the recession, coupled with the Government's tough style and no-nonsense approach, has created an opportunity for reorganization and lasting improvements in efficiency. The achievement may have been to make both managers and workers more aware of economic pressures, but it is too early to say whether underlying social and political attitudes to work have altered.

The trade unions themselves are in a difficult position: they are aware of their weakness not only in the industrial arena but also politically since Labour's crushing defeat at the 1983 election. In the summer of 1983 union leaders were having to decide whether to resume talks with the Government on employment legislation. But Norman Tebbit knew that he had the initiative, in the short term, over the next stage of his legislative proposals. These would require both the holding of ballots for the election of governing bodies of unions and periodic decisions about whether unions should have party political funds, and would curb the legal rights of unions to call strikes without seeking the prior approval of those concerned through secret ballots. In addition, there were more tentative proposals to ensure that trade unions would allow their members to decide for themselves whether or not to pay the political levy (a decision against this would significantly undermine the financial base of the Labour Party). Overall, the union movement was, at national level, in its weakest position for fifty years.

9

Home Affairs

The most disturbing threat to freedom and security is the growing disrespect for the rule of law. In Government, as in Opposition, Labour have undermined it. Yet respect for the rule of law is the basis of a free and civilized life. We will restore it, re-establishing the supremacy of Parliament and giving the right priority to the fight against crime.

Conservative Election Manifesto
1979

Fear of crime in the British inner city has reached levels found in major US cities.

One of the conclusions of the 1982 Home Office
survey of 11,000 people's experience of crime

The failure of the many attempts over the last three decades to tackle the problem of inner-city decline successfully is striking.

Lord Scarman
Report on the Brixton Disorders of April 1981

The Conservatives made the fight against crime a central plank of their 1979 election campaign. Their manifesto was quite specific in promising to spend more on fighting crime by increasing the pay and resources available to the police and by taking tougher action against criminals. Yet the official figures show a sharp increase in almost all categories of recorded offence, especially burglary, theft and violent crimes. Both the promise and the performance highlight some of the conflicts between instinct and pragmatism at the heart of Thatcherism.

Law and Order

There is no doubt that law and order is a very important issue for Conservative activists and in the party's appeal to voters. Respect for the rule of law and authority have always been central to the Conservative tradition, but under Mrs Thatcher's leadership the issue has become more prominent and has taken on a populist aspect. Crime and especially punishment are high on local activists' list of priorities — often particularly in the suburbs, away from the inner cities. Candidates attending the many selection conferences after the constituency boundary changes before the 1983 election reported that they were invariably asked their views on capital punishment and frequently also on corporal punishment. None of this is new. The novel feature has been that many of the rank and file's views have been endorsed by Mrs Thatcher. For instance, she appeared to sympathize with the vociferous law-and-order lobby during a particularly heated debate at the Conservative Party conference in 1981, when Mr Whitelaw was heckled.

What Mrs Thatcher has done, according to one senior critic, is to make the activists' prejudices respectable. Of course, it can be argued that she has merely been more in tune with popular preferences for a tough policy against criminals and in favour of capital punishment than the party's liberal and paternalist wing. But the danger of bolstering popular discontent over these issues is that the problems will be over-simplified. Expectations will be raised of solutions to what are inevitably complicated questions with no ready answers.

Fighting crime has also been an important element in the Conservative Party's wider appeal. Mrs Thatcher's final election broadcast in 1979 included a reference to 'feeling safe in the streets'. Commitment to strong action over law and order featured in the election addresses of 87 per cent of Conservative candidates; it was the second most important topic, just behind tax cuts (Butler and Kavanagh, 1980). This was also the major policy issue on which the Conservatives had the most decisive lead over Labour — plus 72 per cent, according to a BBC/Gallup survey (Penniman, 1981). And the Tories retained a sizeable advantage over Labour (though not nearly as large as previously) during the 1983 election, in spite of the fact that the issue was still less important to voters than unemployment and prices. Nevertheless, Conservative leaders appear to have believed that it was one of their issues, though the public seems to have been sensibly sceptical about how much any Government could do in practice. A survey in April 1979 (quoted in Penniman, 1981) showed that 20 per cent more people thought that the Government would not achieve its aim of reducing violent crime than those who thought it would.

There is no doubt that there has been, and is, a serious crime problem. The official statistics have to be treated with considerable caution because they merely show recorded crime — probably less than a third or a quarter of the total. A large number of offences, such as the majority of vandalism incidents, are not reported to the police. Even with that caveat, there has been a sharp increase in almost all types of offence, particularly violent crime, burglary, robbery and theft. It is also apparent that people are increasingly worried about crime. The British Crime Survey of 11,000 people carried out by the Home Office in 1982 showed that 60 per cent of elderly women living in inner cities felt 'very unsafe' when walking alone at night, while even in the 31-to-60 age group 38 per cent of women also felt 'very unsafe'. About one-third of women generally, and over a half in the inner city, sometimes avoided going out at night because of their fears. However, the victims of street crime such as robbery, theft or attacks have been predominantly not older people or women but men aged between 16 and 30.

Nevertheless, in the inner cities there are few people who either have not been the victim of a crime of some kind or do not know someone who has been. It is something that might happen to you. The problem is therefore real, and the fears are deep-seated. But solutions are not easy. The Conservative approach has, however, at times appeared to be one-dimensional. The views of activists and of some Conservative backbenchers have tended to be direct and unqualified: extend more resources and power to the police;

require the courts to award stiffer sentences, and have more concern for victims than criminals. Of course, this is to some extent a caricature. Any Conservative Home Secretary has to try to satisfy, or at least to appease, the simple demands of activists and backbenchers while implementing a more sophisticated series of policies. However, when he was Home Secretary from 1979 to 1983 Willie Whitelaw's bluff style and no-nonsense phrases about punishing violent offenders failed to satisfy the law-and-order lobby and the more strident Sunday newspapers, for whom he had become the epitome of flabbiness and ineffectiveness by the time of the 1983 election.

Some of the actions that were necessary to head off the law-and-order lobby also often left him in an unsatisfactory position in relation to civil liberties groups. He would anyway never have been able fully to satisfy the latter. His own preference was for strong solutions to some key issues, such as police powers, over which he came down firmly on the side of authority. But he recognized that the answers to many of the crime issues were multi-dimensional, though his instincts, and the pressures of his party and the police, led him to be cautious and to adopt a gradualist approach.

Under the Whitelaw regime the Home Office poured large amounts of money into law and order. The Government's actions included:

(1) an increase in spending on the police of nearly a quarter in real terms between 1978—9 and 1982—3;
(2) a rise in the number of police of roughly 9,500 to more than 120,000 in England and Wales;
(3) a pay increase of over 30 per cent in real terms for a police constable in the 1979—83 period;
(4) a rise in the number of police back on the beat;
(5) the introduction of a 'short, sharp, shock regime' for young offenders in four detention centres and the opening of new attendance centres.
(6) a widening of the range of penalties available to the courts, including the introduction both of community service orders for 16-year-olds and of residential care orders;

(7) an extension of the system of compensation for victims of crime;

(8) the largest prison-building programme for decades, involving the start of two new prisons in each year from 1981—2 to 1984—5, together with more modernization.

The prison programme highlights the dilemmas faced by Mr Whitelaw or any other Conservative Home Secretary. Prison conditions have been deteriorating over the last decade. In 1982—3 the number of people in prisons, hostels and detention centres was nearly 44,000, squeezed into accommodation intended to house 38,700. The result has been not only overcrowding but also restrictions on education, recreation and work. The reports of the Prison Department have expressed increasing frustration about the ability of such institutions to make any lasting deterrent or rehabilitative impact. Not surprisingly, recidivism has been high, and there has been a growing number of prison disturbances. These pressures could be relieved by two expedients — shorter sentences (including non-custodial ones for some offences) and the expansion of prison accommodation. Conservative policies have been an uneasy mix of the two, leading to a further deterioration in an already serious position in the short term.

In view of the crime wave, there has been strong political resistance to any shortening of sentences. Indeed, there have been calls for even longer terms of imprisonment for violent criminals. The Thatcher administration has tried to divert alcoholics from prison, and the Criminal Justice Act of 1982 abolished imprisonment for vagrancy and loitering and soliciting for prostitution, but this has still left in prison many petty offenders, fine defaulters and so on. Instead the main emphasis has been on prison building and renovation. While this is long overdue, the Government's own figures (as contained in the 1983 expenditure White Paper) envisage that in 1985—6 there will still be a gap of 4,000 between the likely prison population and available accommodation, and that will be after an increase of nearly 4,000 in places in prisons since 1978—9.

The impact of the Government's other measures is difficult

to assess, but the indications are that extra resources for the police have dealt with only part of the problem. In particular, relations between the police and the public have been under strain mainly in big cities and particularly in London. There has been a general loss of confidence in the competence of the police. In London the Metropolitan Police has 3.6 officers per thousand people compared with 2.7 in Manchester, spends £69.70 per thousand each year compared with £40, but secures convictions in only 17 per cent of reported crimes, compared with 41 per cent. As often happens when an institution is facing problems, the Met has also experienced a series of scandals – the intruder at Buckingham Palace in 1982, the mistaken-identity shooting in Kensington in early 1983, allegations that corruption has gone unpunished.

Equally significant has been the feeling among both middle-class and working-class people in London that the Met has been unsuccessful in providing protection against burglary – up 43 per cent in its area over five years. There has been little confidence or trust. Middle-class people who would previously have had limited contact with the police have been heard to complain about police insensitivity, incompetence and the harassment of their children. More dramatically, there have been tensions, and in some cases breakdown, in relations between the police and the black and Asian communities in parts of inner London and other big cities. There is little doubt that far-left groups have been exploiting the problem, but the attitudes and style of the police have also been at fault. The argument is not whether crime can be condoned or excused but how it can be contained in ways which elicit widespread consent.

These problems emerged vividly from the Scarman report on the Brixton riots of April 1981, which concluded:

A major cause of the hostility of young blacks towards the police was loss of confidence by significant sections, though not all, of the Lambeth public in the police. The reasons for this loss of confidence included the collapse of the police liaison committee in 1979; 'hard' policing methods which caused offence and apprehension to many; lack of consultation about police operations;

distrust of the procedure for investigating complaints against the police; and unlawful and, in particular, racially prejudiced conduct by some police officers.

Lord Scarman defended the police response after the disorders occurred but recommended that there should be improvements in the recruitment, training and supervision of police, in their methods and in local consultation and accountability. The same points were made after the riots in other British cities in the summer of 1981.

The Government's response, both to the general unease and to the inner-city riots, indicated the tensions within the Conservative approach. Mr Whitelaw was torn between sympathy for the Scarman philosophy and the demands of Tory supporters for even tougher action against lawlessness. His preference was for administrative changes to improve the quality of the police: he accepted Lord Scarman's detailed recommendations, and a number of changes were introduced along the lines suggested. There was also an increase in the amount of anti-riot equipment and training available to the police, prompting accusations about the creation of paramilitary forces. Roy Hattersley, the Labour Home Affairs spokesman, commented that the Government's response to the inner-city riots had been to match violence with violence by adding tear gas, water cannons and armoured vehicles to the approved armoury of every police area.

The reaction to the Scarman report and the inner-city riots formed part of a wider redirection of police effort, reflected in the appointment of Sir Kenneth Newman as Commissioner of the Metropolitan Police in 1982. His approach (as set out, for example, in an interview published in the *Financial Times* on 23 March 1983) has essentially been to put the police back into more direct touch with the community, in the hope that this move will improve crime prevention and detection while helping to defuse racial tension. The measure included the Scarman-inspired consultative committees of councillors, MPs, policeman and other local groups, whose work has been reinforced by the improvement of information flows so that resources can be concentrated on particular crime targets. Yet the

pace at which these changes can be implemented is dependent
on the attitude of junior and middle-ranking police — and
Sir Kenneth was barracked by some of his own officers at a
meeting of the Police Federation in autumn 1982. But the
initial signs suggest some improvement, and there has been
an increase in arrests for muggings in certain areas.

Public doubts have remained, however, notably over the
Thatcher administration's plans to strengthen and extend
police powers. The Police and Criminal Evidence Bill proposed giving the police greater powers to stop and search
people in the street, to arrest suspects, to extend the time
suspects could be kept in police custody and to allow the
police to search the homes and workplaces of people not
suspected of an offence in order to find evidence. Proposals
were also included to establish a statutory framework of
consultation between the police and local authorities and
to introduce an independent element into police complaints procedures. The Bill was based on one part of the
Royal Commission on Criminal Procedure of 1981 but
failed to include some of the suggested safeguards, notably
a prosecution service independent of the police. There was
a case for tidying up the law in this area, but the Bill was
strongly criticized when it appeared in autumn 1982. And
Labour spokesmen argued that what was missing was
provision to make the police directly accountable via elected
authorities.

Doubts centred on the degree of discretion that would be
given to the police, who would be able to use the proposed
powers on 'reasonable suspicion' that a 'serious' offence had
been committed. The worries reflected the experience of
many middle-class people that existing powers could be used
arbitrarily. Criticism not only from established civil liberties
groups but also from doctors, bishops and members of other
professions revealed the extent of the distrust, especially in
the case of the powers of the police to search confidential
records of these professional groups. After public protests
this aspect of the Bill was amended, yet there were still
serious reservations — including among some Tory MPs,
privately — about imprecise nature of the powers being
granted. According to Roy Hattersley, 'The bond that must

be re-established between the police and the public will not be recreated by the introduction of arbitrary and capricious new powers.' The Bill was lost when the June 1983 election was called. And it was significant that Leon Brittan, the new Home Secretary, did not immediately reintroduce the Bill but deferred consideration of the measure until the autumn of 1983. Moreover, both the Conservative manifesto and the Queen's Speech of June 1983 promised the consideration also of the creation of a new, independent prosecution service.

The crime problem did not involve just police behaviour; wider social issues were raised. The Scarman report was clear: 'Any attempt to resolve the circumstances from which the disorders of this year sprang cannot therefore be limited to recommendations about policing but must embrace the wider social context in which policing is carried out.' And within the limits of his terms of reference Lord Scarman stressed the failure of many attempts to tackle the problems of inner-city decline. He called for a better co-ordinated attack both on these general economic and social difficulties and, specifically, on racial disadvantage. He noted that this might mean that 'ethnic minorities will enjoy for a time positive discrimination in their favour', but he felt that this would be justified. There has, however, been a reluctance to go far along this road, in part because of the impact upon race relations and in part also because of a view that it would be wrong to distinguish between young unemployed blacks and whites.

Inner-City Regeneration

The general message was uncomfortable for many Conservatives because of the implied relationship between rising unemployment and crime. Mrs Thatcher repeatedly and specifically rejected this link, arguing that crime had risen rapidly in periods of prosperity and when unemployment was low. For her, as for many Conservative activists, crime was crime irrespective of the research establishing the clear links between social and economic deprivation and lawlessness.

The inner-city riots forced many politicians, however, into a broader reassessment, typified by the energetic involvement of Michael Heseltine, then the Environment Secretary, who was sent up to Liverpool after the serious Toxteth riots. He established the Merseyside Task Force, composed of representatives from government departments and people seconded from the private sector, whose job was to work with local authorities and interests in the area.

Mr Heseltine's approach was based on a partnership between the public and private sectors. Among the innovations that he fostered was the financial institutions group: major banks and representatives of some building societies, insurance companies and pension funds lent twenty-six middle-ranking managers to work with central government for a year in order to develop new ideas for urban regeneration. Various projects related to joint public/private-sector housing and employment schemes have subsequently been launched.

Mr Heseltine argued against a grand strategy to reverse decline. What is needed, he has proposed (Heseltine, 1983), is a revival of the opportunities formerly created by cities:

> The momentum of events stimulated inner-city life. People were attracted to these despite the quite appalling conditions that prevailed. Somehow we have to recreate that sense of attraction and in circumstances where, rightly, people are far more discriminating about the quality of the environment in which they are prepared to live.

Past opportunities

> were not the result of a masterplan. They were the product of unco-ordinated decisions arising from our commercial and manufacturing prowess.

Apart from the specifically Merseyside initiatives, there have been a variety of similar urban schemes. For instance, there has been a derelict land grant (amounting to £30 million initially) to secure the immediate development by

private companies, with £200 million of investment, of land
reclaimed by local authorities, and an urban development
grant (£10 million of public money in the first batch) to
assist projects involving a large input of private finance
(£40 million at first). In addition, the Government has
encouraged the growth of Local Enterprise Agencies and has
set up Urban Development Corporations, along the lines of
New Town Corporations, to help regenerate the docklands
of London and Merseyside. There has been much merit in
these various partnership ideas, but the critics have a point
in arguing that the £270 million spent by the Government
in support of the urban programme in 1982–3 was dwarfed
by the cutback in the Rate Support Grant for many inner-
city local authorities.

Immigration

The Home Office has also faced a delicate balancing act over
immigration. This is another subject on which Conservative
activists have held strong views – notably that immigration
from the New Commonwealth countries should be stopped.
Indeed, this was the one major issue on which the Thatcher
administration was defeated on the floor of the Commons
between 1979 and 1983. A large group of Conservative
backbenchers joined in a bizarre alliance with Labour, SDP
and Liberal MPs in late 1982 to vote down, for entirely different motives, proposed revisions to the immigration rules.

Yet the problem of immigration, if there has been one,
has been of minimal proportions. In the late 1970s total
acceptances for settlement in the UK were in the 70,000–
80,000 range, admittedly somewhat higher than in the
early 1970s under the Heath administration but generally
lower than the rate of emigration. There was certainly no
evidence of a new wave of 'swamping' to use Mrs Thatcher's
phrase in Opposition.

The Conservatives were pledged in 1979 to introduce
further restrictions. The proposals involved a new British
Nationality Act to define entitlement to British citizenship
and residence in the UK; the limitation of entry of parents,

grandparents and children to urgent and compassionate cases; an end to concessions to husbands and fiancés; several restrictions on the issue of work permits; the introduction of a register of Commonwealth women and dependants entitled to entry for settlement; and tougher action against illegal immigrants.

A redefinition of British citizenship was probably necessary in view of the changed position of the UK in relation to its previous colonies and the Commonwealth. But the effect of the British Nationality Act of 1981 was mainly to limit further immigration by creating three classes of citizen. One section of the law, aimed at keeping out Hong Kong Chinese, ironically excluded those Falkland Islanders without a parent or grandparent who had full British citizenship. However, a loophole was quickly created for the Falklanders after the 1982 war. In practice, the law ensured that virtually only whites with close ties to the UK had automatic right of entry and settlement. There were further restrictions concerned with the question of whether children born in the UK could become British citizens and with citizenship registration, which has involved an expensive and lengthy process of naturalization.

In addition, immigration rules have been tightened to prevent the exploitation of marriage as an instrument of primary immigration into the UK. Entry clearance can be refused if there is reason to believe that the marriage is one of convenience and has been contracted primarily to secure entry into the UK. However, under the pressure of actions appealing to the European Convention on Human Rights changes were proposed in the autumn of 1982, defeated and then brought in again in early 1983. The rules were changed to allow women holding British citizenship to bring in husbands or fiancés (contrary to the letter of the Conservatives' 1979 manifesto). But the marriage cannot be an arranged one, and further complicated safeguards were introduced. The bitter row over the issue showed that the original proposals had been discriminatory on grounds of sex, in that men who had settled in the UK were entitled to marry foreign women but not vice versa, and implicitly also on grounds of race, since most of the men affected came from

India and Pakistan. The numbers involved were probably only 3,000 a year at most and possibly even fewer.

Overall, the result of the Government's various actions was to reduce acceptances for settlement into the UK from nearly 71,000 in 1979 to just under 54,000 in 1982 (the number from the New Commonwealth and Pakistan dropped down from 37,000 to 30,300). The cost was strained relations — externally, with Commonwealth Governments and internally with ethnic communities in the big cities.

The Thatcher administration's record with respect to both crime and immigration has reflected the continuing tensions between populist authoritarianism and Whitehall pragmatism. Mrs Thatcher's instincts have undoubtedly been in tune with those of the majority of the public and of her own supporters, and a renewed drive against crime and increased expenditure on the police were necessary in 1979. The Labour Government's policies, especially on pay, had helped to undermine police morale and had led to the departure of many good middle-ranking officers. More resources had to be made available.

The worrying point has been the balance of policy and rhetoric. There is a danger that the emotional forces of vengeance and retribution may have been let loose. Official sympathy for one-dimensional demands for a tough line may have raised false expectations. The issues of murder and immigration have been built up wholly out of proportion. The campaign in favour of the restoration of capital punishment has exaggerated the increase in the number of murders and has failed to provide any convincing evidence of the deterrent effect of the death penalty. But by its very clamour the belief has been created that the return of capital punishment will somehow make people safer. This is a distraction of effort and concern from the real problems and fears — the increase in street crime and burglary — which do require attention. Similarly, the focus on immigration controls by some Tory MPs and activists has been misleading because it has exaggerated the scale of the influx, which has had the result of partially deflecting the debate from the much more pressing problems of the conditions and prospects of those former immigrants who have settled in Britain and of their children.

None of this is to dismiss people's fears and preferences in connection with both issues. However, the job of political leaders is not merely to echo popular opinion but to point to the complexities of the problems and their solutions. There are serious difficulties which require vigorous action. More effective policing methods must go hand in hand not only with closer community links but also with action to deal with the economic problems of both poor blacks and whites in deprived areas. Lord Scarman was right in his diagnosis, as was Michael Heseltine in believing that the public sector can act only in partnership with local communities and the private sector. It is a question not of being soft on crime but of recognizing the need for a cool response and for sophisticated answers.

10

Foreign Affairs and Defence

What has indeed happened is that now once again Britain is not prepared to be pushed around. We have ceased to be a nation in retreat. We have instead a new-found confidence, born in the economic battle at home and tested and found true 8,000 miles away.

Mrs Margaret Thatcher
Speech at Conservative rally, Cheltenham
June 1982

I must be absolutely clear about this. Britain cannot accept the present situation on the EEC Budget. It is demonstrably unjust. It is politically indefensible: I cannot play Sister Bountiful to the Community while my own electorate are being asked to forego improvements in the fields of health, education, welfare and the rest.

Mrs Margaret Thatcher
Speech in Luxembourg
October 1979

British foreign and defence policy since 1979 has turned, almost more than domestic policy, around the personality and views of Mrs Thatcher. Critics, notably in the Foreign Office, argue that there has been a clash between her instincts and outside realities. Her champions claim that she has articulated the real feelings of the British people as opposed to the false internationalism of the Foreign Office. The truth (or the very rough approximation of it that this book represents) lies, as usual, in between. Mrs Thatcher has set a new direction in foreign policy — perhaps more in style than in substance and perhaps less consciously than at home. As a result she has become a figure to be reckoned with in international politics – not necessarily liked but respected. In the process she ruffled the traditional processes of diplomacy and the Foreign Office establishment.

Mrs Thatcher has been described as an English version of the late President de Gaulle. And so she is, though possibly more in her approach to leadership than in her policy views. Admittedly, she is no federalist, and within the EEC she has believed in arguing Britain's case as vigorously as have de Gaulle and his successors on behalf of France. But she has not shared the Gaullist desire to be in a middle position, independent of the super-powers. For Mrs Thatcher the Atlantic Alliance is crucial – indeed, she has seen the UK playing a special role with the USA in fighting Soviet communism. Her hostility to Moscow has almost parodied her 'Iron Lady' nickname. Her Gaullism has been rather an instinctive nationalism, in which the memory of Churchill (at least the 1940 version) has been central. As a young woman in Grantham during the war she was influenced by Churchill's leadership, and she frequently refers to Winston. His influence has been reflected both in her approach during the Falklands war and in her general desire to speak for Britain – referring, for example, to 'my money' in relation to the UK's contribution to the EEC Budget.

This style, with its stark and dramatic choices between right and wrong, has been at odds with traditional diplomacy. Moreover, in the memorable phrase of Conservative MP Julian Critchley, she cannot see an institution without hitting it with her handbag. To her the Foreign Office is like the BBC, full of doubters. Mrs Thatcher has distrusted its very cosmopolitanism, its aloofness and its desire for harmonious relations with other countries in almost all circumstances. To her, and to many of her backbench supporters, the Falklands crisis showed up the principal failing of the Foreign Office – its tendency towards appeasement rather than steadfastness in support of British interests. She was openly critical of the Foreign Office, while her relations with Francis Pym were strained. Indeed, she circumvented official channels in turning for advice to friends like Lord (Hugh) Thomas, the historian. Her doubts culminated in the appointment of Sir Anthony Parsons, Britain's highly successful Ambassador to the United Nations during the Falklands crisis, as a special adviser on foreign affairs in Downing Street.

To a considerable extent the Foreign Office has had only itself to blame for its isolation. Its style has at times appeared arrogant, and diplomats have deliberately detached themselves from domestic influences. For example, the Foreign Office has successfully resisted the pressures towards integration with the home Civil Service which started with the Duncan Report in 1969 and culminated in the provocative Think Tank report on overseas representation in 1977. Its view has been that diplomacy is a distinct skill and should have a different career structure. This separation has broken down somewhat in recent years, notably as a result of Britain's entry into the EEC. The co-ordination of Britain's dealings with the Community is controlled from the Cabinet Office, while home civil servants undertake most of the detailed negotiations in Brussels.

Yet the Foreign Office has remained apart. All Whitehall departments have a house view — Agriculture is for helping farmers and so on — but the Foreign Office philosophy has been almost consciously different. There has been the belief that foreign policy should be separate from domestic political pressures — that there should be a continuity of policy whoever is the political master. According to this view, the Foreign Office has been the guardian of the revealed truth of British interests — strongly in favour of Britain's membership of the EEC, more sympathetic to Arab than Israeli concerns, pro-Black Africa and pro-NATO. It is for the international consensus and, in the words of David Owen, one of the more vigorous and controversial recent Foreign Secretaries, 'Its weakness is a depressing tendency to split the difference in every negotiation.'

These attitudes and style have not commended themselves to Mrs Thatcher: the result has been considerable tension. It is not so much that foreign policy has changed. In classic British tradition there has been little formal doctrine, and the general priorities with respect to NATO, the EEC and so on have remained the same, though Mrs Thatcher has added her own emphasis to relations with the USA and the Soviet Union. More significant has been the response of the Thatcher administration to particular events — notably the independence of Rhodesia, the recurrent rows over Britain's contributions to the EEC Budget and the Falklands.

Rhodesia/Zimbabwe

The negotiations over independence for Rhodesia/Zimbabwe were in many respects the high point of Foreign Office influence — the peak of the Carrington era. The role of Lord Carrington during the first phase of Mrs Thatcher's premiership has been discussed in an earlier chapter. It was a time when she still felt inexperienced in foreign affairs and paid close attention to Lord Carrington. At the time of the May 1979 election there was little doubt that many Conservative MPs and Mrs Thatcher herself were sympathetic to the internal constitution worked out by Ian Smith and Bishop Abel Muzorewa. The Conservative manifesto referred to the possibility of moving Rhodesia to a state of legal independence depending on the outcome of elections being held there in April 1979. The Conservatives had sent a team of observers to Rhodesia under Lord Boyd, a former Colonial Secretary. They concluded that the elections had been conducted in a reasonably free and fair manner.

The result of the Boyd mission encouraged the large pro-(white) Rhodesian lobby within the Conservative Party to believe that economic sanctions would soon be lifted and that the new regime would be recognized despite the absence from the elections of the Patriotic Front of Robert Mugabe and Joshua Nkomo, which was still fighting a guerrilla war. Moreover, Mrs Thatcher herself said during a brief visit to Australia in July 1979 that she doubted whether the annual renewal of sanctions could be got through Parliament, and she hinted at possible recognition of the Muzorewa Government in time.

The Foreign Office view was different. Reflecting the analysis developed during Dr Owen's time as Foreign Secretary, the diplomats believed that the internal settlement would not work in the face of the continuing guerrilla war. Consequently, it was necessary to devise a new settlement covering all groups, including the Patriotic Front, and winning the support of the neighbouring Black African countries. This was also the conclusion quickly reached by Lord Carrington, not least because support for the Muzorewa regime might lead to an open breach with the USA over the renewal of sanctions as well as threatening Britain's large business interests in Black Africa. In his view, these questions were more important than whether the Rhodesian elections in 1979 had been conducted fairly. These were the arguments of power politics rather than of kith and kin.

Lord Carrington then started on the task which had defeated his predecessors for fourteen years. First, he had to persuade Mrs Thatcher, which he did immediately after her return from Australia. According to Hugh Stephenson (1980), Lord Carrington put forward a paper suggesting that if she maintained her position, 'it would be disastrous to the interests of the West in general and Britain in particular. The policy must be changed. The arguments were presented persuasively and Mrs Thatcher accepted them, then and there.' She flew to the Commonwealth heads of government conference in Lusaka determined to launch a broader settlement.

Once persuaded, Mrs Thatcher was bolder than Lord Carrington, recognizing the inevitability of coming to terms with the Patriotic Front. The Foreign Secretary was more cautious and understandably pessimistic in view of the repeated failures of previous negotiations. Yet a settlement was arrived at through a combination of Mrs Thatcher's will and readiness to deal with any internal party problems, together with Lord Carrington's skill in handling the subsequent Lancaster House talks. And the Thatcher administration took the risk, rejected by its predecessors, of sending troops to monitor the ceasefire in the interim period before elections and full independence in spring 1980. The result was to rid Britain of a troublesome problem, to establish a new regime which had international support and to reduce, at least temporarily, the level of bloodshed. The political divisions and violence which developed under Robert Mugabe's rule in 1982–3 were hardly unexpected in Black Africa. They could not really be blamed on Britain, which had poured in considerable support for the new Zimbabwe.

The outcome was at least more favourable than many had believed possible only months earlier. Mrs Thatcher was able to claim in Perth in May 1980, 'We are once more a nation capable of action rather than reaction.' The Rhodesia/Zimbabwe talks had the paradoxical effect not only of establishing Lord Carrington's reputation as a Foreign Secretary but also, in retrospect, of marking the peak of his domestic political influence. The negotiations and the outcome increased the doubts of many Tory MPs about the Foreign Office, and these did not disappear over the following two years. Lord Carrington was criticized in the period for spending too much time travelling overseas and for neglecting his domestic political base. Moreover, while he was initially able to persuade Mrs Thatcher to act contrary to her instincts (over the Vietnamese boat people, for instance), she became increasingly confident about conducting her own foreign policy. And other key external issues touched on more sensitive domestic political nerves.

Europe

Britain's arguments with its EEC partners over its Budget contributions have become a saga with a life and language all of its own. The amounts of money involved have not been large — well under 1 per cent of total UK public spending, though more significant in relation to the balance of payments. Yet the underlying issues have gone to the heart of Britain's place within the EEC. There have been two consistent points in the British case: first, that UK net contributions have been too high and, second, that the structure of the EEC Budget is wrong in its heavy bias towards agriculture. The problem has arisen because of the UK's low level of receipts from the Community Budget — only about one-tenth of the expenditure under the Common Agricultural Policy (in itself around two-thirds of the total).

Britain has been financing 20 per cent of the EEC's gross spending. Its contribution to the 'own resources' of the EEC (that is, taxes belonging to the Community, including a 1 per cent Value Added Tax) has been higher than its share of EEC Gross Domestic Product because Britain's level of trade with other countries has been significantly higher than that of other member states. This has meant that Britain has had to pay more in customs duties, while its lack of self-sufficiency in food has meant higher payment of levies on agricultural imports. Many of the difficulties are the result of Britain's failure to be in at the start of the EEC in the late 1950s and early 1960s.

Consequently, there has been a series of bruising talks, starting with the 'renegotiation' of the terms under Labour in 1974–5. Immediately after coming into office in 1979 Mrs Thatcher made it plain that Britain was not prepared to accept the prospect of net contributions (payments less receipts) of over £1 billion in 1980. As important as the substance of the subsequent talks was her style of approach, which was not exactly *communitaire* in spirit – not cast in the language of a family squabble, as described by Lord Carrington and the Foreign Office. Mrs Thatcher went in with guns blazing. She talked of 'politically indefensible' positions and demanded 'Britain's own money back'. Her approach conflicted with the notion that the Community should have its own resources. Moreover, Britain, with its growing North Sea revenue, appeared to be a strange country to plead poverty at that time of oil crisis.

At the Dublin summit in November 1979 Mrs Thatcher clashed angrily with other EEC leaders. She was unrelenting and irritated them all. Her behaviour was criticized both by the Foreign Office and by strongly pro-EEC politicians like Edward Heath on the grounds that a more accommodating attitude should have been displayed. Her view was that it was necessary to be blunt at first in order to reach agreement later, which is what happened after a further six months of hard talks and some sharp exchanges between Mrs Thatcher and the Foreign Office. The eventual deal, which she reluctantly accepted, was that the other EEC countries agreed to pay compensation for Britain's excessive contributions of 1980 and 1981, with a possible extension for a third year should a long-term solution not have been devised by then.

The rebates of £1.8 billion in the first two years were used to help finance infrastructure projects, especially in the assisted areas. The deal worked out reasonably well in the short term: net contributions in 1980 and 1981 totalled less than £200 million, largely because of difficulties in predicting the Budget outturn. However, it was by its nature a stop-gap arrangement, and it was not long before the talks started again. In 1982 a crisis developed when the British veto on the farm price package was overriden in the council of Agriculture Ministers, in direct breach of previous agreements and of the traditional manner of reaching decisions. The row was defused by an agreement about refunds for the UK in 1982, but with qualifications, and the release of funds was held up until early 1983 by the European Parliament.

Problems also developed over the 1983 rebates; again, the negotiations were protracted. Even the agreement at the Stuttgart summit of EEC leaders in June 1983 that the UK should receive a final rebate of £440 million ran into trouble, with a small cut at a council of Budget Ministers in July 1983.

Overall, the 1980 deal has ensured that the UK's net contributions have been substantially lower than they would otherwise have been. Assuming that the £440 million rebate will be paid for 1983, the total refunds since 1980 will have amounted to over £2.5 billion, equivalent to a rebate of 65.4 per cent of the unadjusted net contributions before rebates.

Nevertheless, everyone was agreed that such ad hoc arrangements were unsatisfactory and time-wasting. The original May 1980 agreement had given the EEC Commission a mandate to submit proposals for the restructuring of the EEC's spending priorities. As these were pursued intermittently over the following three years, the UK took the lead in arguing both for a reduction in the proportion devoted to agriculture and for tight control on the overall level of spending by the Community. The position in mid-1983, in the context of the proposed entry of Spain and Portugal into the EEC, was that the Commission had proposed an increase in the Community's 'own resources' via a rise in the 1 per cent VAT ceiling and via a new Common Agricultural Policy-related tax based on agricultural production shares and on Gross Domestic Product per head.

The British Government had reservations — shared to some extent by West Germany and the Netherlands — about increasing the Community's 'own resources' ahead of restrictions on the Common Agricultural Policy budget. Sir Geoffrey Howe, translated from the Exchequer to the Foreign Office after the June 1983 election, maintained his tough line. He argued that instead of adapting its finances to suit its policies, the EEC would have to change its policies to match the available money — that is, spending on agriculture would have to be reduced. In addition, Sir Geoffrey suggested a safety-net to prevent any member state's burden from becoming intolerable. Britain's resistance to an increase in the overall size of the EEC Budget faced opposition both from other member states, especially those with large farming interests, and from the European Parliament. The latter might reject or place conditions upon any supplementary EEC Budget, including rebates to the UK. Therefore in mid-1983 omens for an early agreement acceptable to the UK were not good.

This row was paralleled by arguments over EEC agricultural policy, notably over the size of increases in farm prices and over the restructuring of the EEC's steel industry. The overall result was to leave the UK a somewhat uneasy partner in the EEC as Budget row followed Budget row endlessly. Mrs Thatcher has seen the EEC essentially as a Europe of separate nations with certain common interests — in bargaining, say, with the USA over economic issues and in trying to develop an internal free market in goods and services. There has been little of the idealism and enthusiasm of the early 1970s.

The vigorous approach of Mrs Thatcher was undoubtedly effective domestically in outmanoeuvring Labour. The EEC issue was not rated as one of the two most important by most people at the 1983 election, but among those mentioning it the Conservative approach was preferred to Labour's by a margin of 50 per cent, according to the BBC/Gallup survey quoted in the *Guardian* of 14 June 1983, compared with an 8 per cent advantage for Labour on the EEC issue at the 1979 election. This turnround did not appear to reflect any upsurge in enthusiasm for the EEC.

Instead the majority view could be characterized as favouring a strong assertion of British interests and accepting that British membership was now permanent after ten years; in addition, there was concern about job losses if the UK left the Community. Even centre/left Labour leaders like Neil Kinnock acknowledged the status quo in their post-election reappraisals, when they argued that withdrawal would not be an issue in any election in the late 1980s. Mrs Thatcher and the Conservatives had won the argument in the UK, if not in the EEC as a whole.

The Falklands

The Falkland Islands have presented a very different kind of foreign policy challenge. In the words of Sir Nicholas Henderson, Britain's Ambassador to Washington during the 1982 war, it is one of 'the residual problems of empire (along with Gibraltar and Hong Kong) which are central to our responsibilities but peripheral to our long-term interests, except in so far as our handling of them affects our standing in the world'. This caveat is important, since that is how Mrs Thatcher interpreted the crisis when it developed. The implications of the events of 1982 for decision-making in the Thatcher administration have been discussed in an earlier chapter, but there is no doubt about their impact on the standing of the Foreign Office.

The report of the committee of Privy Counsellors, under Lord Franks, inquiring into the background to the Argentinian invasion of the islands on 2 April 1982 concluded that the attack could not have been foreseen and that no blame or criticism could be attached to the British Government. Many leading politicians and commentators thought this a surprising conclusion, since most of the preceding report had identified serious failures of policy and of intelligence appraisal, as well as weaknesses in the machinery of government. The burden was that the Foreign Office, both its officials and its Ministers, had failed over the years to present a policy acceptable to either the Falklands Islanders or to Parliament, while misreading the intentions of the Argentinian Government in the crucial months of early 1982. The result was a paralysis of policy, as Britain partly abdicated the initiative and hoped that the feared crisis would be postponed. The difficulty was that the Falklands issue had been an irritant for a long time but had never been sufficiently important in London to force Ministers to consider fully all its implications. Among the failings noted were the following.

First, faced by a vocal but small pro-Falklands lobby in Parliament (in itself partly to blame for its blinkered jingoism), Foreign Office Ministers failed to make clear where alternative policies might lead. The option of ceding sovereignty of the Falklands to the Argentine and leasing the islands back for a lengthy period was only half-heartedly pursued in view of parliamentary and local opposition and waivering among other Ministers. Lord Carrington's decision in September 1981 not to press this option but instead to keep negotiations going was criticized by the Franks Report for putting the Government in a position of weakness in relation to Argentina.

Second, misleading signals were sent to the Argentinian junta about British intentions — notably the announcement in June 1981 of the withdrawal from the South Atlantic of the survey ship HMS *Endurance* (against the advice of Lord Carrington), the denial to many of the islanders of full British citizenship under the 1981 British Nationality Act and the failure to extend the airfield to make the Falklands more self-sufficient (as recommended in Lord Shackleton's report of 1976).

Third, the shift in Argentinian policy, especially after the succession of General Galtieri in December 1981, was misread. The Franks Report described this as a misjudgement, though not one for which any individual should be blamed. An intelligence assessment in July 1981 had warned that if the Argentinians became frustrated about the course of the negotiations, there was a considerable risk that they 'would resort to more forceable measures swiftly and without warning'. One problem was that many British Ministers and diplomats in London did not comprehend the unpredictable and shifting behaviour of the Argentinian junta.

Fourth, no adequate contingency plans were made when

the warning signals increased after the failure of the bilateral talks in New York in late February 1982 and especially following the landing of Argentinian scrap-metal dealers on South Georgia. There was lengthy debate subsequently about whether deterrent military action could have been taken — for example, the earlier dispatch of naval forces — and whether the last-minute warnings to Buenos Aires about the consequences of an invasion were sufficiently clear.

While the Franks Report took an over-generous view of the failings before the invasion, the response at the time was harsher. Lord Carrington and two other Foreign Office Ministers resigned, and Sir John Nott's offer to resign as Defence Secretary was rejected on the grounds that his department was not the one responsible. Despite these pressures the Foreign Office's response to the invasion was adept and successful, notably in New York, where Sir Anthony Parsons organized support for the crucial United Nations Security Council resolution which was used to justify subsequent British actions. This initiative was matched by activity in Brussels, where Britain secured EEC support both for condemnation of the Argentinian action and for sanctions. Over the following two months of tortuous negotiations Francis Pym, the new Foreign Secretary, and his officials examined every path to a peaceful settlement — the Haig shuttle, the Peruvian plan and talks at the United Nations — in part so that Britain should always be seen to be trying to secure a negotiated end to the dispute.

From the start of the dispute, however, Mrs Thatcher seems to have believed — correctly, as it turned out — that the Argentinian military junta, having installed its troops on the islands, would never agree to a compromise deal. Indeed, she and quite a number of Tory backbenchers appear to have grown impatient with Mr Pym's constant peace efforts during April and early May 1982. In the event these talks never had a real chance of succeeding, not for want of British concessions but because of the Argentinians' attitude. There has, however, been controversy about whether peace talks might have succeeded if the Argentinian cruiser *Belgrano* had not been torpedoed in early May, with the loss of 370 lives. The attack was directly ordered by Mrs Thatcher and the War Cabinet.

The campaign for an official inquiry into the affair has been pressed, with characteristic tenacity, by Tam Dalyell, the Labour MP for Linlithgow and a self-confessed member of the awkward squad in Parliament, who has argued his case through hundreds of questions to Ministers and over a dozen parliamentary speeches. He has claimed, first, that the *Belgrano* was on course for home when she was attacked outside the 200-mile exclusion zone around the islands. Second, he has argued that when the order was given to sink the cruiser Mrs Thatcher knew that the Peruvian peace terms might be on the brink of acceptance by the Argentinian junta. The implication, according to Mr Dalyell, is that Mrs Thatcher deliberately ordered the sinking of the *Belgrano* to salvage her political position. These charges have been repeatedly denied by the Government, though sometimes in a broad-brush way that has not taken account of the inconsistencies in past explanations that have been pin-pointed by Mr Dalyell.

The balance of evidence so far is against Mr Dalyell. First, the course of the *Belgrano* at the time of sinking was irrelevant, since she and her two escorts were following a zig-zag course. Moreover, Royal Navy commanders believed that the *Belgrano* and an Argentine aircraft carrier were engaged in a pincer operation against the British carrier group, which was at the time over-extended near the islands. In these circumstances it would have been very difficult for any politician to turn down a request from the service chiefs for permission to attack the *Belgrano*. What would have been the reaction if the British carriers *Hermes* or *Invincible* had been sunk? Second, there is as yet no firm evidence to suggest that the leaders of the Argentinian junta were about to accept the Peruvian terms. They were anyway similar to those which the junta had already rejected when presented by the US Secretary of State, Alexander Haig. But many important questions raised by Mr Dalyell about the incident and the Peruvian peace plan have yet to be answered.

There is no dispute that the retaking of the Falkland Islands by the British forces was an outstanding achievement. It was a tribute to their courage, training, morale and leadership, as well as to a formidable logistical back-up. They were also very lucky in view of the number of near misses. But determination paid off, thanks to the single-mindedness of Mrs Thatcher. As Max Hastings and Simon Jenkins (1983) concluded, since the operation did succeed,

> and did so in large measure because of qualities of leadership, [Mrs Thatcher] is entitled to the credit for both her luck and her judgement. It is doubtful if any other British Prime Minister since Churchill, with the possible exception of James Callaghan, would have sent the task force and supported it right through to victory.

After the recapture of the Falklands there was general agreement that the islanders should be given time to recover and to think before any long-term decisions were taken about their future. In any event, the Argentine refused formally to call off hostilities and was rearming. But what were the future options? Mrs Thatcher was adamant that what had been retaken must be held. There was no question of talks about sovereignty: the islands must be defended. Lord Shackleton was commissioned to undertake a second report, on the economy of the islands. And in December 1982 the Government announced various measures to improve the infrastructure of the islands and their commercial framework at a cost of £31 million spread over six years, on top of £15 million for rehabilitation. Moreover, shortly after the June 1983 election the Government revealed its plans for the construction of a new airfield, which will cut the time and simplify the journey to the islands. Together with associated transport and other installation expenses, the total cost should be about £215 million.

The defence of the islands also involves substantial costs (as discussed below), and this may increase pressures to find a long-term settlement. It was significant that a number of Conservative as well as Labour members of the Foreign Affairs Committee of the Commons felt that a 'Fortress Falklands' policy could not be maintained indefinitely. In discussions before the June 1983 election they recognized, however, that the search for a definitive solution then might prove to be premature in view of the bellicose attitude of the Argentine. A number of MPs questioned the viability of the Falklands' society and economy unless stable relations were eventually established with the South American mainland. A draft report by the committee, which was not completed or agreed because of the election, suggested that a leaseback arrangement should not be discounted by the Government in future negotiations. The proposal probably represented the most promising long-term solution to the dispute, but the time-scale of its implementation would probably have to span several generations.

The Falkland Islands may be marginal to Britain's long-term interests, but as a result of the diplomatic failures and the military successes of 1982 it seems that for some time they will complicate both foreign and defence policy. Mrs Thatcher's single-mindedness, which was so necessary to the successes of 1982, may prove to be a stumbling-block to the early start of talks.

Defence Policy

Britain's defence policy faced considerable problems during the early 1980s, even before the Falklands war. The difficulty was the familiar one of balancing commitments and resources, which had led over the previous generation to a succession of defence reviews and withdrawals from around the world. The Thatcher administration itself undertook a limited review, which was partly reversed as a result of the Falklands war. In 1982–3 defence expenditure was 16.7 per cent higher in real terms than it had been in the last Labour year of 1978–9 and had climbed to over 5 per cent of Gross Domestic Product, the highest proportion since the mid-1960s before the withdrawal from east of Suez and higher, both absolutely and relatively, than that of any other major European country.

The broad aims remained as they had been under the Wilson and Callaghan administrations:

(1)   the provision of independent strategic and theatre nuclear forces committed to the Western Alliance;

(2) the direct defence of the UK homeland;
(3) a major land and air contribution on the European mainland;
(4) the deployment of a major maritime capability in the eastern Atlantic and the Channel.

This policy (as set out in various statements on the defence estimates) was underpinned by the commitment to the NATO aim of a 3 per cent annual growth in real expenditure up to 1985—6. There was little emphasis on non-NATO commitments; expenditure on the Falklands has been on top of this. In addition, the Government came to office pledged to improving the pay of the armed forces, which had fallen behind civilian rates during the late 1970s. The result had been a marked rise in pay and in recruitment.

It was not long before these commitments collided with the Treasury's desire to contain the overall level of expenditure. Indeed, Francis Pym was moved from Defence Secretary to become Leader of the Commons in January 1981 because of his resistance to cutbacks. His successor, Sir John Nott, had a clear mandate to limit expenditure. The consequent debate during the 1981 review was widely seen as a conflict between a Continental and a maritime emphasis in the defence effort. This was true only up to a point. Admittedly, the outcome was more stress on home defence and the rejection of any run-down of Britain's land contribution in West Germany, as the commitment to maintain 55,000 troops there was honoured.

The main change was in the balance of the maritime commitment rather than in the Navy's overall capability. The Government decided that the very large costs of building and refitting surface warships meant that there should be a contraction of the surface fleet. It was proposed that the number of destroyers and frigates should be reduced from fifty-nine to fifty. At the same time it was decided to cut from three to two the number of Invincible-class aircraft carriers. The emphasis was to be shifted to submarines; the number of nuclear-powered attack submarines was to be increased from twelve to seventeen, and there were to be more Nimrod patrol aircraft. One result was the proposed closure of the dockyards at Chatham and Gibraltar.

These decisions angered the admirals, who conducted a vigorous and semi-public campaign against Sir John, notably via the vocal pro-Navy and old imperialist Conservative lobby in the Commons. Keith Speed was dismissed as Navy Minister because of his open opposition to what was happening. In his subsequent book (Speed, 1982) he claimed that the decisions would significantly undermine the strength and capacity of the Royal Navy and pressed for a strong surface fleet, both to meet the growing Soviet maritime challenge and to deal with threats which might develop throughout the world.

The Navy had its opportunity to argue back as a result of the Falklands. Admiral Sir Henry Leach, the First Sea Lord, played a crucial role in persuading Mrs Thatcher that a taskforce could be assembled and sent to the South Atlantic, despite the initial doubts of Sir John Nott and of some of the other services. The conflict provided the Navy with the chance to show what it could achieve, even if some of the lessons were double-edged — there was, for instance, the vulnerability of surface vessels to missile attack. Admiral Leach took the positive view. In a lecture just before the end of the war he said that 'the informed' recognized that the 1981 defence review was 'done in a hurry, involved pre-judgement and was driven by short-term politico-economic expediency rather than long-term strategic sense'.

The Navy secured the restoration of the previous year's cuts. Four frigates and destroyers which would have been placed in the standby squadron in 1984 and 1985 were to be kept fully operational, with the result that fifty-five frigates and destroyers were to be retained until 1985. It was also decided not to sell HMS *Invincible* to Australia, thus keeping three carriers. The major surface ships and the Harrier aircraft and helicopters lost during the war were to be replaced. In addition, more aircraft of various types were bought both for garrison duties in the South Atlantic and to provide cover for those committed there. These orders were presented as no more than a modification of the 1981 review. Indeed, Sir John's priorities were broadly right whatever changes were shown to be necessary to the armament of ships and to particular weapons systems.

All this has cost money. The Falklands war and subsequent garrison duties cost between £700 million and £900 million in 1982—3, while to meet the islands' defence costs the Government's expenditure plans provided for £624 million in 1983—4, £684 million in 1984—5 and £552 million in 1985—6. These figures include the cost of replacing all the equipment lost in the Falklands — roughly a third of the total from 1983—4 onwards — as well as the expense of maintaining a garrison to protect the islands, but there will also be the £215 million cost of constructing a new airfield and the sums spent on rebuilding the local infrastructure. The total cost of the Falklands war up to 1985—6 may be at least £2.75 billion and probably over £3 billion, though some of the re-equipment spending will help to meet the NATO commitment. Critics have questioned not only this expense but also the diversion of a sizeable part of the Navy's ships to the South Atlantic — committing over a fifth of available frigates and destroyers, according to one unofficial estimate. The possible implications for NATO worried members of the Defence Committee of the Commons during an inquiry into the subject in early 1983.

Questions about whether all these commitments could be afforded over the medium term have been expressed by politicians of all parties and by independent defence commentators. Colonel Jonathan Alford of the International Institute for Strategic Studies has warned that Britain may be in 'serious danger of paying far too much to defend the Falkland Islands, of over-insuring and over-valuing the national and strategic interest'. He quoted Stephen Leacock's Lord Ronald, who 'flung himself upon his horse and rode madly off in all directions'. On the same theme David Greenwood of the Centre for Defence Studies at Aberdeen University has argued that the planned expenditure totals up to the late 1980s may not be sufficient to meet all Britain's commitments. In his view the overall figures for this period contain over-optimistic assumptions about both the general rate of inflation and the relative cost of defence equipment. The official plans assume that there will be a slow-down in the growth of the cost of this hardware, of which there has been little evidence so far. The inter-departmental report of officials to the Cabinet on the medium-term expenditure outlook examined the possibility that the cost of defence equipment would grow 2 per cent faster than prices generally, in line with recent trends. By the end of the 1980s the gap could be equivalent to more than a tenth of the total defence budget. Consequently, David Greenwood has concluded, the defence programme for the next five years has probably been under-funded by between 10 and 15 per cent. The likelihood therefore is a further defence review and a fierce argument about whether to extend the 3 per cent NATO spending commitment beyond 1985–6.

Any review is bound to focus on the Trident missile system, which is intended to replace the current Polaris force in the mid-1990s. The four submarines will be built in Britain; the 1983 statement on the defence estimates claimed that the total cost would be roughly £7.5 billion (at 1982–3 prices). However, a fall in the sterling exchange rate against the dollar would, if sustained over a period, substantially increase the cost. At its peak expenditure at the end of the decade the Trident programme will absorb the equivalent of 6 per cent of total defence spending and nearly 12 per cent of the equipment budget, which will be slightly less, relatively, than the cost of the Tornado aircraft programme. Over the whole fifteen years of the project Trident will take up 3 per cent of the total defence budget. The snag is that spending on it will rise in the late 1980s, just when the cost of other programmes, such as the construction of new surface ships for the Navy, will also be at a high level.

The Trident programme has anyway become highly controversial as the former consensus on nuclear weapons policy (at least between the party leaders) has broken down. Ministers claim that the introduction of Trident is a continuation of the British policy of possessing an independent deterrent and follows the highly secret Chevaline programme, under Labour, for modernizing the Polaris system. Yet Trident represents a quantum change in British nuclear capacity. Each missile will have multiple warheads, thus increasing the number of warheads to the maximum possible, so as to demonstrate its lack of interest in a first-strike capability.

The purchase of Trident has been described as unnecessary by some defence specialists and a number of Tory MPs, as well as by Opposition spokesmen and committed unilateral nuclear disarmers. The former's case is that its acquisition is both expensive and superfluous, since the Polaris system has been extended until at least the mid-1990s. If a mutually acceptable reduction in the level of strategic missiles has not been agreed by the end of the 1980s, the Government could consider buying a cheaper alternative. Indeed, it is possible that Trident (and perhaps even the current Polaris system) could be included in arms negotiations, though the Government has insisted that a strategic nuclear force like Trident or Polaris would be out of place in the Intermediate Nuclear Force (INF) talks at Geneva, while the strategic arms talks (START) are anyway bilateral. But there is a strong argument for absorbing the British strategic system, and probably also the French one, in any revamped nuclear talks as a positive sign of intent towards breaking the recent impasse in such negotiations.

The row over Trident has been matched by the controversy over the proposed siting of US cruise missiles in the UK that forms part of the dual-track approach adopted by NATO in response to the build-up of Soviet SS20 intermediate nuclear weapons with multiple warheads from the late 1970s. Fred Mulley, the Labour Defence Secretary, attended a meeting of the NATO Nuclear Planning Group in April 1979, just before the Conservatives came to power, which decided that it would be necessary to maintain and to modernize theatre nuclear forces. NATO Ministers formally decided in December 1979 to deploy US cruise and Pershing 2 missiles in certain Western European countries from 1983 onwards unless a satisfactory arms-control agreement had been reached with the Soviet Union.

Talks eventually started in Geneva in November 1981. The USA proposed the zero option, whereby NATO would agree to abandon its plan to deploy these missiles if the Soviet Union agreed to dismantle its equivalent SS4, SS5 and SS20 missiles. There then followed a complicated series of negotiations in which positions shifted, but by mid-1983 it seemed unlikely that agreement would be reached to prevent the stationing of some, though possibly not all, of the US missiles. Within the UK attention centred on the siting of missiles at Greenham Common in Berkshire from the end of 1983. During 1982 there was a highly effective series of demonstrations against the cruise missile organized by the Campaign for Nuclear Disarmament, the fortunes of which had revived in the early 1980s in line with the wave of marches and demonstrations in the USA and other Western countries against nuclear weapons.

The Government was initially thrown on to the defensive by the impact of this campaign. The need for a more effective spokesman against unilateralism was one reason for the appointment of Michael Heseltine as Defence Secretary in January 1983. His counter-attack, with the aid of a special official unit in the Ministry of Defence as well as unofficial campaigning groups, made a rapid impact on public opinion, but this was partly because the permanent women's peace camp at Greenham Common became identified with some of the more bizarre fringes of the feminist movement, while CND was associated in part with some far-left and Soviet front organizations. Moreover, the Labour Party's unilateralist commitment in the 1983 election was unpopular and lost the party votes, particularly among men, according to all the opinion poll evidence. Furthermore, a confusing impression was given by the conflicting comments of senior party figures about when the Polaris system and US nuclear bases in Britain were to be phased out.

The outcome left the Thatcher administration with the initiative after the 1983 election but faced with divided public opinion. The poll evidence (for example, in a Marplan survey published in the *Guardian* in early 1983) indicated that a majority of the British public was in favour of retaining an independent British nuclear force but against the Government decision to go ahead with Trident and strongly opposed to the stationing of cruise missiles in the UK (by a ratio of 2 to 1). On the issues of both Trident and cruise the opposition has grown since 1981, when Marplan asked similar questions. The opposition to cruise seems to have been associated with distrust of the USA and, in particular, with doubts about the intentions and abilities of President Reagan. This distrust was reflected in demands from some Tory as well as Opposition MPs for a 'dual key' to the US cruise missiles to be sited in the UK, so that Britain could be seen to be involved directly in the firing of any missile. The Government argued that this demand was an expensive irrelevance, since there would in practice be joint decision-making between the UK and the USA.

Mrs Thatcher said during the 1983 election campaign that she hoped to be in a position to do more internationally during her second term. Throughout her first four years in office the keynote had been a more aggressive assertion of Britain's interests; priority had been accorded to high defence spending; a strongly anti-Soviet stance and close identification with US policy had been adopted; and the Third World (apart from India) had been neglected. These views may not, however, be sufficient for the next four or five years. Indeed, it is perhaps not surprising that in his first few weeks as Foreign Secretary after the 1983 election Sir Geoffrey Howe was heard to ask puzzled Foreign Office officials, 'What is our foreign policy?'

Within the Western Alliance there may be pressure for some detachment from President Reagan — not only over his adventures in Central America but also over his attitude to nuclear arms talks. Britain and its European allies could take the initiative in seeking to cut theatre nuclear weapons, for example, rather than merely responding to President Reagan's lead. It was significant that in his first speech from the backbenches after being dismissed as Foreign Secretary Francis Pym urged more top-level contacts between London and Moscow, about which Mrs Thatcher has been reluctant. Within the EEC there is the danger of adopting too negative an approach, however well founded Britain's complaints over its Budget contributions may be. Mrs Thatcher's foreign policy may be in tune with popular instincts, but more than rhetoric will be needed to achieve results in the EEC.

Moreover, it seems that some difficult choices will have to be made soon over defence. There has anyway been international pressure — for example, from General Bernard Rogers, the Supreme Allied Commander of NATO — for an increase in conventional land and air forces in Western Europe in order to reduce the possibility of an early use of nuclear weapons. It will be difficult for the UK to protect its essentially national operations, such as Trident and the Falkland garrison, at the expense of its broader NATO commitments, so something will almost certainly have to give. As one jaundiced former member of the Thatcher administration remarked about the Prime Minister's enthusiasm in 1982 for anything to do with defence, 'It will soon go — after all she is a housewife at heart.'

11

Conclusions

Mrs Thatcher appears to have an intuitive sense of what the lively elements in the nation feel. She has the energy of will as well as the serenity of mind to be able to articulate that feeling.

Lord (Hugh) Thomas
Our Place in the World, *1983*

One other myth too must be laid to rest: that is the notion that our approach to Britain's social and economic problems has its origins in the University of Chicago or even the Free Trade Hall of Manchester. It does not. But let me for my part assert that the Conservative tradition is too rich and vital to be hijacked by advocates of paternalistic interference. The aristocratic tradition of paternal Toryism has a place, and an honourable one. But the Prime Minister's Grantham and my Port Talbot, and the values and traditions which they bred, are just as much the cornerstone of what today's Conservatives believe. Thrift, hard work, independence, the desire to succeed — not just for oneself but for one's family and country too — are and always have been the moral bulwark of the Conservative creed.

Sir Geoffrey Howe
Speech at Hemel Hempstead
30 March 1983

The Conservatives' party dominance may be short-lived. The Thatcherite consensus will be more durable.

Andrew Gamble
Marxism Today
July 1983

Thatcherism has won the political initiative in Britain, but after four years the Thatcher Government has still achieved relatively little. There has been much talk of changed moods and attitudes (the 'new realism') but less of positive results. Crucial issues — such as the competitive position of British industry, the size and scope of the public sector, the future of the welfare state, defence policy, Britain's place in the EEC, Northern Ireland — have not been resolved.

The balance sheet of the first Thatcher term shows a Britain divided between haves and have nots, between north and south, between 'new' industries and traditional manufacturing and between owner occupiers and council tenants. Unemployment has risen considerably; standards of provision in the social services have been increasingly squeezed; sizeable parts of manufacturing industry have disappeared; and relations between central and local Government have been a financial and constitutional mess. Yet, on the other side of the account, the inflation rate has been reduced significantly (in part by accident); a long overdue improvement in efficiency and working practices in industry has been claimed by many companies; tighter financial discipline has been introduced within the public sector; the fourteen-year Rhodesian saga has been ended; and the Falklands crisis has been handled with considerable courage and skill (though only after the Argentinian invasion and up to the retaking of the islands).

The principal beneficiaries have been the already well off — both individually as a result of the cuts in the higher rates of income tax and collectively in the wake of the Government's efforts to help business. Ironically, among the biggest gainers have been companies dependent on Government decisions, such as defence suppliers and those in the City and in business that are involved in privatization and contracting-out programmes. By contrast, the losers have been in the main the trade unions and the least well off, the unemployed and the poor, who have been hit particularly hard by the squeeze on public services. The period since 1979 has been one of growing inequality, yet its political impact has been limited, since most of those with jobs have enjoyed maintained or slightly higher real living standards.

How much of this was planned? The extent of the rises in unemployment and in public expenditure was obviously not in anyone's mind in 1979. About half the increase in the numbers out of work can be attributed to the world recession and was therefore probably unavoidable. Moreover, as indicated in chapter 5, the broad shift in macroeconomic policy from 1975—6 onwards was necessary, and an expansionary fiscal policy would almost certainly not have worked in the 1979—83 period. Yet this still leaves a big rise in unemployment that was the result, or at any rate the by-product, of Government action. A different balance of economic and social policy might, however, have taken some of the edge off the impact of the recession on industry and the poor.

The twists and turns of the 1979—83 period have suggested to some commentators that any overall strategy had broken down well before the end of the first term. There were undoubtedly modifications in the face of the recession — the increased support for industry, for instance, as well as apparent deviations from original intentions such as the growing Whitehall intervention in the affairs of local government. The record indicated only a loose adherence to what was popularly thought of as monetarism and a free-market approach. But much more significant than such theories has been a simpler set of prejudices and values. The dominant vision has been that of middle-class achievement and striving, a world of Victorian values and Samuel Smiles. Its manifestations have been a belief in sound money, the family, private enterprise and a strong assertion of Britain's interests in the world, coupled with a marked dislike of trade-union power and of the public sector. Competition has generally been secondary to mercantilism. Any Government which is as assiduous in protecting both subsidies to owner occupiers and special interests (like the Stock Exchange) as Mrs Thatcher's has been is unlikely to win many plaudits from free-market economists. The criticisms from some of the Institute of Economic Affairs academic types about the Government's slow progress have partly missed the point by confusing their objectives with those of the Prime Minister. Their views overlap considerably, but they are not the same.

Has the Thatcher administration had a strategy? For all the qualifications and apparent lack of coherence − for example, over competition policy − the direction of the economic strategy towards lower public borrowing targets has been clear. Moreover, the privatization programme has gained a new impetus since 1981. Mrs Thatcher knows what type of society she wants, even if some of her methods of achieving it have changed since 1979. Indeed, a hallmark of the Thatcher administration has been its thinking about strategy. As a report in the *Sunday Times* on 18 November 1979 pointed out, a Cabinet committee of Ministers close to Mrs Thatcher (MISC 14, the Ministerial Steering Group on Government Strategy) began considering long-term objectives immediately after the general election. The committee discussed proposals to investigate and publicize restrictive labour practices, to support managerial authority in disputes, to reduce oversensitivity to environmental considerations in planning decisions and to de-privilege the Civil Service. The later discussions on privatization, relaxing planning restrictions, further changes to union law and possible private health insurance schemes have followed this early lead. Similarly, the meetings of the Family Policy Group of Ministers since summer 1982 have turned on a clear strategic theme, the shifting of responsibility away from the state towards parents. So throughout the period there has been a desire to think in strategic terms.

The moral basis of this approach was summed up by Sir Keith Joseph (Joseph and Sumption, 1978): the aim must be to 'challenge one of the central prejudices of modern British politics, the belief that it is the proper function of the state to influence the distribution of wealth for its own sake'. Therefore 'the speed of a society's advance is the speed of its fastest members, and a society in which no one may advance an inch before another will remain immobile.' Increasing inequality has not been an accidental result of the Government's policy but a clear aim of at least some of the more ardent Thatcherites.

The appeal of Thatcherism has, however, been broader than this approach might suggest. It has reached out not only to the established middle class but also to the successful working class. Mrs Thatcher's values — notably reward for effort and owner occupation — have attracted people living outside the inner cities in a new social environment without traditional ties. Some of the ideas of the Family Policy Group, such as making wealth creation more acceptable and training children to manage their pocket money, may seem like common sense to these people, however quaint they may appear to some metropolitan commentators.

After the 1983 election Professor Ivor Crewe of Essex University noted, in the *Guardian* of 13 and 14 June, the phenomenon of two working classes — one, traditional, living in council estates in the north and Scotland and working in the public sector, the other, a new one, predominantly owner occupiers living in the south and working in the private sector. Moreover, the latter group has been growing steadily at the expense of the former. Basing his conclusions on the BBC/Gallup survey of June 1983, Professor Crewe reported that there are almost as many manual workers owning their own homes as council tenants, and among these owner occupiers the Conservatives had a 22 percentage point advantage over Labour. Similarly, of the two-thirds of manual workers who have jobs in the private sector Labour had only a one percentage point advantage over the Tories. More than a third of manual workers live in the south, and they preferred the Tories by a sixteen percentage point margin over Labour. These figures explain why only 38 per cent of manual workers voted Labour in the 1983 election, compared with 62 per cent at the time of the Tories' last big victory in 1959.

The splitting of the working-class vote shows that Thatcherism may have appealed to the 'lively' — or, more crudely, the affluent and aspiring — elements of the nation, as suggested by Lord Thomas in the quotation at the beginning of this chapter. The other view is that the less successful element — those living on council estates or in the big cities of the north and Scotland — may feel that they are being ignored and are inferior citizens. The Thatcher Government has identified with the ambitions of this 'new' working class more successfully than Labour, not only by being seen as the party of the owner occupier but also by presenting economic values which have a wider appeal. On the basis of a Marplan survey in April 1981 Professor Richard Rose of Strathclyde University (Rose, 1983) showed that while the British public was critical of many aspects of capitalism, more than three-quarters wanted a system of private enterprise with only enough government controls and regulations to curb business abuses. Moreover, when presented with various definitions of a reasonable wage settlement the preference was overwhelmingly for an agreement that gave higher wages to workers and left money on the table for employers rather than one which squeezed employers for all they were worth or was based on conventional comparability.

Most fascinating — and most frustrating to Opposition politicians — has been the extent to which Thatcherism has altered popular expectations of Government responsibility for economic problems. While, according to the Marplan survey, over two-thirds of the public believed that the Government could control unemployment, only one-fifth blamed its policy rather than other factors such as unions, management, workers and international competition. A separate Marplan poll for the *Guardian* during the 1983 election (published on 3 June) showed that less than a third of the public thought that the problem of unemployment affected the UK more than other industrialized countries (the actual position) rather than that it affected most industrialized countries equally. When asked specifically how much the Government was to blame, just over a quarter of the sample said 'mainly' against 50 per cent who 'partly' and less than a quarter who answered 'not very much' or 'not at all'. A major result of the 1979—83 period has been the generation of widespread scepticism about how much any Government can achieve. Only a third of the sample in June 1983 thought that under a Labour administration unemployment could be restored to the 1979 level within five years. On other policy issues — stricter laws regulating the activities of unions, the sale of parts of British Steel and BL to private companies and defence policy — the Thatcher Government was also more in tune with the public than Labour, according to the BBC/Gallup survey.

But does this amount to a new Thatcherite consensus? The

evidence of the 1983 election suggests that the Conservative victory reflected the fragmentation of the Opposition parties and a dislike of Labour's policies rather than any upsurge in support for Thatcherism. The assessment of policy preferences above was based on a choice between Conservative and Labour, not on an absolute measure. The BBC/Gallup survey showed that 59 per cent of voters disliked other parties more than they liked their own. This hit Labour most, but it applied only slightly less to the Conservatives. The decline in the attachment of manual workers to Labour has not been matched by any greater underlying identification with the Conservative Party. There has been a general loosening of party ties, but Labour has been affected more than the Tories because of the declining number of the traditional working class and because the party's policies have moved further away from the opinions of voters. Thatcherism has cleverly exploited these social changes, yet has not generated any great enthusiasm. The Conservatives' share of the vote fell by two percentage points in the 1983 election compared with that of 1979. The Tories may have had a small lead over Labour among skilled manual workers in the 1983 election, while they were behind in 1979, but this was solely because the Conservative share of the vote of skilled manual workers fell by less (minus seven percentage points) than did the Labour share (which was down twelve percentage points). The gainer was the Alliance, up sixteen percentage points on the Liberal share of the skilled manual workers' vote in 1979.

The rise of the Alliance to challenge Labour for second place has exaggerated the dominance of Thatcherism. It does not yet represent the new popular consensus. The electorate − and particularly the 'new' working class − is too volatile in its behaviour to justify such a claim, as the ups and downs of party fortunes in the 1979−83 period show. The consumer view of voting behaviour is more persuasive. Those sections of the electorate that have looser class ties than in the past and have suffered least from the recession have tended to vote for the party offering most. And in the short term that has meant the Conservatives − for facing up to Britain's economic problems, for offering strong leadership at home and abroad, for selling council houses, for being tough with the unions and, above all, for not being the Labour Party. The first-past-the-post electoral system and divided support for the Opposition parties allowed the Conservatives to turn a slightly smaller share of the total vote into a landslide victory in terms of parliamentary seats. (Excluding the results produced by the different party system in Northern Ireland, the share of the vote in Britain was 43.4 per cent for the Conservatives, 28.2 per cent for Labour, 25.9 per cent for the Alliance and 2.5 per cent for others.)

This victory has given the Thatcher administration an opportunity to create a new consensus in its second term. The first necessary ingredient is clearly economic success. The electorate may have low expectations of any early large fall in unemployment, but by the time of the next election, in the late 1980s, the Conservatives will presumably have to offer more positive evidence of a recovery and of cuts in taxation. By mid-1983 output had certainly picked up considerably from the low point of the recession, but the outlook suggested steady, not spectacular, growth and at best probably only a stabilization in unemployment over the following year or two. Much would depend on the world economy and particularly on US policies and interest rates.

A further uncertainty concerns how much of an improvement there has been in Britain's underlying industrial performance. There are indications of changes in working practices in some companies, and management morale is reported to be higher than it has been for some time, but the real test of whether there is a new mood on the shop floor will come only when order books fill up and companies are seen to be doing better. Income Data Services (IDS), which conducts research into pay and conditions, has noted (according to the *Financial Times* of 15 August 1983) that more and more businessmen are talking about the novel problem of 'managing success'. IDS has pointed out that 'employees are as quick to see changed circumstances in production as the most adept accountant is to forecast profitability.' Many mainstream economists remain sceptical about whether sustained economic growth can be combined with a low inflation rate. A large number of businessmen are also far from buoyant about the economic outlook. A pessimistic analysis of Britain's industrial performance compared with that of its competitors, undertaken by the National Economic Development Office in February 1983, prompted Sir Campbell Fraser of Dunlop and the Confederation of British Industry to comment that people reading it would want to take the first boat leaving the country. Indeed, the general view was that the analysis was so gloomy that discussion about its conclusions should be deferred for two months.

The Thatcher administration also faces difficulties over achieving its hopes of cutting taxes. As Mrs Thatcher herself pointed out in an Independent Television News interview on 28 July 1983:

> The long-term problem of public spending always concerns me because there is a natural tendency for it to rise. People are always asking for more, and when it comes to the Budget and you say it has got to come out of the taxpayers' pockets, the taxpayer does not like it, so you have got to look forward to the longer term.

What this means is that existing public spending commitments with respect to the social services and defence are incompatible with holding down the overall level of expenditure and thus permitting tax cuts.

The other necessary ingredient for any new consensus will have to be an agreed view of the frontiers between the public and the private sectors. A dislike of the public sector in almost all its forms has been a keynote of the Thatcher administration. In some respects — such as obvious frustration with the remoteness of local authority housing management and with the inefficiency of public-sector utilities — this has struck popular chords. To that extent the sale of council houses and such liberalization measures as the removal of licensing controls over long-distance coach routes have won approval. Other measures in the first term were limited. Selling off shares in British Aerospace, Britoil, Cable and Wireless and various ancillary activities of other corporations is not going to make much difference to the lives of most voters or to the running of the economy.

Yet these moves are only a beginning. The proposals for the second term are more far-reaching and would strike at the heart of the post-war 'settlement' if put into effect. The sale of shares in the core utilities like telecommunications, gas and electricity and the possible injection of private capital into parts of other nationalized industries, coupled with a more extensive contracting out of ancillary operations, would substantially shift the balance between the public and private sectors. The angry response of public-sector unions reflects their fears about the weakening of their power base.

These proposals also raise issues of direct concern to the consumer. At present there is a cross-subsidization in most utilities between profitable services for business and less profitable operations for the domestic consumer. These transfers are generally hidden in the present accounting systems of nationalized industries, but they would have to be explicit if the businesses were to be run as independent commercial operations, and this might alter the balance of charges. The debates over the privatization of British Telecom have indicated that the public utilities would probably retain substantial social obligations to the domestic consumer while at the same time remaining virtual monopolies. Any competing suppliers, such as the Mercury Consortium in telecommunications, are likely to be at the margin, involving only profitable business operations.

The Government may be in danger of creating independent private monopolies. One argument for doing so is that at present it is virtually impossible to give the industries freedom to raise capital because of the difficulty of separating off projects which can be financed by the private sector without Government guarantee. So, according to this view, the answer should be to sell the industries off and to regulate the mono-poly aspects. Even for British Telecom it has proved very difficult to devise an appropriate method of regulation and price fixing.

The problem would be much greater for gas and electricity, the prices of which are the product of political bargaining. The privatized utilities would be monopolies just as powerful as the public corporations are now. One answer would be to sell off not whole industries but just parts of them. The chairmen of the nationalized industries generally argue that their operations are integrated and cannot be broken up, though the case against dividing the express coach and local bus operations of the National Bus Company or the domestic and international parts of British Airways seems unconvincing.

The chairmen of the industries appear at times to have formed a curious alliance with Ministers to accept wholesale privatization even when this does not obviously promote consumer interests. Competition should be the priority, not selling for the sake of it. Yet the Government's desire to shift as many as possible of these activities out of the public sector has led to a confusion between privatization and competition. The two are not identical.

Similar points apply to the contracting out of ancillary work such as cleaning and maintenance. This is now leading to increasingly frequent rows with public-sector unions and to questions about standards of service, such as have already been raised in the case of the contracting out of local authority refuse collection. There is a good case for opening up such work to competitive tender so that costs can be compared, but such a programme should be developed on an ad hoc basis. The private sector is not always the best (or the cheapest) provider of a public-sector service, as the fiasco over the contracting out of the Department of Transport's road design work showed.

The Government is on even trickier ground over the future of the welfare state, to which the public appears to remain strongly attached. A series of Gallup polls (quoted in Rose, 1983) has shown that the proportion of voters favouring tax cuts, even though this might mean some reduction in government services such as health, education and welfare, fell from 34 to 23 per cent between May 1979 and March 1983. And despite the rising personal tax burden over the period, the proportion arguing that these government services should be extended even if it meant some increase in taxes rose from 34 to 49 per cent during the four years. Broadly, the same conclusion was reached by the BBC/Gallup survey in June 1983. Only 20 per cent of the sample thought that it was a good idea to cut taxes at the cost of reducing these services, and 80 per cent believed that it was a bad idea. As Professor Crewe has concluded, 'Keynes has been rejected; Beveridge has not.'

Yet at the same time several Institute of Economic Affairs studies (notably Harris and Seldon, 1979) and other surveys – for example, an NOP poll commissioned by BUPA in May 1983 – have shown that a majority of the public believes that there should be an alternative to the NHS, that people should be allowed to pay for private treatment and private health schemes should not be abolished. Support for the NHS and for private provision are not incompatible. People can both want to maintain existing services and believe that a private choice should be available. There may be a case for expanding the private and voluntary sectors, but there is a danger of creating a two-tier system comparable with that in the USA, which is more expensive overall and can leave the poor to rely on state services deprived of necessary resources. Moreover, there is no evidence that the expansion of private medicine or greater emphasis on community care for the elderly within families would make any significant difference, in the short to medium term, to the needs of the NHS.

Current expenditure plans would almost certainly not be sufficient to maintain existing standards of provision in the NHS and in education. Various opinion surveys have shown that the public is already worried about the squeeze on services, and the Government will find it difficult to shift much of the burden to the private sector without alienating voters. A similar point applies to social security; a genuine problem is posed by the question of how to finance the rising number of retirement pensioners, especially as the new state pension scheme reaches maturity over the next two decades. The Government may have to persuade people to accept changes in the scheme, involving either reduced entitlements and/or higher contributions.

The Government has not, however, discussed many of these options in public. There have been hints, generally since the June 1983 election, of difficult choices ahead, but the alternatives have not been spelt out and the Conservative manifesto was completely bland on the subject. The main revelations have come from leaked Think Tank and Cabinet committee papers, and the focus has been on the most controversial and 'politically unacceptable' of the options. This is largely the Government's own fault. Secrecy is the enemy of balanced debate, since anything which does emerge tends to be distorted.

The Government's record has been indifferent in the area of open government. The principal exception has been the establishment in 1979 of the departmental select committees of the Commons at the instigation of Norman St John-Stevas, then the Leader of the Commons; the move was later regretted by many of his ministerial colleagues. This has been an innovation of the greatest importance in forcing departments to justify and to explain their policies. While the committees have been of varying quality, they have changed the way in which policy has been discussed. Yet MPs have faced difficulties in finding out about, and in questioning departments about, options which have not yet appeared in Green or White Papers. The Government has so far been reluctant to discuss major choices over public spending and the welfare state, though it may be forced to do so during its second term.

There are therefore many obstacles to the creation of a new consensus — the uncertainty about sustained economic recovery, the incompatibility of existing public spending plans and the desire for lower taxation, the public's attitudes to the welfare state. But where does this leave the strategy? Ralf Dahrendorf, Director of the London School of Economics during the period and high priest of Euro-centrism, has argued (Dahrendorf, 1982) that 'there is every sign that the new Conservative theory will have a short life in political practice.' He claims that the Thatcherite approach is not in the British tradition. In his view, only in the USA are tax cuts likely to lead to higher investment rather than higher consumption. 'In combination with the evident cost in terms of unemployment, bankruptcies and decline, it is the cultural alienness of this approach which is most likely to defeat it.' But Dahrendorf exaggerates the extent to which the Thatcher Government has followed a supply-side approach. In practice the British priority has been fiscal rectitude rather than gambling on the impact of tax cuts in the manner of the Reagan administration.

The result is that borrowing has fallen in the UK, while the Budget deficit has soared in the USA.

A more pertinent point is Dahrendorf's comparison between Mrs Thatcher's deliberate and radical break with tradition and the consensus approach followed in his own West Germany. The difference between the tight counter-inflation policies followed on the Continent — including France to some extent, even after President Mitterrand's election in 1981 — and in the UK is that in the former case there has been a broader base of political support for the measures. There has also generally been little desire for a radical shift in the frontiers between the public and the private sectors, with the partial exception of France. On this theme Professor Samuel Beer (Beer, 1982) concluded in October 1981: 'The failure of Mrs Thatcher's efforts to mobilize consent for many of her principal measures, even within the leading echelons of the Government and the economy, casts doubts on the chances of the neo-liberal strategy to dominate the future.' He questioned whether Mrs Thatcher's administration could gain consent on a sufficiently wide and sustained basis to shift to a system of market rather than public choice.

Similarly, at the time of the 1983 election some centrist commentators argued that radical Thatcherism was dead and that there was now a new consensus Thatcherism which would avoid major changes. The Conservative manifesto in 1983 was certainly not a radical document in its presentation. The appeal was essentially for a doctor's (or perhaps head-mistress's) mandate — 'Trust us to finish the job we have started.' Admittedly, the Thatcher administration has become more pessimistic about achieving any significant cuts in public spending in real terms below current levels, and that has led to some down-grading of expectations about tax cuts. Sir Geoffrey Howe's last speeches as Chancellor indicated caution about the scope either for reining back spending on the social services or for reducing significantly the problem of the overlap between the tax and the social security systems — the unemployment and poverty traps.

These constraints do not, however, imply any retreat into mere management of the present structure, without attempts to change it. Mrs Thatcher is not President Eisenhower.

The Thatcher administration's radicalism may be of a gradualist kind, pushing forward step by step — in privatization, in contracting out, in undermining union power in the labour market and in taking power away from local authorities. But there is likely to be movement none the less. In this sense the Marxist commentators (Gamble 1983a, b) have been right to argue that the Thatcher administration has aimed to undermine the institutions on which the political strength of the Labour movement rests — big-city local authorities, council estates, monopoly nationalized industries and trade unions. In their view, the new Thatcherite Britain will be founded not on the traditional sources of trade union and Labour Party power but on owner occupiers living in the suburbs and new towns, in small new technology and electronics companies, in the service sector, with weak unions or none at all. Some of these developments, such as the decline of the traditional working class in large-scale manufacturing, were taking place before 1979. But the Thatcher administration has encouraged their acceleration by selling council houses and by ensuring that the development of new industries like cable broadcasting occurs primarily in the private sector.

How far Thatcherism will go down the road towards eliminating the collectivist approach is open to question. So far the frontiers between the public and the private sectors have not been shifted significantly; the trade unions are battered, but their power has not been destroyed; and no lasting improvement in the performance of British industry has been confirmed. In future there is likely to be strong resistance to any substantial change in the structure of the welfare state; the growth in public spending will be difficult to contain; and the privatization programme will take a long time to implement. The likelihood is that neither the optimists nor the pessimists will be proved right. During the second Thatcher term the economy will improve slowly and patchily. The personal tax burden will fall only slightly. Standards of provision in the health and education services will decline but not to the point of breakdown. And Britain's defence commitments will have to be cut back yet again. It is likely to be the familiar story of the management of Britain's continuing decline rather than of either triumph or disaster.

The Thatcher Government could remain in a strong position because the battle between Labour and the Alliance for the role of principal challenger will rumble on. The 1983 election showed that Thatcherism had been more successful in identifying the aspirations of the 'new' working class than Labour, but the rise of the Alliance indicated that the endorsement was only partial. As Peter Jenkins pointed out (Kennet, 1982), the Social Democratic Party was 'a child of Britain's decline. The new party was not so much the cause of the "breaking of the mould" but rather an expression of it, one of the pieces.'

It has been one of the ironies of recent politics that the forces behind the creation of the SDP consisted both of those rejecting the post-war 'settlement' and those wanting to recreate it in a slightly modified form. The jibe about wanting to build a 'better yesterday' was not far from the mark in describing the views of Roy Jenkins and Bill Rodgers on economic and industrial policy. It applied also to the attitudes of establishment groups of policy-makers and professionals who disliked both the populism and narrowness of Thatcherism and the sectarianism and dogma of Labour. It was as if these people's views had been set permanently in the framework of the late 1960s and early 1970s. In many ways it was Roy Jenkins's personal tragedy to have been away from Britain during the late 1970s, when the shift in economic policy occurred and when it became clear that the post-war 'settlement', with its deals over incomes policy and interventionist strategies, had broken down. The views of Roy Jenkins did, admittedly, change but he still appeared to be a man from the past.

The SDP included those who rejected the previous approach. David Owen's comment (Owen, 1981) that 'corporatism is a recipe for choosing the lowest common denominator for the stifling of initiative and innovation' could have been echoed by Sir Geoffrey Howe. Ironically, David Owen, the strongest advocate of the independent identity of the SDP within the Alliance, has held views on economic and industrial policy which have been most closely shared by the Liberals. However, in part because of their predominant origin in local politics, some Liberals have appeared naive about the role of central government in macroeconomic policy and about the importance of growth.

What has happened in the last few years, which only the Thatcher administration has fully appreciated, has been a move away from a collectivist approach towards lower expectations of government. This has involved more than just a shift in monetary and fiscal policy, as has been pointed out, significantly, by a Social Democrat economist, Nicholas Bosanquet. He has argued (Bosanquet, 1983) that public services have become more bureaucratic, more inflexible and too orientated towards producer groups rather than consumers, while expenditure decisions have been divorced from fiscal consequences.

Bosanquet's conclusions naturally differ from those of the New Right in urging the reform of, rather than necessarily a major reduction in, the role of government. To him the NHS and public education still have greater merits than the alternatives. The Government still has a major role to play in redistribution through the social security system and in acting as a countervailing force to private coercion and to oppressive actions by bureaucracies. Yet many of his detailed suggestions follow lines strikingly similar to those of the Conservatives — the notion of creating more competition in the supply side of local government through competitive tendering and of expanding the market element in the public sector by weakening monopolies in nationalized industries. The emphasis is, however, on the consumer and competition rather than on private enterprise versus the public sector, as it has tended to be with the Thatcher administration.

These ideas show the extent of the change in thinking in the political world since the late 1970s, which Thatcherism has stimulated but not created. Indeed, even within the Labour Party the size of the defeat in June 1983 has forced a few leaders to rethink their views on the role of the state, if not their commitment to Keynes. But it is still uncertain whether it will be possible to broaden Labour's appeal to the 'new' working class once again.

There has been a parallel development in the USA, where some leading Democrats — for example, Senators Gary Hart, Bill Bradley and Paul Tsongas — have been questioning their party's former commitment to the unions and to big government. This group, confusingly known as the 'neo-liberals', has argued for a greater role for the market, for decentralization and for fewer government controls, welcoming the deregulation of the airlines under the Carter administration. The closest non-Conservative parallels in the UK so far have been a few Social Democrats like David Owen and some Liberals.

To date, the Thatcher Government has proved skilful in exploiting these new forces in British politics, and it has also enjoyed a remarkable run of luck. But it has not yet succeeded in creating a new consensus and may find that hard to do, given the problems that it is likely to face over unemployment, public spending and the welfare state. Moreover, the honeymoon period after a big election victory often lasts only a short time as unexpected or inherent problems begin to appear.

Mrs Thatcher at present seems to admit of no such doubts. However, she frequently listens to Enoch Powell, the errant Cassandra of Conservatism. Perhaps she should read his own revealing epitaph for Joseph Chamberlain (Powell, 1977): 'All political lives, unless they are cut off in mid-stream at a happy juncture, end in failure, because that is the nature of politics and of human affairs.'

Bibliography

Bacon, Robert, and Eltis, Walter (1976), *Britain's Economic Problem: Too Few Producers*, London, Macmillan

Baker, Kenneth (1982), *New Jobs from New Technology*, London, Conservative Political Centre

Barnett, Anthony (1982), *Iron Britannia*, London, Allison & Busby

Barnett, Joel (1982), *Inside the Treasury*, London, André Deutsch

Beer, Samuel (1982), *Britain Against Itself*, London, Faber & Faber

Behrens, Robert (1980), *The Conservative Party from Heath to Thatcher*, London, Saxon House

Bosanquet, Nicholas (1983), *After the New Right*, London, Heinemann

Brittan, Samuel (1982), *How to End the Monetarist Controversy*, London, Institute of Economic Affairs

Brittan, Samuel (1983), *The Role and Limits of Government*, London, Temple Smith

Bull, David, and Wilding, Paul (eds.) (1983), *Thatcherism and the Poor*, London, Child Poverty Action Group

Burns, Sir Terry (1981), 'Economic Policy and Prospects', reprint of a lecture given in Washington DC, September 1981, *Public Money*, December

Butler, David, and Kavanagh, Dennis (1980), *The British General Election of 1979*, London, Macmillan

Campaign Guide 1983, Conservative Research Department

Changing Gear: What the Government Should Do Next (1981) (Proposals from a group of Conservative MPs), London, Macmillan

Could Do Better (1982) (Contrasting assessments of the economic progress and prospects of the Thatcher Government at mid-term), London, Institute of Economic Affairs

Dahrendorf, Ralf (1982), *On Britain*, London, BBC

Dalyell, Tam (1982), *One Man's Falklands*, London, Cecil Woolf

Dalyell, Tam (1983), *Thatcher's Torpedo*, London, Cecil Woolf

Defence Committee of the Commons, Session 1981–2, First Special Report, *Strategic Nuclear Weapons Policy*, House of Commons Paper 266

Defence Committee of the Commons, Session 1982–3, Third Report, *The Future Defence of the Falkland Islands*, House of Commons Paper 154

Defence Estimates, Statement 1983, Cmnd 8951, London, HMSO, 1983

Donnison, David (1982), *The Politics of Poverty*, Oxford, Martin Robertson

Economic Outlook (1982), Organization for Economic Co-operation and Development, Paris, December

Edwardes, Sir Michael (1983), *Back from the Brink*, London, Collins

Environment Committee of the Commons, Session 1981–2, First Report, *The Private Rented Housing Sector*, House of Commons Paper 40

Falklands Campaign: The Lessons, Cmnd 8758, London, HMSO, 1982

Fforde, John (1983), 'Setting Monetary Objectives', *Bank of England Quarterly Bulletin*, June

Financial Statement and Budget Report, 1983–84 (1983), London, HMSO

Foreign Affairs Committee of the Commons, Session 1982–3, Fourth Report, *Overseas Development Administration's Scientific and Special Units*, House of Commons Paper 25

Franks, Lord (1983), *Falkland Islands Review: Report of a Committee of Privy Counsellors*, Cmnd 8787, London, HMSO

Gamble, Andrew (1974), *The Conservative Nation*, London, Routledge & Kegan Paul

Gamble, Andrew (1983a), 'The Rise of the Resolute Right', *New Socialist*, January/February

Gamble, Andrew (1983b), 'Thatcher: The Second Coming', *Marxism Today*, July

Gilmour, Sir Ian (1977), *Inside Right*, London, Hutchinson

Gilmour, Sir Ian (1983), *Britain Can Work*, Oxford, Martin Robertson

Glennerster, Howard (ed.) (1983), *The Future of the Welfare State*, London, Heinemann

Government's Expenditure Plans 1980–81 to 1983–84 (1980), Cmnd 7841, London, HMSO

Government's Expenditure Plans 1983–84 to 1985–86 (1983), Cmnd 8789, London, HMSO

Gretton, John, and Harrison, Anthony (eds.) (1982), *How Much are Public Servants Worth?*, Oxford, Basil Blackwell

Hall, Stuart, and Jacques, Martin (eds.) (1983), *The Politics of Thatcherism*, London, Lawrence & Wishart

Harris, Ralph (Lord), and Seldon, Arthur (1979), *Over-Ruled on Welfare*, London, Institute of Economic Affairs

Hastings, Max, and Jenkins, Simon (1983), *The Battle for the Falklands*, London, Michael Joseph

Hastings, Sue, and Levie, Hugo (eds.) (1983), *Privatisation?*, Nottingham, Spokesman

Heald, David, and Steel, David (1982), 'The Privatisation of Industry', *Political Quarterly*, July/September

Henderson, Professor P. D. (1983), 'Mrs Thatcher's Old-Style Dirigisme', *Journal of Economic Affairs*, January

Heseltine, Michael (1983), *Reviving the Inner Cities*, London, Conservative Political Centre

Hood, Christopher, and Wright, Maurice (eds.) (1980), *Big Government in Hard Times*, Oxford, Martin Robertson

Howe, Sir Geoffrey (1983), and four economists, 'Agenda for Liberal Conservatism', *Journal of Economic Affairs*, January

Jones, G. W., and Stewart, J. D. (1983), 'The Treasury and Local Government', *Political Quarterly*, January/March

Joseph, Sir Keith, and Sumption, Jonathan (1978), *Equality*, London, John Murray

Kaldor, Lord (1983), *The Economic Consequences of Mrs Thatcher*, London, Duckworth

Kay, John (ed.) (1982), *The 1982 Budget*, Oxford, Basil Blackwell

Kennet, Wayland (ed.) (1982), *The Rebirth of Britain*, London, Weidenfeld & Nicolson

King, Anthony (ed.) (1976), *Why is Britain Becoming Harder to Govern?*, London, BBC

Lawson, Nigel (1981), *The New Conservatism*, London, Conservative Political Centre

Lawson, Nigel (1982), *What's Right with Britain?*, London, Conservative Political Centre

Layton-Henry, Zig (ed.) (1980), *Conservative Party Politics*, London, Macmillan

Likierman, Andrew (1982), 'Management Information for Ministers: The MINIS System in the Department of the Environment', *Public Administration*, Summer

Matthews, R. C. O., and Sargent, J. R. (eds.) (1983) *Contemporary Problems of Economic Policy*, London, Methuen

Minford, Patrick (1983), *Unemployment, Cause and Cure*, Oxford, Martin Robertson

Murray, Tricia (1978), *Margaret Thatcher*, London, Star

Norton, Philip, and Aughey, Arthur (1981), *Conservatives and Conservatism*, London, Temple Smith

Owen, David (1981), *Facing the Future*, London, Jonathan Cape

Patten, Chris (1983), *The Tory Case*, London, Longman

Penniman, Howard (ed.) (1981), *Britain at the Polls, 1979*, Washington DC and London, American Enterprise Institute

Pliatzky, Sir Leo (1982), *Getting and Spending: Public Expenditure,*

Employment and Inflation, Oxford, Basil Blackwell

Powell, J. Enoch (1977), *Joseph Chamberlain*, London, Thames & Hudson

Pratten, C. F. (1982), 'Mrs Thatcher's Economic Experiment', *Lloyds Bank Review*, January

Public Accounts Committee of the Commons, Session 1981–2, Tenth Report, *Department of Industry: Sale of Shares in British Aerospace and Sales of Government Shareholdings in Other Publicly Owned Companies and British Petroleum*, House of Commons Paper 189; Thirteenth Report, *Department of Transport: Road Construction Units, Transfer of Work to Consultants*, House of Commons Paper 20

Rose, Professor Richard (1983), 'Two and One-half Cheers for the Market in Britain', *Public Opinion*, June/July

Särlvik, Bo, and Crewe, Ivor (1983) *Decade of Dealignment: The Conservative Victory of 1979 and Electoral Trends in the 1970s*, Cambridge, Cambridge University Press

Scarman, Lord (1982), *The Scarman Report: The Brixton Disorders, April 10 to 12, 1981*, Harmondsworth, Penguin Books

Seldon, Arthur (ed.) (1981), *The Emerging Consensus?*, London, Institute of Economic Affairs

Shackleton, Lord (1982), *Falkland Islands Economic Study 1982*, Cmnd 8653, London, HMSO

Speed, Keith (1982), *Sea Change: The Battle for the Falklands and the Future of Britain's Navy*, Bath, Ashgrove Press

Stephenson, Hugh (1980), *Mrs Thatcher's First Year*, London, Jill Norman

Thatcher's Britain: A Guide to the Ruins (1983), London, Pluto Press and *New Socialist*

Thomas, Lord (1983), *Our Place in the World*, London, Conservative Political Centre

Townsend, Peter, and Davidson, Nick (eds.) (1982), *Inequality in Report of a Research Working Group set up by the Department of Health and Social Security* (the Black Report), Harmondsworth, Penguin Books

Treasury and Civil Service Committee of the Commons, Session 1979–80, Second Report, *The Budget and the Government's Expenditure Plans 1980–81*, House of Commons Paper 584; Fifth Report, *Provision for Civil Service Pay Increases in the 1980–1 Estimates*, House of Commons Paper 730

Treasury and Civil Service Committee of the Commons, Session 1980–1, Second Report, *The Government's Economic Policy: Autumn Review*, House of Commons Paper 79; Third Report, *Monetary Policy*, House of Commons Paper 163; Fifth Report, *The 1981*

Budget and the Government's Expenditure Plans 1981—2 to 1983—4, House of Commons Paper 232; Eighth Report, *Financing of Nationalised Industries*, House of Commons Paper 348

Treasury and Civil Service Committee of the Commons, Session 1981—2, First Report, *The Government's Economic Policy: Autumn Review*, House of Commons Paper 28; Third Report, *Efficiency and Effectiveness in the Civil Service*, House of Commons Paper 236; Fourth Report, *The 1982 Budget*, House of Commons Paper 270; Fifth Report, *The Government's Expenditure Plans 1982—83 to 1984—5*, House of Commons Paper 316

Treasury and Civil Service Committee of the Commons, Session 1982—3, First Special Report, *Civil Service Manpower Reductions*, House of Commons Paper 46; First Report, *The Government's Economic Policy: Autumn Statement*, House of Commons Paper 49; Third Report, *The Government's Expenditure Plans 1983—84 to 1985—86*, House of Commons Paper 204; Fifth Report, *The 1983 Budget*, House of Commons Paper 286; Second Special Report, *International Monetary Arrangements*, House of Commons Paper 385

Waldegrave, William (1978), *The Binding of Leviathan*, London, Hamish Hamilton

Wapshott, Nicholas, and Brock, George (1983), *Thatcher*, London, Futura

Whitfield, Dexter (1983), *Making it Public: Evidence and Action against Privatization*, London, Pluto Press

Index